Art/Museums

International Relations

Where We Least Expect It

CHRISTINE SYLVESTER

Paradigm Publishers

Boulder • London

Copyright © 2009 Paradigm Publishers

Published in the United States by Paradigm Publishers, 3360 Mitchell Lane, Suite E, Boulder, CO 80305 USA.

Paradigm Publishers is the trade name of Birkenkamp & Company, LLC, Dean Birkenkamp, President and Publisher.

Library of Congress Cataloging-in-Publication Data

Sylvester, Christine, 1949-
  Art/museums : international relations where we least expect it / Christine Sylvester.
    p. cm.
  Includes bibliographical references and index.
  ISBN 978-1-59451-464-7 (hardcover : alk. paper) — ISBN 978-1-59451-465-4 (pbk. : alk. paper)
  1. Art museums—Political aspects. 2. Museums—Political aspects. 3. International relations. I. Title.
  N430.S95 2009
  708—dc22

                                    2008039111

Printed and bound in the United States of America on acid-free paper that meets the standards of the American National Standard for Permanence of Paper for Printed Library Materials.

Designed and Typeset by Cheryl Hoffman

13 12 11 10 09   1 2 3 4 5

to a wily coyote and a pumpkin on the gill

Contents

Acknowledgments

Here is the real location of any curator's egg: in the room with the acknowledgments and heartfelt thanks. Among many people, studios, artists, and galleries that helped me along the way, gave me encouragement, or inspired me with their work, I especially want to thank, in alphabetical order: Brooke Ackerly, Tina Balmer, Anthony Burke, Stephen Chan, Kathryn Cramerei, Sharon Daugherty, Mervyn and Lola Frost, Gagosian Gallery (Los Angeles), Gerry Davies, Lene Hansen, Cheryl Hoffman, Brigitte Holzner, Vivienne Jabri, Alyce Jordan, Jennifer Knerr, Peter Larmour, the Leverhulme Foundation, Tim Luke, Erin Manning, Chris May, National Gallery London picture library, David Paletz, Elina Penttinen, Karen Pugliesi, Henriette Riegler, Tricia Smith (Art Resource), Kezia Storr (PAP photos), Tate Modern picture library, Ann Tickner, Helen Topliss, Jeff Wall Studio, Michael E. Weil, and Joseba Zulaika.

With enormous appreciation, I also thank: the Institute of Social Studies, The Hague, for the study leave that kick-started his book; the School of Oriental and African Studies, University of London, Department of Politics and International Relations, for inviting me as visiting professor under the auspices of the Leverhulme Foundation (2003–2004) and keeping me on as an honorary affiliate for two more years; and my wonderful colleagues at Lancaster University UK, especially the Department of Politics and International Relations.

Photographs

CHAPTER 1

Can International Relations and Art/Museums Come Together?

Can we talk about art/museums and international relations in the same breath or is the relationship too fugitive—or trivial? This book digs into that question guided by the strong hunch that there are layers of significance that huddle in the intersections of activities, institutions, and academic fields that do not usually have much to say to each other, at least not directly. Facing up to art/museums as institutions of power and reach takes the field of International Relations (IR) into new areas of analysis and strengthens work in art history and museum studies that ranges internationally, but somewhat naively, because it does not look at the world through any IR lens.

International relations, where the field of IR says it is and therefore expects it to be, conducts diplomacy over a fine state dinner, moves weapons and development advice between states or tries individuals in an international criminal court. It spies, secures, and sends personnel to the United Nations and its expanding agencies. Most noticeably, international relations conducts wars—everywhere and frequently. War is its traditional forte. But international relations where IR least expects it is furtive too, seemingly invisible, and thus can be missed by the field. It walks calmly through domestic airport security screenings on September 11, 2001, undetected. It darts nervously, hungrily across borders on a regular basis. It mingles international terrorism with tourism in a Bali nightclub or mixes into an artistic performance by entering a Moscow theater with bombs, shifting attention from the drama on the stage to a terrifying performance of interloper international relations in the stalls. Gory dioramas of massed toy soldiers can turn up in a London art gallery; or art can be taken from a Baghdad museum while combat-ready troops across the street look elsewhere for the real international relations of war.

This book focuses on institutional locations of international relations where IR would least expect it: in major art/museums and galleries. IR claims neither art nor museums as traditional bona fides of international relations. The field might glimpse art looters in the context of a war in Iraq, but it will be slow to incorporate that kind of activity into its studies of war. It will most likely not notice that the groups rushing in to save looted and damaged artifacts are international art teams and institutions. The saga of New York's twin towers will not usually be talked about in terms of architectures suddenly fallen and replaced, after intricate politics, in ways that concretize and museumify an event of international relations. The worldly Guggenheim, at once art foundation, set of international museums and governance practices, and organizational network, operates peacefully, although not uncontroversially, in places thick with international relations. The Getty Museum and Center in Los Angeles is so wealthy it can conduct private art diplomacy, while the British Museum is diplomatically adept at warding off restitution claims on the Parthenon sculptures it exhibits and other objects acquired through imperial skulduggery. Interesting, all this, but not particularly so for IR—traditionally, and even now, when IR queries where an international that seems omnipresent resides (*Millennium,* 2007).

Analysts from the world of art and museums are more regularly attuned to the international in their midst. "It" appears unmistakably around the museums and archives of Iraq and Afghanistan. Art restitution claims often arise out of the international relations of wars and imperialist acts of the past and present. Globalization increasingly influences where museums locate, the architectures they build, and the visitor amenities they offer. International political economy enables large art museums to become international bazaars that sell ersatz art as neckties, scarves, jewelry, mugs, dinnerware, and vases: in 2003, the Metropolitan Museum of Art turned a profit of around $39 million from its house-managed retail operations (Schneider 2006, 31); its rug department alone seems a cross between a smart Fifth Avenue shop and a market in Dubai.[1] Such money-spinning activities, promoted by museum managers, can be viewed askance by culture critics and artists, who can think the art/museum has lost its way. The Guggenheim has been blasted for its alleged profit-seeking ambitions. Major art institutions like the Getty and the Metropolitan Museum of Art can land in foreign courts for violating local cultural-heritage laws in their acquisitions. Big museum architectures and blockbuster exhibitions attract crowds but can leave critics apoplectic about tacky shows and crass commercialism.[2] Even the field of museum studies can be critical of art museums as cultural superpowers ruthlessly ensuring that their art holdings are not "lost" to overseas competitor museums.

The bigger and more internationally esteemed the art institution, the more critical the views of it can be, from the outside and the inside. James Cuno (cited in McClellan 2003b, 36; also, Cuno 2004a, 2004b), who has been director of the Courtauld Institute in London and the Chicago Art Institute, insists that "an art museum's fundamental purpose is to collect, preserve, and exhibit works of art as a vital part of our nation's cultural patrimony." He laments aspects of the new museum and would like to see art museums spend more time debating the direction of collecting and displaying art, research capacity, and future special exhibitions. Recent obsessions with attracting visitors, providing state-of-the-art security, and filling tills emerge from the international management models that major art museums are adopting. Somewhere in between traditional and reformist concerns lie the many discussions taking place about architectural spaces and how to use them, achieving the correct balance between art and nonart offerings, and establishing the kind of ambience to encourage—hushed, dignified, and reverential or noisy, busy, and more like an international air terminal than a traditional art museum. In the midst of these debates, it is not easy to work out what an art museum definitively is about today.

I want to say that a major art museum today is an institution that is heavily political, often involved with or implicated in international relations, and savvy about power. It is an intricate, multivalent, internationally implicated / socially situated social institution that seems to be growing in popularity and influence. Attendance at American art museums catapulted from 22 million in 1962 to more than 100 million in 2000 (Cuno 2004b, 17–18). Similar attendance jumps occurred across Europe, although this might not be historically unique.[3] According to an American survey, visitors rank museums of all sorts higher than government institutions when it comes to providing trustworthy sources of objective information (Cuno 2004b). Most surveys also indicate time and again that the well-educated, affluent and/or upwardly mobile classes choose museum-going as their leisure pursuit (Wallach 2000; Falk 1998); when other groups come to an art museum, they report being very glad they did (Rice 2003, 84). Class concerns can even mean that the important high-end collectors, and the young audiences art museums like to court and who tend to prefer contemporary art, are not entirely catered to (Taylor, Spero, and Higgins 2007). Middle classes and middlebrow tastes can be seen in the endless repackaging of popular Impressionist works and artifacts from Pharaonic Egypt. Other forms of non-Western art bring out Western audiences largely when lashed to current international events; Islamic and Chinese art shows draw considerable media hype in this moment of international relations.

The museum sector is also expanding—dramatically. Large and small, urban and rural, private and public, art museums and galleries have sprouted from Las Vegas to Liverpool, from Marfa, Texas, to Naoshima, Japan, and from Kinmen Island to the Orkney Islands. Many are new: "more than half of our art museums were founded after 1970" (Cuno 2004b, 17). Established art museums try to keep up via ambitious architectural projects, such as the glass pyramid at the Louvre; the Sainsbury Wing of the National Gallery, London; and the new additions to the Denver Art Museum, the Los Angeles Country Museum of Art, the Phoenix Art Museum, and the Royal Ontario Museum, Toronto. Sometimes nothing will do except an entirely new building, such as those that house the Weisman Art Museum in Minneapolis, the New Museum in New York, and the Institute of Contemporary Art, which cantilevers over Boston Harbor. New complexes of museum buildings define the Getty Center in Los Angeles and the High Museum of Art in Atlanta, and major renovations have reworked the Yale Art Gallery in New Haven. Museum expansion and reshaping can also be geospatial. The Tate has branches in Cornwall and Liverpool, and the Guggenheim is now in New York, Venice, Berlin, and Bilbao; it has tried to be in Las Vegas and will soon showcase another Frank Gehry creation in Abu Dhabi. The historically conservative Louvre is also going to Abu Dhabi, clad in a Jean Nouvel creation. Paris's Pompidou Center was planning to manage a new contemporary art museum bearing its name in Shanghai until talks suddenly failed. Start-stop international collaborations are common, but it is also common for museums to fire up media attention before the negotiating process is very far along. The migrating art museum is a phenomenon these days.

International relations and art/museum practices blend into each other. The art world sees this, but its writings can be naive about international power and politics, largely because it has not taken on board relevant theories or ideas of IR. For its part, IR asks itself where the international is at a time when "it" seems to be driving politics and economics; and yet IR can hesitate to enter the art museum to find more of it. One field increasingly becomes an instance of the other, but academic work on art/museums does not reference works in IR, and the field that studies international relations does not load art/museums into its can(n)ons. There is a certain irony in residing in a shared black hole. Each field endeavors to be au courant even as changes around it push its boundaries and challenge its expectations. "More than ever," says one specialist, "museums may be many things to many people and no one theory or discipline can do them justice" (McClellan 2003a, xviii). The same type of comment can be made about international relations. When significant activity recurs where it is not expected by academic overseers, it is possible that the field in question is at a certain end. It carries on as though nothing is amiss, but it misses much, reacts more than it anticipates, and risks becoming merely academic.

IR AT THE END?

Take IR as an example. As an academic field, IR has developed through three discipline-defining debates and a less-disciplined tumbling-in of new topics and field entrants in recent years.[4] Controversy has been seen as keeping IR on its toes and attuned to trends in other social sciences and to changing relations of the international in the world. The field began as a peace-oriented discipline in the years immediately following World War I. It then shifted in the main toward a conflict-and-threat emphasis in the interwar years as aggression inched forward in Europe and Asia. The postwar cold war ensured that IR would stay on a conflict course rather than angle back to peace. Large swaths of IR also came under the influence of America's postwar technocratic superpowerdom: North American scholars found science the promised road to description, explanation, and prediction of international relations. The British and Australians did not surrender to science, preferring to retain their more historical, philosophical, theoretical, and normative orientations to methodology. All sites of IR, however, became absorbed, each in its own way, in the struggles against the Soviet Union. It was only in the waning years of the cold war that spaces and people outside the frame of the East-West conflict climbed the fences of IR and claimed ground for their concerns. By then the soil had been prepared a bit by the oil shocks of the 1970s and by confrontations in the United Nations over postcolonial demands for redistributions of international resources.

In the end, IR's debates and methodological plurality could not save it from the spectacular disciplinary failure to anticipate the peaceful demise of the Soviet Union. No branch of IR believed that a powerful state—a superpower—would declare itself out of business one day. And, given that superpower relations had been IR's favorite topic, this fundamental failing weakened the field and enabled a plethora of new topics, people, and interests to stretch its small constellation of knowledge and awareness. Women, racial minorities, migrants from the poorer Southern Hemisphere and Eastern Europe, trafficked people, workers in shifting globalizing factories—all came into IR, in the flesh or as subjects of research. Through the 1990s they not only rearranged IR's boundaries but also introduced new methodologies associated with critical theory, feminism, postcolonial analysis, constructivism, and poststructuralism. And then even more locations, people, actors, processes, and ways of knowing became possible, multiplying the possibilities of realizing the many places international relations was operating.

The narrow field of IR needed this broadening. Indeed, a continued bringing-in process is still required in IR before the subject area can begin to settle again into a distinctive field, if ever it does. As is often the case when change occurs, however, the upsurge of relevance also ushered in new problems. The too-tight field loosened to the point where it configured anew into a fragmented camp structure. IR is now a field of discernible and lively camps, each organized around a fairly narrow set of research interests, identities, geographical locations, and/or methodologies. Feminists have a camp and, in Britain, so do poststructuralists. There are European networks of critical IR scholars and American networks, each impelled by a different understanding of security. Some camps correspond to schools of thinking linked to locations: the English, Welsh, Copenhagen, and Paris schools. Some camps focus on the international politics of economic relations, and others grab hold of terrorism studies, peace studies, feminism, or international law[5]. It can be the case that the camps are relatively self-satisfied and disinclined to interact more than minimally or superficially with other camps, particularly camps that seem to have a very different take on the issues they also study. Debate, once thought of as disciplinary sport, is now more or less confined to within-camp issues. This means that each camp carves out specific areas of interest, uses a particular vocabulary to express that interest, upholds a different set of revered personages, and holds to canonical texts that camp followers read, reread, and cite incessantly and other camps might never even know of, let alone read or cite. The structure of IR confines art/museums to a small camp located in the British International Studies Association (BISA) that calls itself "art and politics." Other camps ignore it.

The camp structure boosts diversity and widens purviews, but it does not disperse all the new knowledge evenly around the field. If you specialize in critical approaches to the study of international relations, you might be reasonably comfortable sharing some fire with scholars from feminist IR, European critical security studies, postcolonial analysis, or poststructuralist studies.[6] But given that many IR camps have their own journals today, it is easy to concentrate on preferred topics and orientations and nearly ignore the rest. IR has become a field of differences rather than similarities, the differences often sneering at each other through camp fences.

There have always been groupings and schools of thinking in academia. The major change in today's IR is that no camp is strong enough to set the parameters of the field or to knock out any other camp through brilliance, fiat, or control over academic positions and publishing. Publishing outlets proliferate and academic posts have globalized. One camp might accuse another of not studying the real international relations, but words cannot hurt today like they used to—not fatally. There is space for everyone within some camp zone where identity and knowledge fragments reign in a mise-en-scène that is nothing if not camp (Sylvester 2007a).

We might say that with IR specialists agreeing on very little today, including what the field is about, where it draws the line between itself and other fields, and what methods of analysis it should employ, IR is at a certain end. Obviously, the field carries on: classes are taught about "it," articles are published about aspects of "it," and students go on being trained in "it." It is a field hard-pressed, though, to bring its considerable accumulated resources to bear on a troubled world where bombs sit in theaters, art empties into the streets of war, and the National Gallery of London fusses over saving a painting from the clutches of a distinguished art institution located in a foreign country. Art/museums are part of IR and yet are not seen to be part of camp IR. They are part of a field that for good or for ill—and the jury is out on this—is at the end of its capacity for common narratives of any sort. Some say art is in the same boat.

ART AT THE END?

Columbia University emeritus professor of philosophy Arthur Danto (1997) has argued since the 1980s that art is at an end. It ended, or rather the field of art history ended, in the 1960s, when Andy Warhol gave us Brillo boxes. By the time the likes of Damien Hirst arrived with sharks in formaldehyde, art had been at an end for nearly thirty years. It is not that the activities of art making ended or the writing about it wrapped up. Rather, at the end of art, "art" refuses to be the art that professional art historical narratives and norms say it is. Hans Belting (2003, 3), whose work on the same topic from a more European angle is coterminous with Danto's, talks about the current period in art history as the age of the epilogue. In his view, it is not that art history is entirely flat-footed in its demise. Rather, in place of one canonical art history there are now, as in IR, "many art histories that exist side by side" (Belting 2003, 7). The frame has been shattered.

The art history frame had been largely Eurocentric pretending to be universal; so was IR in the "debates" phase of its existence. Art history traces its subject area to a period around 1400 when found images and forms from Greek or Roman times started to be designated as art and admired aesthetically by spectators who obviously were not themselves the artists (Belting 1987). By the nineteenth century, academic art history was flourishing around activities that included identifying art forms and materials, cataloging artworks, and periodizing history around distinctive styles or schools of art. The relationship of art making to art history has since been one of the chicken and egg, with the egg winning. As one art theorist puts it, "what artists make as art depends upon the context of intentions possible for a given era and culture—whatever the culture theorizes as art" (Freeland 2001, 57). That is to say, artists have innovated, customized, or become avant-garde with respect to art historical culture narratives rather than according to other standards, such as genius, talent, and quirkiness (Hickey 1997). And until recently, art historians, philosophers, and museum curators have written the scripts of art; the rest of us have been "Sunday spectators" meant to follow the lead of the experts (Hooper-Greenhill 1994).

These experts agreed early that fine visual art objects could come in only a few forms—painting, sculpture, architecture—using materials associated specifically with those forms. Objects put to use in life, such as pottery and fabrics, or even lawn ornaments, might look like art but could not be art; they were crafts or mass-produced kitsch items passed off as art (Greenberg 1985). As for styles and periods of art, art history periodized on the basis of composition, materials, and techniques, as well as subjects depicted. Danto believes that the end started when Warhol made simulacra of Brillo boxes and called that art. Was an enlarged and dreamlike but nonetheless exact reproduction of an everyday object found on grocery shelves and used in household cleaning really art?

By blurring the lines between the fine and the prosaic object, between the distanced aesthetician and the viewer as consumer or housewife, between art and advertising, Warhol violated sacred codes of aesthetics and then drove the revolt further by doing "portraits" of Marilyn Monroe and other celebrities as silkscreen replicas of common media photographs. Roy Lichtenstein continued the trend by basing his work on popular cartoon characters and exaggerated comic-strip adventures. On it went from there. And then came counterparts to IR's opening-up period: feminist, postcolonial, black, globalist, and non-Western artists and academics, each with a challenge to pose to an exclusionary history that had missed as much art as it had included. Art history professionals were so hamstrung by their principles that they could not readily fit these new types of art to older traditions. They could not tell us "what makes the difference between an artwork and something which is not an artwork if in fact they look exactly alike" (Danto 1997, 125).

Danto's answer is . . . nothing. Post-Warhol, there are fewer and fewer principles of art or, as he puts it, fewer "constraints on what a work of art has to look like. Works of art can look any way at all" (Danto 2002, 31). Abstract expressionism, minimalism, conceptualism, and installation take drawing out of the picture altogether. Modernism in architecture gives way to postmodern nostalgia and whimsy—a little of this and a little of that. At the moment, art can be someone's messed-up bed (Tracy Emin), a diamond-encrusted skull (Damien Hirst), cartoon heads drawn onto Goya etchings (the Chapman brothers), words running up poles (Jenny Holzer), recitations of flawed memory (Emma Kay), or sculptures of negative space (Rachel Whiteread). The 2003 British Turner Prize awarded to Grayson Perry shows that distinguished art today can even be pottery. All of this is art outside the art historical box—art where it's not supposed to be. It is staged by museums with new agendas, signaled by Tate Modern's disinclination to display artworks traditionally, by schools and eras, preferring thematic groupings showcasing color, form, and materials.

Danto claims that today's art is without aesthetic ambitions. We cannot see within it time-honored principles about art as a thing of beauty, good taste, significant form, or emotions of pleasure detached from the usual activities of our lives. As "art" bypasses the classic canvas for video, mixed-media photography, installation, performance, and computer-generated images, much of it comes out willfully abject, ugly, revolting, de-formed. Or it is incomplete until viewers finish it for the artist—by adding our handprints, gazing in the provided mirror, throwing something at the piece, or tearing something off it. Art making can be a "collectively authored process" (Jones 2003) of artist and viewer, which is different from the tradition of an art studio finishing a master's work. If the viewer's contribution to art is awkward or utterly pedestrian—because we may not have any feel for art making—then, Viva pedestrian art! That is art, too. So is "art" that appeals directly to particular and politicized identities of viewers, such as gender, race, age, nationality, ethnicity, and class, which violates older aesthetic norms demanding that art hold to universal standards. The end of art not only breaks down rigid categories of all kinds, it also lets art making "philosophize by visual means" (Danto 2003, 31), using unconventional materials like old newspapers, meat, used clothing, found snapshots of an average family, blood, rusted steel, rope, semen, paint on fabric, computer designs. It can come up with something grand or something trivial. Art after art is liberated.

Or is it? Jean Baudrillard (2005, 62–63) has labeled contemporary art banal, mediocre and worse: null—apparently with no raison d'être. He has accused the art world of colluding with society's worst tendencies, including rampant consumerism, crass politics, and even aspects of terrorism. By elevating value over form, contemporary art has lost the ability to be an illusion of the world. It has degenerated into celebrating (al)ready-mades, prosaic things arted up to look like art, as though Disney make-believe worlds could exercise artistic imagination. This is the overaestheticizing of culture: "images without imaginary" (Baudrillard 2005, 47)—too many images, too much ersatz art that goes anywhere and everywhere through globalization and the neoliberal market. Almost anyone can get into the game, even a man like himself, who is without art training or art aspirations. Being an artist equates with being a celebrity. The Baudrillard name is enough to get him an exhibition of photographs at legitimate art galleries. There is no one to say what he does is not art.[7]

The upshot of overaestheticization is that "art" today gets away with the trick of pretending to be art, like the terrorists of September 11, 2001, got away with pretending to be ordinary air travelers. We colluded in that pretense then and do so now, standing in line at the airport with our little plastic bag of personal items on momentary exhibition. We wait interminably to go through stepped-up security procedures that render us manhandled, exposed, shoeless, coatless, and nearly naked. Artistic/travel imagination is gone and rote is here. The result, claims the editor of Baudrillard's oeuvre, is that "the 'end of art,' so often trumpeted, never happened. It was replaced instead by unrestrained proliferation and cultural overproduction. Never has art been more successful than it is today—but is it art?" (Lotringer 2005, 18–19, emphasis in original).

Danto might see this attack on art specialists, who alone think they know who and what makes art, as part of the end of art. Baudrillard, though, sees art infiltrating all spaces, whether it makes sense to be where it is or not. As he puts it, "art does not die because there is no more art, it dies because there is too much" (Baudrillard 2005, 64). "Art" is everywhere, which means it is nowhere. Sometimes he agrees with Danto about the end of art as the end of art history's power to pronounce art, and sometimes he talks of the end of art itself and not just of the narratives about it. His positions can seem contradictory but are not quite; nullity is not about nothingness or worthlessness but about illustrating our nullifying world. Baudrillard can seem well in step with Danto when he says that "we should be able to have an awareness that things have reached a certain end, an end that does not mean everything is finished" (Baudrillard 2005, 59). Danto is exuberant about ungoverned possibilities of art, however, and Baudrillard is disgusted with the banal self-referentiality of the so-called art imagination.

Donald Kuspit (2004) is another naysayer. He takes Allen Kaprow's (1993) term "postart" and embellishes it into a time of willful destruction of high art and aesthetics. Art today is often shallow, he insists, because it has no important function any longer. "Art has been subtly poisoned by social appropriation, that is, the emphasis on its commercial value and its treatment as upscale entertainment, turning it into a species of social capital" (Kuspit 2004, 8). The viewer, the buyer, is in charge of art now, not the art historian, the artist, or "standards" of aesthetics. What that viewer wants is something of immediate value, like the news in today's newspaper. Never mind, says Kuspit, that the art is woman-hating, manners-hating, beauty-hating, and full of ressentiment and joylessness. One looks at Duchamp's *Fountain* (1917) and feels nothing, says Kuspit. That is the point: it is a urinal with all its banality, absent specialness. *Fountain* appeals, to the degree it does, to one's reason instead of the parts of the brain that engage the senses. Today, Duchampesque logics of art contra art reign. Tracy Emin, of the not-so-young-now Young British Artists, parades the mundane bed, the list of boyfriends, and artless dance steps twirled into a video. She is Duchamp's postmodern alter ego, taking the everyday and manipulating it into something meaningless that the chattering classes will nonetheless exclaim over and flock to see. Her "art" momentarily shocks the eye but never disturbs viewer sensibilities, lifestyles, or expectations. Rather, the message is that art is the prosaic and the artist herself is the thing of importance. The point is to be hollow and shallow, sleepwalking through the death drive, just like the society Baudrillard describes in the West.

Kuspit laments the end of art as the end of concerns with aesthetics in art. Art where it was expected, according to the art historical narrative and most art practice, once reflected aesthetic sensibility. From the perspective of an eighteenth-century ordering system, to be aesthetic meant that an object could inspire rapt attention from educated viewers. Later aesthetics took on connotations of spiritual investment in the truth and healing power of beauty (Abrams 1989, Shiner 2003). In a vast and contentious literature, art philosopher Cynthia Freeland (2001, 8) slices through to say, simply: "When you call a thing beautiful, you thereby assert that everyone ought to agree. Though the label is prompted by a subjective awareness or feeling of pleasure, it supposedly has objective application to the world." What is that awareness, that application, and who has it? Is it intersubjective (Hume 1757) or universal and constant (Kant 1790), engaged or disinterested, trained or natural, issuing from form and design or separate from these?

The most common aesthetic approaches of art history posit that art objects are separate from art making and best viewed through the lenses of schooled evaluators, who concern themselves only with the universal, formal qualities of the work (Bell 1969; Bullough 1969): experts guide us to appropriate art inter-subjectivities. Writers outside the field of art history see other influences at work. Sociologist Pierre Bourdieu (1984) has considered class influences on the content of "good taste." Gilles Deleuze (1994) asks whether the faculties of viewing required to attain aesthetic appreciation operate in tandem or at odds with one another. Walter Benjamin (1992) claimed there was an "aura" in Old Master artworks that was lost in the viewing histories of them; as we look, we all lose a certain critical awareness. To Baudrillard, Kaprow (1993,103), and Kuspit art has become anything you can get away with, and that is not the good news Danto touts, but rather bad news all around.

Although aesthetics is complex and insinuating, it is not the main concern here and is not treated systematically in the following pages. The issue at hand is art as international relations, in the sense of art as an institution loose from aesthetic and disciplinary foundations and carrying on in ways that violate narratives about materials, forms, innovations, progressions and pleasures. And it is not just art that turns aesthetics away. Some argue that the art museum is such an agenda-imposing thing in its own right that it is impossible to view art in a museum in anything approaching detached aesthetic contemplation (Carrier 2006). Art/museum rebellions against canons and aesthetic norms occur at the exact moment IR becomes a camp structure devoid of a disciplinary narrative. Kuspit (2004, 53) might call it IR's period of entropy, as he does in speaking of art today. We have become restless, easily bored, searching for new kicks along with new power sources and sensations, all of which quickly disillusion us. The two fields struggle to pinpoint the respective art or meaning in and among other types of objects, actors, artifacts, and concepts that each used to esteem. Standards have been blown away. Beauty and order are out the window. Aesthetic and diplomatic admirations have been taken to the laundry. Art history and art aficionados and museologists struggle to make sense of a range of phenomena that are not where and how experts and philosophers thought and ordained them to be. So do we.

THE END OF ART/MUSEUM?

Who gets to say what art is after art? We all do, says Baudrillard (2005, 80); with too much "art" around, "we're living in a giant museum." Traditional art historians and museum specialists would present the art museum as a more particularistic, structured entity: "Art is what is shown in museums. Art may also exist outside of museums, of course, but its status as such may be questioned in a way it never is inside a museum" (McClellan 2003a, xiii). With or without walls, museums command a space, have missions, and select their contents and management staffs. "Museums and galleries are where the great majority of people today experience art" (Arnold 2003, ix), and that is still the case at the end of art, however we characterize that period. Indeed, it has already been noted that art museums have proliferated during endist days and so have their audiences. Bustling interest in visual culture has led to a new subject area by that name, which compensates in theory and practice for art history's narrative end (Elkins 2003); and there is some disparagement of it as offering a thin substitute for art culture, nothing more than a commercial engulfing of art that turns museums into staging grounds for mass entertainment.

Paul Virilio (2003; 2007) takes the critical view of the art/museum, suggesting that art has been defeated by its own contemporary forms and its complicity in granting approval to art-unsettling social changes. One thing that has changed is the ambience of the museum. Art museums used to be quiet places where we went to see art. Now art noisily comes to us as audiovisual installations, media presentations, sound-and-light shows, and screeching scenes of abjection. The museum can be a banal, scatological place or, in the extreme, a place that resembles a death camp, an Auschwitz of charred, decapitated, wounded, sightless parts serenaded by eerie metallic sounds. It can seem to Virilio that Nazism, defeated in war, now reappears as art aping those horrors: the contemporary art museum as concentration camp (Virilio 2003, 28). Virilio does not think this trend is mere coincidence. His favorite target is the Australian body artist Stelarc, who mutilates his body through "medical operations" carried out against the backdrop of earsplitting sounds. Virilio sees Stelarc's "art" as a form of the end of art that is the end of humanity and the end of vision. It is terrorist death at the end of art, played out, mimicked, in the art/museum. Virilio thinks that all this is a shame as well as an outrage: "In a decidedly fin de siècle world, where the automobile questions its driver about the functioning of the handbrake or whether the seat belt is buckled, where the refrigerator is gearing itself up to place the order at the supermarket, where your computer greets you of a morning with a hearty 'hello,' surely we have to ask ourselves whether the silence of art can be sustained for much longer" (Virilio 2003, 76). This is an important question for Virilio. He argues that when the silence of art ends, we have art without pity and museums as sick-making places that assault our senses and leave us feeling battered—and wondering whether we liked that.

Pierre Bourdieu (1991, 112), by contrast, has been suspicious of the silence expected in an art museum. When he conducted a study of art and its publics in the 1960s, he named the imposition of silence as a norm used to set the world of art in opposition to the world of everyday life, along with "the untouchability of objects, the puritan asceticism of the amenities, always sparse and rather uncomfortable, the quasi-systematic absence of any information, the grandiose solemnity of décor and decorum" and so on. Larry Shiner (2003) might disagree, but possibly only about the sources of silence in the museum. He writes that it was only in the eighteenth century that the familiar categories of art versus craft developed, only then that haute art became entombed in museums instead of being part of church services, bourgeois homes, or government buildings. The rise of the international art market had much to do with this; in replacing patronage, it separated salable from usable art. A power system of gender relations also enabled the divide, for who were the usual western artisans if not women who sewed quilts in groups, did needlepoint pictures in the home, knitted sweaters, made rugs, and often threw pots? Similarly, it was the working class rather than the heroic or educated individual artist who made iron and leather works. When art was pulled apart from its noisy roots in functional life, says Shiner (2003, 7), we learned "the ideal of silent and reverential attention in . . . art museums."

And yet, early art museums could be very noisy places (McClellan 2003b). The London National Gallery was described by art connoisseurs in the mid-nineteenth century as overrun by ill-attired, smelly, and uncouth members of the public. The Whitehall Gallery, which started up in East London late that century, sought to attract and "uplift" residents of slums, who were presumed to know little about formal art or the decorum of the museum. The Victoria and Albert Museum in the West End of London concentrated on the industrial era, its founder, Henry Cole, hoping that "the largest masses of people may recreate themselves, even in the neighbourhood of London, with propriety and freedom from moral harm" (quoted McClellan 2003b, 10). And they did: over a million visitors clamorously entered the Victoria and Albert in 1870, up from a little less than half a million in 1857. Cole was one of the first to liken the popular appeal of new museums to the enthusiasms that old churches and cathedrals of Europe once generated. Of course, those early uplifting churches combined the spiritual with the bustle of commerce, as the pilgrimage businesses around the sale of food and mementos remind us. It is the same today except that, as Virilio asserts, spectators have been rendered mute in a world where, overall, "remaining silent now [is] a discreet form of assent" to noise (Virilio 2003, 69). It is assent to commerce, amusement, infotainment, theme parks, and virtual experiences of all kinds (e.g., Baudrillard 1982; Jameson 1991; Featherstone 1991). David Carrier (2006, 41) says that the modern public art museum is simply at an end, for its originating purpose—to "show the power of aggressive cultures to move precious objects great distances and organize their public display in grand buildings"—no longer stands as the raison d'être of the museum.[8]

What is being moved and displayed in museums today? Highbrow entertainment is less about showing off the king's treasures to an envious audience than about mixing media, as in offering the possibility of seeing a film before, after, or instead of seeing fine art (e.g., at New York's Museum of Modern Art [MOMA] or the Institute of Contemporary Arts [ICA], London), having interactive exhibits, and encouraging children to play at the museum. Little wonder that art museums are popular with middle-class audiences, who still want to be taught art appreciation but also seek a changing room for the toddlers they bring along—to give them an early start on culture. Museums know that contemporary visitors also like to shop for items that remind them of what they have consumed culturally; small Mexican tin skeletons dressed for the ball, which I bought at the Phoenix Art Museum years ago, lean against an oil painting in my own dining room. A seamless entity, the museum is a place of retail and a place of proclaimed art, a place austere and raucous, punctuated throughout, whether officially allowed or not, by piping cell phones. It is an eccentric space (Harbison 1977).

Of course, corporations have an acknowledged influence on art/museum trends, as do wealthy collectors—so much influence that critics accuse today's art/museums of dancing to the tune of business (Wu 2002). Those "tastemakers" (Millard 2002) rain on the art history enterprise by establishing idiosyncratic standards of good art collecting, which not only distort the art market but also shift public tastes; recall the Japanese mania for van Gogh and Charles Saatchi's single-handed boost for British contemporary art. By buying and displaying what they like in their own museums and corporate headquarters, businesses put pressure on major art museums to follow their lead. There are also private clubs in London that cater to "creative entrepreneurs" from the arts, media, and business, who might have gone their separate ways in earlier times but now network for mutual benefit. And increasingly the spectator is called upon to consider the art in what might not have been intended as art, or in proclaimed artworks that are unseemly or difficult to comprehend. Is that black bench in the gallery meant to be art or is it a place to sit down and view art— or both? And who says? With no guidelines in the end-of-art era, says Danto (2002, 31), "everyone is required to be a critic, and must learn to put together the thought embodied in the work."

True; but some art critics find Danto's optimism about the end of art misplaced. They argue that art is whatever corporations, gallery owners, and museum curators currently say it is , leaving artists tethered to or outside the critical and museum loops (Hickey 1997). Signaling the end of art might also divert attention from the ways that "art" outside the frame of art history gets into revised and reformed art histories, just as it gets into the museums. Art as narrative may end, but there is real staying power to the art system of ideals, practices, and institutions (Shiner 2003, 8), just as IR's staying power is in its departments, courses, and PhD training programs. Danto, for one, is not unaware of these arguments but rejoices in an era when art must be "dealt with on its own terms" (Danto 2002, 31). He feels unburdened of arcane terms and standards set by what Fred Orton and Griselda Pollock (1996, iv) have termed "the institutionally dominant art history," which has difficulty seeing beyond the Roman figure, Christopher Wren's architecture, or the cubist moment. A democratic forum rules with the end of art; for Danto, there is no other option.

Baudrillard wonders whether it is democracy we are experiencing in the art/museum world or something far more cynical, mercenary, and possibly stupid. Are museums simply supermarkets of culture that robotic visitors roam in search of something that just might keep their interest for more than thirty seconds? The Pompidou Center in Paris attracts upwards of thirty thousand people at a time. They move up and down the exterior escalators or gather outside in the square, agitated, distracted, and always seeking diversions that the art inside the museum does not seem to provide (Baudrillard 1982). His sense of that contemporary museum is that it is something on the order of a rock festival—Glastonbury every day, or Woodstock updated—where people assemble and move about for dayslong concerts in muddy, trampled fields. Baudrillard (2005) now thinks that the Beaubourg effect he referred to in the early 1980s—the mingling in, filling up, and emptying of the entire area around the Pompidou—is the sign of a certain violence of dense mass saturation, which can implode on itself.

Perhaps, though, there is no such thing as an undifferentiated mass that congregates at large art museums. Elites are still there: "the more successful a museum grows, the more elitist it tends to become" (Cotter 2007, H35)—as gauged by some increased admission charges (e.g., MOMA) and by exhibition strategies that still showcase conventionally defined genius, almost invariably male. No matter how much fun museums seem to be today, the fun presumes some knowledge of art, some familiarity with the need for the presence of so many security guards, and some sense of what one does in front of artworks. As Nick Prior (2003, 61) puts this: "What people bring to the museum in the way of 'cultural capital' is as important as 'supply side' issues." He does not want to paint "museums" and "publics" in monochrome. Some museums are run by enterprise culture managers, "whose sole purpose has been to bring museums into line with the 'for-profit' sector of the economy" (Prior 2003, 55). Others are traditional or virtual, multilocated geospatially, and/or specialized and catering to particular audiences within the public. For all the changes we have seen, art/museums "still on the whole, celebrate values worked up by nineteenth-century aesthetics, including ideas of genius, expression, and cultural transcendence; but to these they have added new approaches, technologies, and flamboyant modes of exhibition more suitable to a hypermodern era" (Prior 2003, 67). Avoiding an either/or position, Prior (2003, 52) offers the view that museums are double-coded institutions: they do cater more to noisy and restless audiences seeking one spectacle after another to consume; but they are able to pull people in by combining elements of traditional art and museum practice with "consumer populism, drawing on, whilst transforming, cultural modernity." That is to say, art/museums do not wait to pick up the latest media and consumer trends. They retain the power to guide and reassure people that what they see in the museum has been judged to be of quality.[9]

There are clear parallels here to the end of IR. A field and its institutions are overrun by events. Customs and rules and principles begin to lose ground to new practices and new explanations. Adaptations are tried, IR through its camp structure and art/museums through admixtures of old and new institutional practices and art philosophies. There is considerable feeling of one's way to new notions of what constitutes a work of art or proper frame of international relations, while old traditions continue to have considerable pull in practice, in the museums and in the policy circles surrounding presidents and prime ministers. Meanwhile, the art and the international relations can become uglier and uglier and the experts more and more contentious, even as the social institutions in which they work continue on flexibly, dynamically, and, for the moment, as though the crowds they attract will always be there and the problems will always be where we expect them to be rather than rudely interloping.

A RELATED END/BEGINNING

These endings join others. There is a sense in many academic fields that cherished, or at least traditional, ways of thinking and analyzing have been outrun by events, and outrun to such an extent that it is possible to speak of those fields too as being at an end of some sort. Along with the end of art and IR, we hear of the end of architecture (Noever 1993), the end of history (Fukuyama 1989), the end of nature (McKibben 2001), the end of science (Horgan 1997), the end of geography (Camilleri and Falk 1992), and the time after theory (Eagleton 2003). We also hear endism scorned as one of those mumbo jumbos that afflict our time; Francis Wheen (2004) calls it a fin de siècle delusion, and Steve Smith (2003, 8) lists it among the ten core features of IR theory that helped us get to September 11. As a final glimpse into the end, and to bring some comparative sense to our previous discussion, consider "after theory" trends in the humanities as captured in a special "town meeting" on theory that editors of the journal *Critical Inquiry* convened in 2003.

In April 2003, the University of Chicago–based journal *Critical Inquiry* called the board together for the first time in the journal's thirty-year history. W. J. T. Mitchell, the chief editor, wanted the journal's body of distinguished critical thinkers to evaluate the interdisciplinary criticism and theory that *Critical Inquiry* had showcased over the years. The part of the meeting that was open to the public attracted a standing-room-only crowd, with others outside watching closed-circuit TV alongside journalists from the *New York Times* and the *Boston Globe*. Mitchell remembers an atmosphere charged by events of international relations: the plunge of the United States into war in Iraq in the face of considerable local and international opposition, and the sense of perpetual emergency that had arisen around a seemingly boundary-less war on terror.

Several distinguished members of the board proceeded to suggest that academic critical theory was now dead or impotent. It was a strong sentiment to express at a time when critical social theory often presented itself with a capital T and came laden with Continental stars and "difficult" terminologies: the harder to understand, the better it was often thought to be. Stanley Fish declared to the assembled: "I wish to deny the relative effectiveness of intellectual work and especially to advise people against going into the academy if they hope to be effective beyond it. . . . If you want to do that, you should in fact *be* beyond it" (Mitchell 2004, 327, emphasis in original). Henry Louis Gates said he had missed the part of the theory revolution that had supposedly liberated the colonial subject. Sander Gilman declared that "for the last 4000 years intellectuals have not only been wrong almost all of the time, but they have been wrong in corrosive and destructive ways" (Mitchell 2004, 327–28). Harry Harootunian (2004, 399) described theory today as "simply jumbled like numbered balls bouncing around in a circulating chamber before they are spit out in random but winning combinations in the great game of academic Lotto, while history of the present and past, here and there, is reduced to mere rumor." Like his colleagues, Harootunian was exercised by the seemingly non-existent relationship that filled the spaces where theory and political and social worlds informed one another.

Clearly, as Mitchell (2004, 328) put it, the tone of pessimistic endism reflected a time of "profound political anxiety. And insofar as criticism and theory in our time have been closely associated with progressive political thought and action, this meant that the *CI* [*Critical Inquiry*] symposium was meeting in a moment of crisis for its own mission, understood as an intellectual, interdisciplinary microcosm of a global crisis." Mitchell (2004, 332) asked his colleagues to consider the merits of working now with "medium theory." By medium he meant theorizing that is neither high nor low but can focus on the various mediums by which we come to know our troubled time: cinema, TV, the mass media, communities of the Net—all those things that make up (or could be seen as making up) "a middling compromise, a middle-class meliorism, a bourgeois bromide" (Mitchell 2004, 334). Nothing too radical in what Mitchell is saying, more of "a principled resistance to ideological clichés" (Mitchell 2004, 335).

The argument most directly relevant to art and international relations at the end of IR came from the historian Mary Poovey (2004, 431). Not happy to stand in a theory void, she asked the group to consider conjoining humanist and social science approaches into a study of interactions among social collectives, individuals, and institutions. A project of that nature would make demands on all participants, revitalize all our fields, and change views of evidence and power. Poovey's research intentions resonate with some of ours:

> If we could study such institutions [as government or religion] in a way that would enable us to describe the active roles they play in subject-formation, geopolitical relations, and imaginative productivity, then we might be able to begin developing new theories about abstractions like nationalism or globalization. This might enable us to understand the sense in which literature and painting can be understood as social institutions that work alongside (but sometimes counter to) other social institutions.

Perhaps now that IR has shattered into the light of many campfires, we can step back and look at the many kinds of possibilities that Poovey urges on us, having to do with social processes of art and government bureaucracies. We can contemplate a field that includes art/museums, schools of art and architecture, and international coalitions that shift, save, conserve, store, and sell art internationally. If Poovey is right, then rather than generating another new camp, connecting these dots could construct any number of afterlives of art/museums / international relations/IR. IR has been a social science discipline, and the social sciences have sharply demarcated themselves from the study of drama, literature, music, and the plastic arts. Other divisions of the university are meant to specialize in those areas while IR explores war and peace, trade and finance, development aid and humanitarian intervention. This is not to say that IR scholars are unmindful of art; there is a small art and politics camp, after all. Moreover, art as hobby can mix well with IR as profession, with some practitioners drawn to naval seascapes, Renaissance depictions of the great trading city-state of Venice, or the many artifacts that have found their way from the colonies to western museums. To say IR does not generally do art would never mean that those within IR scorn art or refuse to publish pieces on it. Indeed, some around the field already know the value of the arts of international relations, having sighted these partners in some museums (Luke 2002c; Sylvester 2002b, 2006b; Lisle 2007), running through novels and poetry (e.g., special issues of *Millennium* 2001, and *Alternatives* 2000; Sylvester 2006a, 2004), speaking lines in ancient and contemporary plays (Jabri 2003; Odysseos 2001; Chan 2003; Frost 2003), and taking up considerable space in (auto)biographies of a factual or fictional sort (e.g., Inayatullah 2003; Sylvester 2002a; Solway 2003; McCann 2003). There have even been special issues of two IR journals dedicated to aspects of visual art and IR topics (*Millennium* 2006, *Alternatives* 2006).

And, of course, no matter which camp one follows in the field, art is in the air whenever we speak of the art of politics, the art of diplomacy, the art of war, and the art of peace. Such references are expressive throw-ins designed to dress up dull sentences. Nevertheless, the fact that IR writes "art" in at all suggests that it is more than a decorative feature of our work. Art is what we appeal to when we cannot satisfactorily explain international relations using the field's—and now the camps'—concepts and methods. Art is the space we cannot put our fingers on, cannot quite grasp, and cannot really see: it is the missing bit in the explanation. Art anchors a worry about elusive meaning. It signals to the reader that some things pass by all of us. It is a code word for unquantifiable, immeasurable, and unclear dimensions of an international relations beyond reach. Art is the space before and after and always somewhat eluding language, as Gadamer (1999) might put it. Even as we have learned over the years to note the voices of women and disadvantaged or war-affected people and to take on board languages and philosophies that help us read and analyze texts better, we have neglected to link international relations with art institutions. We do not see the Guggenheim as a key nongovernmental organization of our time. We do not see the Parthenon sculptures as a story that traces paths of international relations from Thucydides' time to the Napoleonic era of the state system to today's international relations of national identity. If we were to trace the journey of Jackson Pollock's iconic painting *Blue Poles* from a Long Island barn to the National Gallery of Australia, we could slice into the cold war in new ways; but the field camps are not likely to be intercamp enough to see this. Looking at the looting of art across Iraq in the wake of the 2003 invasion reveals culture being militarized in and around a war on terror: we see an outside (art) come inside international relations (tanks guarding museums) right before our eyes. But we do not know where to put this picture within IR.

Steve Smith might know. He incorporated paintings into his where-it's-not-expected-to-be presidential address to the International Studies Association in 2003. Drawing first on the Belgian surrealist painter René Magritte, who also intrigued Michel Foucault (1983), Smith considered how we in IR draw conclusions about what we (think we) see. Magritte presents us with a naturalistic looking pipe. Above the pipe, he writes the words "Ceci n'est pas une pipe." Although we should be aware that we are not looking at a real pipe, rather at a composition in oils of something that reminds us of a pipe, Magritte's bold surrealist trope demands that the viewer focus directly on the representational issue. His painting invites viewers to think about what we take to be real and whether it is real or a version of the real, with other versions possible. Central to the surrealist mission (Sylvester 1999a), this type of problematic reminds us in IR that the world we believe we know and understand might not be quite as it appears.

Diego Velazquez's famous painting *Las Meninas* also intrigues Smith, again as Foucault (1966) before him, for its play on viewing the inside and the outside of a problematic. It initially appears that Velazquez painted the daughter and entourage of Philip IV of Spain (including the painter himself) enjoying a private moment. The king and his wife appear in the mirror in the background of the painting, giving the impression that the assembled look up at the royal couple as they enter the room. On close examination, the figures in the mirror seem to be positioned more to reflect a picture the artist is in the process of painting than the entrants to the room. If that is the case, there is another viewer arriving, a viewer the family sees but those of us beyond the frame cannot make out. Is that viewer where he or she is expected to be or not? It is not easy to say. Does that viewer "cause" the scene to appear as it does, with everyone looking up and out at him or her? By focusing attention on this mystery viewer, does the artist steal the moment from the king and queen in the mirror, or are they really the ones who are attracting the attention? It is not easy to say. The composition looks at us and we look at it with no certainty about who the real viewers and the real subjects are. The point exactly: what one (thinks one) sees determines what one takes as reality. This is a position associated with feminist-standpoint thinking in IR (e.g., Enloe 1989; Tickner 1992), but even there the references to artworks or optical puzzles are scarce.

I want to take the fascinating emergent discussions of art and politics further here, incorporating concerns with representation that animate much of what has already been done at the intersection of the social sciences and art into direct studies of art/museums as instances and enactments of international relations. This fugitive set of relationships can complicate narratives of power, nationalism, competition, war, peace, trade, and terrorism, casting something we have looked at many times, such as the cold war or globalization, in a different light that throws a different range of shadows. IR might be at an end now, but its aftermath or afterlife is surely in the making. Think of "after" in two senses, suggests Jacques Derrida (2003, 9): "'after' as in coming after, or 'post'; and 'after' in the sense of 'according to'—*d'après* . . . following without following." We have seen the field move "after" as in "post" its narrower vision of the past through numerous recent additions of peoples and topics. Now there is need to go d'après, as in turning toward a variety of newly included knowledges while keeping an eye on what lies beyond the camp structure. D'après follows skeptically rather than in the manner of disciples. After the end, there is the possibility of art and its institutions taking places among the many commodities, diplomatic maneuverings, wars, and technologies we study, yet going beyond them. Put a bit differently, at the end of IR, art/museums are "after" subjects of the field that could become important contributors to a robust but flexible "according to."

COLLAGING ART/MUSEUMS/IR

IR and art/museums: parallel and fascinating fields of activity grappling with disciplinary changes and with various challenges of international relations. One way to think about their intersections is in terms of the art-making technique or methodology of collage. Collage revels in difference, in the sense of putting seeming incoherences or incommensurabilities together in ways that illuminate hidden meaningful connections. I like Max Ernst's description of collage as "the meeting of two distant realities on a plane foreign to them both" (Danto 1997, 21). Think of works by Braque or Picasso, where painted violins occupy space on boards filled with real newspaper pages, onto which packages of cigarettes have been pasted. Imagine cloth affixed to cement, pornography engraved onto household pottery, or an *haute* Guggenheim museum sited in *bas* lowbrow Las Vegas. Gaze at a tank affixed to the steps of the National Museum of Iraq in 2003. Think of the National Gallery of Australia purchasing *Blue Poles* at the exact moment Australia breaks with the U.S. mission in Vietnam and brings its troops home, the last ally to do so. Consider art/museum as one engine regenerating the international relations of Bilbao. Picture Ground Zero as a museum of early-twenty-first-century international relations. The juxtapositions might seem too odd to imagine until we see them on a plane, in a context, that itself seems odd. Then they can "make sense" in wholly new ways.

A collage reworks and remakes a reality. It is not a fantasy about remaking reality but the actuality of remaking "it" visually, materially, and concretely. Collage has us cutting up and rearranging familiar images in jolting and shocking ways, in ways that exhibit a sense that nothing is quite where we expect it to be. It is exactly that quality of the unexpected that can help a viewer see and experience the shrouded relationships and connections that we often overlook or fail to see, such as the child pornography painted onto graceful Italianate vases by Grayson Perry; from a distance, the vases look lovely, upper-class, elegant, but viewed at closer range, the unsettling juxtaposition suggests what can go on in the underbelly of ever-so-polite social circles. Collage mixes things up, launches objects out of assigned places and into spots we least expect them to be but where they nonetheless work to provide insight into our often unimaginative imaginations. Collage also refuses to present a coherent story line of itself and can resist smoothing the edges between oddly juxtaposed pieces. The viewer must make all the connections, theorize the transitions, and do the reinterpretations. We must remake reality with and beyond the artist.

Each camp of IR thinks it knows where and how to look for international relations. Inured to the bizarre and unexpected, as though there could not be any plane foreign to us any longer, we can juxtapose weapons of mass destruction and suicide bombers, airplanes and skyscrapers, war and humanitarianism, obesity and starvation. Yet we still get caught looking the wrong way or not looking penetratingly at the international relations that faces us. Timothy Luke (2002, xxiv), writing on American exhibitions, says that we lack the appropriate "style of interpretive criticism." To understand odd pairings turning up where they are decidedly not expected requires visual acuity, impossible narratives of connection, and sightings of power and institutions off piste. It requires thinking "collage," and little in a collage is where rationality says it should be. It helps to know this.

Like Danto, I see in IR today opportunities to probe relations international instead of constantly being pulled "back" to a small set of established basics. I share the concern of *Critical Inquiry* to foreground the issues we might be losing sight of as our middle-class scholarly existence becomes ever more the flip side of someone else's impoverishment: we would not want to subordinate life and death, war and peace, and trade and development to studies of colors and styles. That Mary Poovey can see the potential in investigative exercises that link the arts and humanities with the social sciences is good news. Perhaps it is also the best story line to pursue after the various ends we have noted.

WHERE THE BOOK GOES

On then to our "living artistic options" (Danto 1997, 5) for redoing IR at the end as art. I hold the curator's egg (Schubert 2000); but having only the space of a smallish gallery to show the bounty of art/museums and international relations, choices must be made. I focus mostly on major fine arts museums and galleries rather than bring in all the arts and their institutions, although I do make reference here and there to literature and drama. At one level this is a simple matter of preference and manageability. At another level it is a choice to exclude much of the popular arts (film, cartoons, video games, TV, etc.) that are important to cultural/visual studies and to some camps of IR, as well as to W. J. T. Mitchell of *Critical Inquiry*. Popular arts are of and for "the people," and I have certainly not shied away in the past from driving some light into the "people corner" of IR. I want to make the point here, though, that we need not move away from the kind of art that has sustained states and wars and international theft in order to do something radical to old IR. Because the art museum is often historically implicated with royalty and statecraft, it makes some sense to face fine arts of international relations, knowing, of course, that art/museum debates can come up undecided.

I select works and institutions that illustrate a variety of ways that art/museums and international relations exist in parallel and intersecting universes. The guiding image before my eyes is the one mentioned earlier in the chapter: troops watching out for the real international relations in Iraq and ignoring, or being told to ignore, the museum across the street—until an international uproar occurs over looted treasures. Having seen that particular museum shadow international relations where it is expected to be, to the point where it knocks on the war core of IR (Sylvester 2005), I concentrate on particular cases of art both *within* and *of* the art museum as instances of international relations. Western art museums get most of the attention here. This choice reflects a certain chronological development of formal, institutionalized museums, which I find useful for IR to consider. It also reflects my locations in the world when this book was being researched and written: in London at the invitation of the University of London's School of Oriental and African Studies, in The Hague at the Institute of Social Studies, and in the Cumbrian Lake District of Britain, where I now live. These personal locations, although more conducive to certain research foci and less conducive to others, do not mean that all the best or most important art museums in the world are in the West. There is frequent mention throughout of challenges to western museums raised by critics and institutions located elsewhere, an interest I hope to pursue in a subsequent volume. The emphasis here, however, is principally on the British Museum, the National Gallery (London), the National Museum of Iraq, the Museum of Modern Art (New York), the Getty, the Guggenheim Bilbao, and the museum of international relations in the making at the World Trade Center site in New York City.

The British Museum starts us going in chapter 2. A determined early "collector" of what we now think of as third-world art and archaeology, it has been a player in international relations since at least the Napoleonic era. Controversies over "saving" the Parthenon sculptures by transporting them to, and showing them in, London provide entrée to an examination of the politics of a nation-building institution of the European colonial period that struggles today to keep its sometimes ill-gotten collection from apology and restitution. It says it is "saving art for the world," a challenging claim to make in today's climate of exquisite identity politics.

Chapter 3 continues and extends that discussion by considering two rescue-and-save operations in the museum world of the moment, one at the National Gallery, London and the other at the National Museum of Iraq. Flying the banner of saving art for the nation, the National Gallery put up a strong effort in 2003 to keep a small Renaissance painting by Raphael that was being sold by its rightful owner to the Getty Center in Los Angeles. Who the National Gallery was saving the painting for is the issue here, as is the competitive international environment that frames its struggle. We then travel halfway across the world to consider herculean efforts to save Iraq's art and artifacts from loss and destruction in a war of international relations. Saving art in that context involves an armada of western museum staff and armed culture troops waging a war for art within the war for Iraq. Yet the question remains: saving what for whom and from whom?

In chapter 4, we shift to museums of modern and contemporary art and focus on the progenitor of them all, the Museum of Modern Art in New York. Revisiting the modernist period and its predilections, we then dig into an art historical controversy about MOMA's alleged role in the cultural international relations of the Second World War and subsequent cold war. Considered in the discussion are a number of exhibitions MOMA mounted during that period, including the famous Family of Man photographic exhibition of the 1950s and its shows of American art abroad, organized, some insist, to establish abstract expressionism as the symbol of the free world. An extraordinary time in the museum's history and in international relations has been undergoing reinterpretation by art/museum scholars who, in their way, engage with the international relations of the time.

In chapter 5, the Guggenheim comes into its glory years as the neoliberal globalist with ambitions as big as its director's ego, or so the usual story goes. Our concern is with the ways art/museum–based narratives about the Guggenheim often simplify its role in international relations in the interest of denouncing a particular museological approach. When we consider the crown of Guggenheim's overseas empire, Guggenheim Bilbao, from Basque rather than art-world perspectives, a different international relations of development and regeneration emerges, putting superpower Guggenheim in a revealing and more positive light.

The museum cases close in chapter 6 around the absent twin towers. Massive architectures leave one foot in the cold war and reach forward to footprint Ground Zero as a museumifying space. In an architectural absence there is mostly politics—of landlords, architects, and survivor groups with purposes and designs broader and narrower than any World Trade Center. Located on the terrain of old-world and new-world colonial histories, modern business, urban redevelopment, and struggles between titans of finance and art, this spatial project is the direct result of an unexpected event that occurred on September 11, 2001. One might say that Ground Zero in its entirety—more than its sixteen acres—is a new museum of early twenty-first century international relations.

Chapter 7, the final chapter, considers the power of art/museums and the art of international relations. Collage comes into sharper focus in this chapter as a methodology for putting together art/museums/international relations in ways that can make new sense of all the elements without staging an amalgamation. Several artworks help us with this demanding task by presenting imagined and real collages that juxtapose pieces of a picture without overdetermining the connections. It is too early to decide whether fragments and juxtapositions build into something like theory. Suffice it to make the case that art/museums are international institutions that IR will want to enter more often if its aficionados seek pertinent afterlives beyond the camp structure of the field. Similarly, the art and museum world will hopefully wish to enter into conversation with the field of international relations in order to be truly worldly actors. IR or art? Both.

CHAPTER 2

Cultures, Nations, and the British Museum

I am standing before the Reading Room desk at the British Museum. Uncertain of the protocol, I approach the woman there and inquire about procedures for using the room and the museum's archives. She whispers that the newly opened Reading Room, which had been the seat of the British Library, is now a public space. Anyone can use the books lining the walls, although the materials cannot be taken out of the room. Somewhat distractedly she asks, "What archives do you have in mind?"

"I'm looking into the issues surrounding the Elgin/Parthenon sculptures for a book on art and international politics. I'd like to see museum archives that contain documents, debates and museum position papers, if that's possible."

"Are you from Greece?"

"Umm, no."

"Have you been to Greece, then?" She doesn't raise her head from the computer in front of her.

"Excuse me?"

"This is a difficult area for the museum right now. Everyone's making a fuss about something that doesn't warrant it."

"I'm interested in international politics surrounding the sculptures and not about making a fuss."

"There are far more important objects in this museum, you know," she answers sternly. "Have you been to the map room? There are hundreds of maps from all over the world. People should be looking at where those maps came from."

"Maps. Okay. Right. I'm not looking at maps just now, though. Is there an archive here on the sculptures, or should I inquire elsewhere?"

"You can look on the shelves over there, the 733.3 series. You won't find much, though. This is difficult, as I said. I'll give you a recent statement from the director of the museum. That's the best we can do."

While she copies the statement, I peruse the indicated shelf and find a few dog-eared copies of the most easily accessible books on the topic.

"There you go, now," she says briskly, and hands me the statement.

Dated 11 November 2002, the document header screams, "'The British Museum is the best possible place for the sculptures from Parthenon in its collections to be on display,' says Neil MacGregor, Director." I read this headline several times. Is it that the British Museum is the best place for the sculptures to be when they are on display, or as part of its other collections, or when the museum decides to display them, or what? The rest of the short text has a crystalline clarity that the header lacks: the British Museum claims unqualified entitlement to the sculptures. Among the reasons cited: they fit properly with a collection that has global range and a mission to cover millennia of human history; the Parthenon is damaged and its restoration is an unachievable goal; half the sculptures are in Athens already; the sculptures are in the core collection of the British Museum and cannot be lent; entrance to the British Museum is free and five million visitors come yearly. The most imperial of the claims is this one: "Only here can the worldwide significance of the Parthenon sculptures be fully grasped." This is an international art relations of considerable audacity.

THE BRITISH MUSEUM

My experience in the Reading Room of the British Museum turns out to have a long historical pedigree. The museum was founded in 1753 and is considered the oldest independent museum in the world, but not the first public museum (an honor that goes to the Louvre). Comprised at that time primarily of reference books and archives plus some objets d'art, the British Museum was, in fact, a difficult place for the British to visit. Only "gentlemen" could access it until the nineteenth century, and even for them, gaining admission was a serious business of applying and waiting out a process that, in the words of one writer, "was governed by the rules of court protocol and aristocratic etiquette" (Schubert 2000, 17). As with my experience in late 2003, a visitor allowed entry to the British Museum in its first century could only move about within it in tow to a staff member. There was always drama attached to a visit, with staff sometimes pulling viewers away from an object just as they showed interest in it. A contemporary brochure put out by the British Museum tells us the museum "is free and open not only to scholars, but also to the 'curious' amongst you." Unless one wants to look at certain archives, it seems.[1]

The British Museum was less dramatically royalist in the first half of the nineteenth century, though, than its large French counterpart. To begin with, the museum building was not a former royal palace, as was common on the Continent, nor were its first collections bequeathed from royal or ecclesiastic patrons. The initial endowment of books and some art came from gentlemen scholars. Then, while other museums of the time were exhibiting mostly Old Masters (Haskell 2000, 8), the British Museum became keen on showing the range of scientific and naturalist interests associated with the Enlightenment. Along with its books, it tended over the early years to display stuffed birds, shells and fossils, ancient hieroglyphs and medals, navigational instruments, religious artifacts, and trophies of trade and discovery in the Americas, the antipodes, Africa—specimens all, each carefully classified in that characteristically Enlightenment way of ordering the world. It was a jumble of objects of all sorts until the 1880s, when the natural history components of the museum were relocated. Henry Cole founded the South Kensington Museum (now the Victoria and Albert), primarily because he found the British Museum too exclusive and decidedly unfriendly to families (Flanders 2006). Even though art and artifact were then separated from science, MacGregor (2004a, 22) suggests that the British Museum carried on with its distinctly British "empirical path to knowledge, about learning through looking." This, he asserts, stands in contrast to the French approach to knowledge at that time: "The British Museum is often contrasted with Diderot's Encyclopedia. Where the conceptual French characteristically wrote a book, the empirical British collected things and put up a building. Surely the key difference is that Diderot was put in prison and the Encyclopedia banned, whereas the British Museum was created by parliament specifically to promote intellectual inquiry, and to encourage the discovery of new kinds of truth" (MacGregor 2004b, 5).

"Discovery of new kinds of truths" can come about in a variety of ways. In the middle years of the British Museum, much discovery would arrive via international relations of imperialist acquisition. Initially, the Louvre was the museum stocked with items won on the battlefield and the British Museum was mostly full of bequeathals. When Britain joined the continental contest for national greatness through possessions and trade, arts and artifacts played a role. The European nation that could claim the largest and best collection of pieces from the classical world would possibly be the rightful heir of ancient power and empire. Archaeological competition in the European balance of power could be as fierce as competition in munitions and trade. The Rosetta stone, for instance, was first in French hands and then relinquished to the British after Napoleon's defeat. Upon learning that Greek sculptures were en route to the British Museum, the French tried to intercept them at sea. There was also a rush on all sides to take the treasures of Sumerian palaces before rivals could (Russell 1997). International competition helped forge a link between nation building and art/museums.

The Cultured Nation

Nation building is central to IR studies of historical state power. It generates a literature as vast and plentiful as ripe apples on an autumn tree. Any major review of that literature would take us too far from the art/museums / international relations ensemble that is our focus. A shortcut that makes sense focuses only on the relatively few sources that do connect these themes to the endeavoring nation.

We can begin with Benedict Anderson's (1991) well-known point that nations are built on imaginary, though not false, bonds of identity and solidarity, which cement diverse social groups into large collectivities. The ideal nation combines well with apparatuses of governance over a territory. That is to say, the ideal nation is a nation-state. States can exist in the absence of properly imagined national identity and solidarity—much of Africa has been in that situation—and nations can exist in the absence of internationally recognized statehood—Palestine, Israel before 1948, Chechnya today. Anderson posits that European nation building was promoted by the invention of bookmaking. Replacing book copying with bookmaking enabled much of Europe to break gradually with a sovereign Catholic Church that conducted its international relations in the language of elites and ecclesiastics, Latin. Bookmaking enabled cultures of secularity to grow, accumulate sources about their histories, and communicate these through a print medium that was vernacular and cheap and therefore accessible. In his view, nation building was likely as more and more people in a given territory could read and identify each other with the stories they read. Literacy was the "magic bullet" of nation building.

Anthony Smith (1999, 50) questions the link between print materials and the building of nations, because he thinks of bookmaking and book reading as elite activities through much of their history. Why, he asks, would "so many people (the 'masses') . . . be impressed by, let alone ardently identify with, the literary musings of an intelligentsia?" Is it not more likely that interaction between print innovations and other products of capitalist industrialization—technology, transport, urbanization, factory work, and leisure time—forged the new collectivities we think of as modern nations? Most of those processes would be concrete and visible on a daily basis, bringing ordinary people together through material and visual means as well as through language. Before the Industrial Revolution, for instance, Britain was composed of three distinct nations tethered by historical acts of union and often undone on the ground by acts of devolution and fierce regionalism.[2] The Industrial Revolution, and its accompanying markets for mass production, made the nation and many of its cities. Manchester, where it all began, still offers an architectural record of fortunes, misfortunes, and identities forged out of an international economics of cotton. Its warehouses and factory assembly lines were reached by the tramlines that also forged and linked neighborhoods into wider communities. Grim communities they were, to be sure, as the early paintings of Manchester's L. S. Lowry unfailingly portray.

It was not only work and material consumption that provided average people with common reference points about their time and their identity. Victorian leisure venues, such as fairs, exhibitions, and museums, did so too. Starting with the Great International Exposition at London's Crystal Palace in 1851, a tide of exhibitions swept New York, Paris, and numerous smaller cities across the United States. Curtis Hinsley (1991, 344) calls these "carnivals of the industrial age, communal activities undergirded and directed by corporate boards and interests of state." Their point in Britain was to show the superior nature of manufactured goods, most using raw material from the colonies, as against craft products. French expositions were differently pitched to display archaeological artifacts from the country's overseas territories. The two types of themes conjoined in the Franco-British Exhibition of 1908 held in London. Annie Coombes (1994, 187) describes the "painstaking elaboration of a series of 'differences,'" rather than the collectivities that Smith proposed, which were exhibited to show, according to the exhibition guide, that "natural fitness underlies the Entente Cordiale: the highest results are obtained when leading racial characteristics and prominent industries are not opposed . . . when Anglo-Saxon energy blends with French savoir faire, when British empiricism is ordered by French method, when British solidity is adorned by French grace, a combination is reached which embraces the highest achievements of the human race" (Franco-British Exhibition Guide 1908, 2). The assignment of low and high place meant that although art commentators could see the artistic skill shown in the Benin bronzes, they could also go on to declaim the "cannibalism and other unpleasant habits" of the society that produced them (*Daily Mail* 1908, 18). The exhibition paraded differentiation and hierarchy, a nation-building syndrome that has changed its spots over time but not its message.

Ernest Gellner's (1983, 57) ideas on nation building shift us from the popular culture of exhibitions to the high culture of art/museums. He maintains that the key to building a nation lies in imposing "a high culture on society, where previously low cultures had taken up the lives of the majority, and in some cases the totality, of the population." In his view, it was mass education in particular that made people aware of who they were and who they wanted to be, by narrating a common history, culture, and set of civic obligations. Museums complemented the educational process by showing and interpreting tangible objects as "our" history, "our" arts, "our" crafts, "our" scientific discoveries, "our" books, and so on. Going along with this, Jessica Evans (1999a, 2) remarks that "nations have to be imagined in a particular and selective style, which . . . achieves tangible and symbolic form in the traditions, museums, monuments and ceremonies in which it is constructed." Tate Britain offers a good example of how such a tradition of national education through museums works. Walk into designated rooms and see numerous patriotic paintings by the iconic artist of atmosphere and battles, J. M. W. Turner: British navy ships pound the French, dipping perilously in storms, or retire gracefully from service (Sylvester 2001). Return in the autumn months and see works by contemporary British artists short-listed for the prestigious national award called the Turner Prize. A nineteenth-century artist continues to educate ordinary people to recognize things British and to claim an identity stake in creations and prizes they had no hand in effecting then or now.

We should take care not to equate contemporary understandings of nation building, which emphasize creating citizenship or a people, with orientations of late eighteenth- and early nineteenth-century Europe. Carol Duncan (1999, 322) tells us that it was common then to think of the "nation" as constituting only certain parts of the larger society. There was a "nation" of gentlemen from the landed aristocracy that museums catered to until at least the mid-1820s. The British elite, in particular, associated "the people" with a dangerous "French" threat to privilege. Lower classes were expected to be patriotic but not nationalist in sentiment. They were certainly not expected to be cultured. Culture was for the nation not the people. It was only when Benthamite reformers insisted that the "nation" had to refer to broad segments of society, and museums should be institutions that helped form the nation, that art/museums became accessible. Before that, the great majority of us would be thought cheeky for requesting information at the British Museum on the Parthenon acquisition.

Parenthetically, there is still something of that elite-public tension in the air at the British Museum. In celebration of 250 years of existence, the museum decided to display a range of objects from the Enlightenment period (roughly 1620–1750) that shaped it. These have been placed in the recently renovated King's Library, which was originally built in 1828 to house the seventy-thousand-volume library of King George III. Off the Great Court, the gentlemen's nation now mingles with contemporary museum audiences to see the new permanent exhibit, Enlightenment: Discovering the World in the Eighteenth Century. Leaving aside the boastful terms "discovering" and "world," the exhibit provides insights into eighteenth-century priorities and predilections for labeling and categorizing everything in nature and in arts, from owls to Chinese porcelain—the latter because Enlightenment thinkers tended to be cosmopolites, who did not believe that "nations and local cultures have value to their members over and above a universal community of citizens" (Gillman 2006, 34). Many museum directors, MacGregor among them, continue the Enlightenment tradition of cosmopolitanism.

The various views of nation building surveyed here portray a sense of intentionality and unity of knowledge and power that undoubtedly overstates the nation-building process. Art/museums, like the earlier exhibitions, provide ways for elites to impose culture and identity on masses, but that is not the only process at work. Museums have a place in the larger nation-building processes of Foucauldian governmentality. That is to say, they interact with the myriad other economic and cultural institutions that regulate and shape "forms of conduct amongst the broader population" (Evans 1999b, 365). Museums instruct, edify, guide, impose, and differentiate peoples through visual means rather than through statutes, laws, classrooms, or sacred texts. Displaying objects, as well as knowledge about their value and origins, helps people to see what their society has accumulated and come to claim as its heritage. The items they see might be local or not; that does not matter. Indeed, one stream of museum-skeptical thinking has it that art dies once it leaves whatever its context has been and enters a museum—any museum (see Carrier 2006). What matters for nation building is that there are reference points that people can begin to identify, talk about, and return to see over and over, knowing that others like themselves are exposed to these, too.[3]

The Nation Is Let In

The British Museum bourgeoisified considerably in the mid-nineteenth century, finally taking on a governmentality role as civic educator of the masses in the manner Gellner suggests. And here the technological innovation that Anderson claimed was key to nation building did aid that mission. In the 1830s and 1840s, a spate of cheap papers in common circulation pictured, described, and informally labeled many of Britain's historical institutions as "national monuments," the British Museum among them. Parliament saw the papers and seized the opportunity to imagine a more open and prideful approach to important national institutions. Public education was to nurture "laudable curiosity in the hitherto misinformed mind, as well as a greater respect for works of art and antiquity" (quoted in Altick 1999, 244). Heretofore, enlightenment was reserved for people like William Hazlitt, who described his visit to the new National Gallery in 1824 as "a cure (for the time at least) for low-thoughted cares and uneasy passions. . . . Here is the mind's true home" (quoted in Duncan 1995, 15). Many of those who worried about "low-thoughted cares and uneasy passions" in the working classes urged Parliament to move quickly to enable the many to enter and enjoy the uplifting monuments of Great Britain.

But there were some stumbling blocks at the doors. Britain did not stand up well in the arts institutions when compared to continental Europe, particularly to France, Italy, and Germany. To open up its museums entirely would be to broadcast their deficiencies as well as their strengths. Moreover, British monuments tended to be in a filthy state. As late as the 1840s, the walls of St. Paul's were defaced by scribbles, often vulgarities, and the interior was strewn with rubbish. Statuary and stones had disappeared from Westminster Abbey. The British Museum was better maintained, but it was cluttered with objects and stacked with poorly archived papers and books. Before any art institution could open to the public, it had to be scrubbed and put in order. Seventy years after it was established, and following a strenuous cleanup, the British Museum invited the general public inside—but only on holidays. On "the first Easter Monday under the new policy of 1837, 23,000 persons jammed the building" (Altick 1999, 247). The museum's popularity was both instant and troubling to aristocrats, who feared "the crowd" could become unruly and nationalist.

Once visitors were inside the British Museum, the most spectacular pieces to see were from ancient empires of the Middle East, Greece, and Rome. Mac-Gregor (2004b, 5) has said that having "objects from many different places provides visual 'proof' that other societies exist, have equally impressive ways of showing identity, and have important ways of contradicting our own myths of superiority." But his assertion opens up postcolonial counterassertions about the international relations of these and other acquisitions. Victor nations grab art as war booty and colonials take souvenirs as a right and entitlement. Travelers pocket what they can while making their "heroic" way through dangerous and exotic places. Scientists claiming special knowledge of ancient cultures relocate bits of those cultures for their own study. Once the British Museum itself embarked on overseas excavations and removals, it would be hard-pressed to deny its stake in an imperial game. An institution that sets about to "represent both itself to others and those others to themselves" (Dodd 1999, 88) cannot avoid the wholesale impression of orientalism (Said 1978). The objects on display might come from "our" overseas territories or "our" corporations, whether the Dutch East Indies Company in the seventeenth century or the art-loving Sara Lee Corporation today. They might appear in art histories as derivatives or not of "our" traditions, as inspirations or not for "our" artists. The local simply expands and becomes "a relational, and relative, concept" (Robins 1999, 23).

At a time when apologies are demanded for all manner of historical removals, from taking Aboriginal children from their families in Australia, to forcing Korean women to give sexual "comfort" to Japanese troops, to slavery in the United States and Britain, it is a bold move for major museums to hold steadfastly and often unapologetically to what they have amassed by hook or by crook. It is all "held in trust for the world," as MacGregor (2004b, 6) angelically puts it. Thus are we soothed into reverence for the art/museum: the art is where we expect it to be. But such comments mask intense debate in museum circles around who can own ancient art and artifacts. Is the nation-state a reliable or unreliable owner of art? Is national identity today wrapped up with the material culture of the pre-nation, or is fealty to "our" past in fact a past that was not always "ours" or is not "ours" today? The destruction of Bamiyan Buddhas by the Taliban government of Afghanistan shows without a doubt that the country, state, or population that holds ancient art on its territory today can turn against it after a regime change. It happened across England and Wales during the Cromwell years and in erstwhile Yugoslavia during the recent Balkan wars, when historic areas of Sarajevo tumbled in the space of months.

Save the art for humanity, says the British Museum. It scores many points with that argument, even though saving art inside any museum is a far cry from saving it in situ. In 2006 the New School University in New York hosted a discussion, moderated by the art critic Michael Kimmelman (2006), on the question of who owns antiquities. Princeton philosophy professor, Kwame Anthony Appiah (quoted in Kimmelman 2006, 17), born in Ghana, opined that many nation-states "have very conflicted and sometimes odd relations with the cultures that happened to be on their territory" (see also Appiah 2006). Philippe de Montebello (Kimmelman 2006, 17), then director and chief executive of the Metropolitan Museum of Art, suggested that an object cannot return to its original context when it is returned to its modern country: "It's not in its original context in either place." Only Elizabeth Stone of the State University of New York at Stony Brook consistently maintained that art must be returned to countries that ask for it, arguing that "what we're talking about is how people create identities" (Kimmelman 2006, 17). Against the backdrop of this ongoing debate, the Parthenon sculptures loom as the case that keeps coming back and keeps embroiling the British Museum in an international politics of art diplomacy and identity.

WHOSE PARTHENON SCULPTURES?

The Parthenon sculptures are the most famous of the seven million British Museum holdings, and the most contentious. These pieces of large marble friezes, sculptures, and metopes adorned the Parthenon on the Acropolis, but now the British Museum has "247 feet of the original 524 feet of the frieze, 14 of the 92 metopes, 17 pedimental figures, a Caryatid and column from the Erechtheum, four slabs of the frieze of the Temple of Victory, the statue of Dionysus from the monument of Thrasyllus and a number of Greek reliefs and fragments from Mycenae" (Caygill 2002, 22). All reside in Britain thanks to Thomas Bruce, Earl of Elgin and English ambassador to Constantinople from 1798 to 1803, his then wife, Mary Nisbet, and his chaplain, Phillip Hunt, who are the parties responsible for the physical removals. Parliament played a key role in authorizing their purchase for the nation, after being confronted with the pieces as a fait accompli. The British Museum bought them and displays them lavishly.

Considerable ink has been spilled in arguments for and against the removals and the retention of the pieces in Britain. Classicist Mary Beard (2002, 16) claims that the works "have attracted as much attention as the Parthenon itself, if not more." Certainly they have embroiled the British Museum in a national and international politics of high emotion and intermittently high politics since at least 1816, when Elgin sold the several shiploads of sculptures to the Museum. Since then, the "marbles" and Britain have been linked, no matter how awkwardly and defensively. MacGregor expresses no qualms when he proclaims that they reside at the core of the British Museum's collection. They occupy a large, purpose-built gallery that is softly lit and reverential in feel. The third edition of a British Museum publication calls the sculptures "the Elgin Collection" (Caygill 2003, 79). They are "ours."

At the time they arrived at the museum, however, it was not clear who exactly wanted them there. Parliament established a special select committee to investigate both the legality of the removals and the quality of the pieces as art. Elgin, Hunt, and noted art historians of the time gave the committee conflicting stories on both counts. Elgin waffled about the Turkish terms for removing pieces of the Parthenon. One art historian insisted that the sculptures bore Roman marks, and others reported disappointment in Elgin's sculptures compared to the Roman pieces they knew; the latter were, in fact, derivatives of the Golden Age Greek tradition. In the end, Parliament authorized the purchase for the low sum of £35,000. Elgin had wanted and had requested more, £74,270 to be exact, to cover his costs of removing the sculptures and shipping them to London. Included in that figure was a recovery operation he launched after the French sank two ships en route, causing their marble cargo to sit at the bottom of the sea for two years. Nevertheless, archaeologists of the time, most of whom had never seen artworks from ancient Greece, thought Elgin's price excessive. Elgin's timing was also bad in terms of international relations and government expenditures: it was the eve of the Battle of Waterloo.

Once the sale was finalized, the popular press ridiculed "John Bull buying stones at the time his numerous family want bread" (Caygill 2003, 23). Yet it was commonplace then to question in some manner all British Museum acquisitions from abroad, on the grounds of a vague anti-imperialism. A popular caricature of a polar exhibition depicts an elaborate procession bearing dead bears and red snow to the museum doors. Within less than ten years, however, the sculptures had taken off with the public and the media. A cartoon of 1822, entitled "Tom and Bob in Search of the Antique," shows spectators in fine rural hunting garb taking an admiring look at the sculptures and other antiquities (26). British aestheticians would soon pronounce the "Elgin" sculptures the ideal of classical beauty, and by 1852, the professor of sculpture at the British Royal Academy could confidently tell Parliament that the sculptures "are the finest things in the world; we shall never see anything like them again" (cited in Jenkins 1992, 199).

The sculptures are indeed fine, depicting human and animal forms with enormous bodily frankness, emotion, and movement, qualities the Romans often tried to copy without the same success (plate 1). But it is also the case that many objects associated with various Western cradles of civilization came to be admired by art specialists for qualities that were supposedly superior to anything achieved elsewhere in the world. In the mid-1800s, there was such frenzy over ancient art that British Museum expeditions regularly traveled to the Middle East to bring back biblical antiquities, such as the notable ruins of Nimrud. As that professor of sculpture who extolled the virtues of the Parthenon sculptures went on to say, "no man would think of studying European art" (Jenkins 1992, 199). At the time, the British Museum's entire cache of art from Britain and Gaul could be displayed in just four cases in one room. "Even as late as 1870 a 391 page guide, *A Handy-Book of the British Museum*, covered the Celtic, Roman and Saxon collections in 6 pages, the prehistoric and ethnographic collections in 3 pages, the Medieval collection and Coins and Medals in 8 pages each. This compared with 80 for Assyrian antiquities, 144 for Egyptian and 129 on classical" (Caygill 2003, 34). "As for cultures on the fringe even of Oriental barbarism, such as the Chinese, the fewer artists who looked at their art the better" (Jenkins 1992, 199). Art historical hierarchies soon put the classical era of Greece at the pinnacle, followed by other "civilizations" feeding European heritage. All the other continents and civilizations trailed behind. Thus were the vast geospaces of the world marked in the international relations of art history.

The British Museum has long since become more balanced in its collecting strategies and careful in its designations. It courts public support now for the collection it knows can seem ill placed in the world and also too ancient to be relevant to modern or postmodern times.[4] Under MacGregor, the museum has taken to hosting public discussions on art and politics, focusing on how pieces in the collection can shed light on contemporary international relations. The June 2004 discussion, cohosted, as is usually the case, with the left-leaning *Guardian* newspaper, was called "Babylon to Baghdad: Can the Past Help Build a Future for Iraq?" Rather boldly, this topic was showcased at a time when people across the country were protesting the government's commitment to the 2003 war. MacGregor led off with a short and brilliant synopsis of how the museum's Assyrian pieces illustrate the cultural politics of regime change in our time. He pointed to the ways national monuments were politicized then and now, arguing that in the heyday of the Assyrian civilization, when one leader ousted another—and this was usually done in brutal ways—artistic renderings of the outgoing head of state were defaced. The head would be scratched out on reliefs, with particular concern to blot out the eyes. In the wake of the American overthrow of Saddam Hussein, scores of that man's self-tributes were similarly defaced, reminding us not only of ongoing traditions in the region but also of the ways that monuments to overblown power often meet their end. Public political actions can determine that certain edifices will not be saved as historical documents, whether the Berlin Wall or some of the gargantuan monuments to Hussein.

Panelist Ghaith Abdul Ahad, a young journalist for the *Guardian*, applauded the popular defacements in Iraq and repeatedly called for all monuments from the Hussein era to be destroyed outright by Iraqis. They are nothing, he insisted, but symbols of our oppression. Kanan Makiya, a Harvard professor involved in nation building in Iraq today, could agree with the journalist's views only to a point. He suggested that monuments to exaggerated power and imperial aims should be removed, yes, but they should go to a museum, so that the nation can remember its excesses as well as its triumphs. As the discussion went back and forth, it was a surprise to me that no one on the panel or in the large audience queried the presence of Assyrian art in the British Museum or its "right" to host a discussion of this sort. The power of the museum was palpable, alive, agentic. From the point of view of the British Museum, the evening was a resounding success: the audience affirmed museums as keepers of monuments from far-flung places and grew in appreciation of the Assyrian holdings in the British Museum. The director came across as brainy but in tempo with the times. All was well.

Yet all is not always well at the British Museum. More than three-quarters of Britons polled in 2003 said the Parthenon sculptures should be returned to Greece, up from the fewer than 50 percent who held that view in a 2002 poll (Brooks 2003, 7). A new British nongovernmental organization (NGO) called Marbles Reunited declared that the continued display of overseas antiquities in the British Museum was both embarrassing and unethical. With the Olympics looming in Athens, the British Museum found itself prodded by international relations into a defensive game of marbles, not for the first time. Over the years, it had parried concerns and investigations about the motives for removal and acquisition of the Parthenon sculptures, about how the British Museum was treating the sculptures, and about the respective rights of Greece and Britain to them. Each point of contention is a minidiscourse on art/museums as instances of international relations.

Removal, Acquisition, Preservation

The view from the British Museum has been that the removal of sculptures from the Acropolis was fully justified. Lord Elgin, a British public servant, may have arranged the removals privately or through his ambassadorial connections, but the official line is that he was motivated by concern to preserve treasures that were rapidly decaying. Many, many centuries had intervened between construction of the Parthenon, which started in 447 BC and finished in 433 BC, and the removal of the sculptures on it. The toll on the condition of the frieze, metopes, and pediment was considerable: war, fire, vandalism, fortune hunting, and pollution. Over the course of its long history, the Parthenon had been a temple, a mosque, a church, and a military camp. Many of the sculptures had withstood the kind of indifference that found the Ottoman authorities storing ammunition in the buildings depths, which exploded under attack by Venetians in 1687. The blast tore apart most of the Parthenon, rendering it from that point on a ruin rather than an actively used structure. By the time Lord

Elgin and his wife got there, the Parthenon had been colonized, encroached upon, and "despoiled by locals and visitors alike" (Beard 2004, 88).

Whereas other foreigners simply took what they could, Elgin asked permission of the Ottoman authorities before proceeding. Whether he was actually given authority to remove, as opposed to study, examine, and excavate the sculptures, is a perennial question mark. There is no surviving document except for an Italian translation of the original letter of permission (a firman, or decree) that the Ottoman court sent to Elgin. That letter does give Elgin rights "to draw, to measure, to put up ladders and scaffolding, to make plaster casts, and to dig for what sculptures and inscriptions may lie buried. But its language is ambiguous and its terms contradictory. It is silent on what has always been the main topic of controversy" (Beard 2004, 90). As one professor of classical archaeology asks that key question, "Did the Ottoman officials in Athens interpret the firmans too broadly, possibly helped by a generous bribe" (Settis 2004, 15)? In other words, was the "deal" an illegal act of transfer? That issue lies at the heart of the debate and the international relations of Parthenon ownership, irrespective of any good intentions that may have influenced the original removals.

There is also the question of damage done to the sculptures and the main building during the removals. Not only did Elgin's team scavenge pieces lying about, they also extricated whole or partial sculptures from positions on the Parthenon building; indeed, they chiseled and sawed off most of the standing sculptures on display in the British Museum collection. These activities of dismemberment were said to have caused irreparable damage to the main structure. It is also known that several pieces were lost entirely when the pulleys and ropes used to lower the heavy marbles were not up to the task. And then, as noted earlier, en route to England, one ship bearing some of the marbles was sunk by the French, tipping many pieces into the sea, where they stayed for two years until Elgin could raise the funds to mount a recovery expedition. When the British Parliament was considering the purchase, several MPs voiced strong reservations about the international ramifications of all this. Might not the Turks in control of Athens be more cautious now in admitting northern European officials to their sphere of international power? Sides lined up on the political-cum-cultural/arts issues of nation and international relations and persisted in doing so. Lord Byron depicted the removals as an act of British chest-thumping in his poem, "Childe Harold's Pilgrimage." Even the French coined the term *Elginisme* to signify plunder of cultural artifacts, although their hands were hardly clean in this regard (Greenfield 1995, 56).

Controversy about damaging the Parthenon in order to save it later merged with concerns about damage done to the sculptures through cleaning efforts carried out at the British Museum in 1938. It seems the latter-day patron of the sculptures, Joseph Duveen, unilaterally decided to have several of the best sculptures cleaned before being rehung in the new gallery named after him. In a tale of "money talks," he commandeered museum workmen, rather than conservation specialists, to scrub the (admittedly filthy) marbles with copper tools at night in the museum basement (Jenkins 2001; Hitchens 1998). Although there was a hue and cry when the director discovered the midnight cleaning sessions, and an accounting before Parliament, all was seemingly forgotten in the scramble to safeguard all museum treasures from the pending war with Germany; many of the marbles spent a fair period in the Aldwych tube station. The cleaning issue resurfaced in the 1990s, though, and the British Museum was forced to convene an international conference in 1999 to air a range of concerns about damage done to the sculptures while in British safekeeping. Since then, the argument that the sculptures had to be removed from Athens to London in order to save them from mistreatment and destruction—known as the global custodianship or stewardship claim—has had a somewhat hollow ring.

A thin justificatory base, propped up by imperial international relations, does not prevent the British Museum today from aligning with other self-proclaimed universal museums to claim unique capacity to safeguard treasures of humanity. On December 8, 2002, an NGO that nearly no one in IR will have heard of issued a statement of some international importance. The International Group of Organizers of Large-Scale Exhibitions (also known as the Bizot Group), a powerful forum of the forty leading museum directors in the world, declared that "museums serve not just the citizens of one nation but the people of every nation" (*Art Newspaper* 2003a, 1). This is the universalist, Enlightenment position, which MacGregor staunchly defends. He sees the British Museum as globally unique in providing one place where many of the world's cultures can come to write their narratives of history against the backdrop of other cultural achievements in the world. In other words, availability and access at the British Museum guarantee that these artistic resources can continue to exist for cultural communities worldwide. This argument downplays the colonial and imperialist activities of Britain that enabled the museum to gain such resources and seeks to establish the value today of having a safe central repository for all ancient cultural artifacts. Those who argue for a return of the artifacts run up against the realities of today's international relations. The remaining holdings of the National Museum of Iraq in Baghdad were sealed behind concrete walls in the museum basement to save them from further looting or outright destruction in the interventionist and now civil war. The upshot of what in IR would be termed a securitization move—the bringing of artworks into a framework of national or international security discourse—is that no one, local or international, could view those pieces for several years, not even the country's leaders.[5] Culture commentator Bryan Appleyard (2007, 5) declares that "for the time being, the national museum of Iraq is the British Museum." Had the British Museum decided to atone for its colonial looting by returning the Assyrian holdings to that museum, many of the pieces would very likely have been stolen or destroyed during the 2003 war.

The cosmopolitan position of the Bizot Group and the British Museum can sound archaic and naive to many, as can the British Museum Act of 2005 and the Regulatory Reform Act of 2001, which constrain deaccessioning activities by the museum (Gillman 2006). Yet the art of imperial and postcolonial international relations is rarely straightforward. In late 2000, the former South African president Nelson Mandela spoke at the British Museum. He delivered a message that was clearly not politically correct in the context of arguments that large Western museums are vestibules for stolen art worldwide. He said, "This great museum may have begun as the beneficiary of British imperial power, but it has become a truly international institution supported by global donors and attracting scholars and tourists from across the world to its unique collection of artistic treasures in which every continent is represented" (*Art Newspaper* 2003a, 2). One may read Mandela's argument as false consciousness or as an apologia for imperial art practices of international relations. The point is that the culture of fine arts lends itself to myriad power/knowledge/viewing combinations. It therefore enables us to resist, as some postcolonial scholars ask us to, any too easy equation of the West with an unreconstituted, self-centered grabbiness that can overwhelm all interpenetrations of power and knowledge (Chakrabarty 2000).

Greek Claims?

The immediate impetus for the Bizot declaration on the value of universal museums came from repatriation pressures placed on the British Museum by a Greek government preparing for elections and for an Olympics in 2004. Most return and restitution claims (the latter term signifies illegal possession) result when former colonies or war victims call powerful nations on their imperial practices of international relations. Then director of Amsterdam's Rijksmuseum Ronald de Leeuw recalls that Napoleon took Dutch national collections as war booty and that France still holds that art illegally. There are numerous restitution claims for paintings taken from Jewish owners during the Nazi sweep through Europe. In the case of the Rijksmuseum, de Leeuw avers that "we see this as history and are not going to claim them back from the Louvre" (*Art Newspaper* 2003a, 6). The Greeks depart from this general viewpoint. They began insisting on their prior national rights to the marble friezes in the 1970s, after the fall of the fascist junta, most probably as a way of orchestrating a new nationalism, for no Greek nation per se existed at the time the sculptures were removed.

How central is the Parthenon to contemporary Greek national identity? This is both a historical and a philosophical question. Historically, Greece became an independent country only in the 1930s, and then only at the intervention of Europe's Great Powers of international relations. Prior to that point the area had seen a variety of masters, including the Romans, the medieval

Catholic Church, and the Turks. Having rousted the last, Europe added another layer to "Greece" by installing Bavarian king Otto as head of state. That was in 1934, and shortly thereafter the Acropolis became an official archaeological site under the administrative authority of the Greek government. For the first time, it was called the Sacred Rock of Greek spirit and identity, and remnants of the previous civilizations were carted off the hill. Visitors to the Acropolis today see the aftermath of a stripping exercise that artificially purified—or, in the language of contemporary international relations, ethnically cleansed—a multicultural historical site into something always already Greek.

Some argue that to return the British-held sculptures and friezes to Athens would be to come down on the side of a distorting (Westphalian) logic rather than on the side of historical realities. It would turn an architecture of fluid use and living adaptation over centuries into a monument locked into only one of its many moments, the current national moment. This is one way to tame the disorder of history: the Parthenon spent less time as a Greek temple than as a Turkish mosque. And, apropos of the question the Reading Room librarian posed to me in December 2003, one can ask why these particular artifacts of the Acropolis draw so much attention when thousands of Greek archaeological pieces appear in the museums of the world. A noted classicist reminds us of one other cost that would be incurred in freezing a moving frieze in time: "This tendency to select totem-like works, which in themselves synthesise an entire culture, unfortunately implies devaluation not only of all other works but of the contextual nexus that links such works to one another" (Settis 2004, 15). Thus, even if the sculptures were returned to Greece, would not their sojourn in London also affect their many identities?

The philosophical questions around heritage are just as thorny and persistent. Marbles Reunited, the contemporary successor to the British Committee for the Restitution of the Parthenon Marbles, was established to promote a UNESCO recommendation of 1982 that the sculptures be returned to Greece and reincorporated into their original structures. That cultural property argument is premised on the view that "things of value are best (or most) valued where they were originally made, or with the people most associated with their manufacture" (Gillman 2006, 116). The Greeks, through the offices of a national government today, are thereby often represented as the people most associated with the manufacture of the Parthenon and all things attached to it, irrespective of how many other cultures adapted, used, expanded, or resided in and around that building. Some even argue that the sculptures are part of the personality and well-being of the Greeks, which means that their absence is "irreparably diminishing an integral part of the celebration of being Greek" (Moustakas 1989). Many Greeks would like to see the sculptures returned to Athens, just as many British want to return them as a way of atoning for an era of imperialism in their nation's international relations. Indeed, there is a view that all countries should have the right to recover aspects of their cultural heritage lost to colonialism or war. But when does a wish for cultural property become a right to it that can be incorporated into international laws and conventions? It has been argued that the fact the sculptures are absent from present-day Greece does not mean that Greeks have a diminished understanding of their historic culture, as their nation is not on the verge of disappearing or being conquered (Gillman 2006, 127–28). A point can also be raised about which Greeks identify with the sculptures and strongly wish them back—the native born; immigrants; government officials; all educational, generational, and class groups; art institutions? Who/what are the Greeks today compared to who/what they were then? These are unanswerable questions.

The Parliamentary Assembly of the Council of Europe has argued since 1983 that there is a unity to European cultural inheritance that makes it far more indivisible than the current debates about repatriated art allow. The Council of Europe came down on the side of unity and declared that claims for art repatriation *within* the European Union would not be of the same order of significance as claims for repatriation coming from *outside* the new Europe. To reach that point, UNESCO thinking had to switch over time from a strict cultural property position on heritage to a somewhat more universalist picture of cultural "Europe." The European culture perspective tries to advance the argument that there is something culturally similar about European societies today, whether Greek or British, Italian or Polish. The heritages are linked with each other through migrations, intermarriage, continental alliances, trade, and even wars. If they were not, the European Union could not exist or persist. Thus John Merryman (1986b), who counterpoises the two ways of thinking about cultural property and then comes down in favor of the universalist view, argues that it is just as reasonable today to say that the Parthenon sculptures are part of British identity. "They help define the British to themselves, inspire British arts . . . civilize and enrich British life, stimulate British scholarship" (107).

Ratchet up that argument a level and notice the ambiguity successively presented in the preamble to UNESCO's 1970 Convention on the Means of Prohibiting and Preventing the Illicit Import, Export, and Transfer of Ownership of Cultural Property and then, a mere two years later, in the 1972 UNESCO Convention Concerning the Protection of the World Cultural and Natural Heritage. The first sets forth the returnist position, stating that "cultural property constitutes one of the basic elements of civilization and national culture, and that its true value can be appreciated only in relation to the fullest possible information regarding its origin, history, and traditional setting." The second establishes the principle of the heritage of mankind, also called world heritage. Sharon Williams (1978, 202) could see within the latter the possibility of fleshing out international cultural heritage, "a sort of property, owned by the international community as such, administered by an international agency." To MacGregor, acting with the Bizot Group, however, the British Museum is, in effect, or should be, something akin to an international agency for ancient world art.

The ball is tossed back and forth in a complex arc of art/museums and international politics that sees all sides of the issues seeking to enact their favored narrative of nation and Parthenon sculptures. The Marbles Reunited campaign to join the Parthenon sculptures in the British Museum to those still held in Greece in time for the August 2004 Olympics was backed by prominent British politicians, former Olympic athletes, academics, and up to 90 percent of the museum staffs across Britain. Feelings were so strong in Britain that former Labor foreign minister Robin Cook stepped forward and argued, more pointedly than he did when he held office, that the sculptures should not just be returned but be reinstalled on the Parthenon building. The Parthenon today is so decrepit, though, that it would be impossible to reattach the sculptures without endangering the entire structure. A milder form of the returnist argument has it that if a full reinstallation of the marbles is not possible, then the British Museum should lend part of the collection to Athens until new museum facilities are operating beside the Acropolis. In a complicating move, the newly elected Greek government of 2004 decided to halt work on an Acropolis museum on the grounds that the construction process would damage remains of Byzantine structures beneath it. As Athens is literally full of archaeologically significant ruins—there are at least seven layers of remains where the new museum's foundations had already been built—that perspective could have held up the one local art institution that could make a claim for the reliable and safe housing of the Parthenon sculptures. It would also suggest a particularism within particularisms. That is to say, the area of the Acropolis would thereby belong only to social collectivities of the past, prioritized according to the layer they occupy under the soil. Against the past, the present could make no claims.

Refusing to budge, and growing increasingly testy about the issues, the British Museum kept "its" marbles during the Olympics and still has them.[6] A new round of debate is already starting. The business of finishing the Acropolis museum was like a traffic light in Athens that changes from red to green and back every few minutes. But now the museum is finished and it is indisputably state-of-the-art. It is also joined at the hip with international relations, not just in terms of old games of marbles, but also because the architect of the museum, Bernard Tschumi, found that his bid had been successful moments before the first plane hit a twin tower. He watched from his New York office as the second plane hit. In his words, "it wasn't a particularly good start" (quoted in Glancey 2007, 23). The finish, however, is spectacular. The Greek- and EU-funded project is sited below and in view of the Acropolis and its Parthenon, a building so perfect that it would shame anything imitating it. Tschumi's New Acropolis Museum is a relatively straightforward rectangle, like the Parthenon, albeit made in glass, concrete, and marble set on columns rather than ringed by columns. On top of the building, a smaller rectangle twists off center to afford an intriguing architectural geometry and a glorious view of the Acropolis. On that rooftop level, the marbles from the British Museum are meant to be displayed whenever, if ever, they arrive. Plaster copies of the missing sculptures are on view for now. They were initially to be covered with gauze masks, as if meant to be in storage, but they have all since been unveiled. Tschumi claims that "a visit to the top floor [is] a journey into the world of cultural politics and propaganda, as well as great art" (25). So is a visit to the ground level, where visitors can peer through the glass floor to see the ancient ruins that held up and continue to ballast the New Acropolis Museum.

In the international relations of ancient art, architecture, and imperial history, all sides claim that the past must be kept and saved exactly where it is supposed to be. Descendants of the Enlightenment want it saved at the major museums of the West as the heritage of all humanity. Cultural property advocates want it saved within original national boundaries as local heritage. Both sides suffer from myopia, but that fact, plus the passion the claims can ignite, keeps the debates open rather than closed. Perhaps this fascinating set of historical, legal, economic, and diplomatic issues, once ignored by IR's camps and by its precamp structure, can be taken up at IR's end as one of its areas of afterlife.

IR AND MARBLE POWER

MacGregor (2004b, 6) is fond of saying that the Parthenon sculptures embody many aspects of the ancient and contemporary world, from "Egypt and Mesopotamia, Turkey, India, Rome and the whole of Europe." He seems to suggest that the significance of the sculptures seeps out of ancient stone into our time. What are some of those ancient art-to-IR connections?

Which Parts of Thucydides Should IR Remember?

For one thing, there is a "roots" issue here for IR. In the field's long-standing realist camp, the notion of the transhistorical nature of interstate conflict is routinely footnoted to the Peloponnesian wars of fifth-century-BC Greece. But there was more than war going on at the time; international politics was unmistakably tangled up with the arts.

In Thucydides' accounts of the wars between the city-states of Athens and Sparta, Pericles emerges as a military man, a general. We learn that he was brave in battle and in his support of Athenian democracy. He was equally capable of cruelty and folly in international relations. It was Pericles who goaded Sparta into wars that Athens would lose disastrously in 404 BC, twenty-five years after his death. What we do not learn from the writings of Thucydides most favored in IR is Pericles' architectural ambitions for the Acropolis and the collision course this would chart with Athens's allies. We must get this from Plutarch, who wrote biographies of leading Greeks and Romans from a vantage point in the first century AD. His account shows Pericles as the political mastermind of what some historians call the "Periclean building program." It included, indeed featured, the Parthenon (see, e.g., Finley 1981).

Thirty years after earlier architectures on the Acropolis had been destroyed by the Persians, Pericles worked with the architects Ictinus and Callicrates, as well as the sculptor-designer Pheidias, to draw up plans for temple complexes at that location. The resultant buildings were typical of their time culturally, although more decorative when completed than most buildings. The plan was not uncontroversial politically. There were concerns that such a lavish building project would require a deep dip into the accounts of the Delian League, the formal military alliance between Athens and various Greek cities aimed at the time (it started up in 477) mostly against the Persians. When the treasury for the league was suddenly moved in 454 from the island of Delos to Athens, at Pericles' bidding, Athens was thought to be exposing its expansionary agenda. Meetings of the Delian alliance suddenly ended and the politics came clear: "allies" were, in fact, "tribute payers" to an imperial lead state. Although Plutarch's version is not definitive—there are some who claim the alliance would have fallen apart anyway[7]—these events of early Western international relations suggest to classicists that "the building and funding of the Parthenon are inseparable from the Athenian empire, its profits, its debates and discontents" (Beard 2004, 39). The imperial knife of international relations cuts many paths.

This means that there is a deeper history of international relations to probe, which coincides with, and also starts a bit earlier than, the Peloponnesian wars—a history of international conflict, national architectural ambitions, and multivectored imperialist diplomacies. To do the probings requires an expertise on ancient civilizations that I simply do not have. One might suppose, though, that such a study would be a project some in IR could undertake to correct a disciplinary tendency to bow to accounts of the Greeks that emphasize war strategies apart from other values, norms, forms, and facets of Athenian international relations. There has also been a notable disinclination in realist IR circles to elevate the study of imperialism to the stature of interstate conflict and power balances (see Hardt and Negri 2000).[8] Neorealists have especially emphasized a Westphalian state system compelled by the absence of international government. Its resulting structure of anarchy in international relations encourages self-help strategies that can lead to war. Taking into consideration the idea that colonial conquests projected power, met with power, and shaped the system would take us down a different path (Darby 1998). If nothing else, it would help IR camps see the types of forces and logics that made international relations and imperialism codeterminants from an early time, much as art history and art/museums produced each other.

That some in IR today do take ancient Greece seriously as a pre-Westphalian signpost of international relations throws challenges to a field that has been accused time and again of being ahistorical (e.g., Constantinou 2001, 1996; Odysseos 2001). Our sweeping, gestural, and inherited wisdoms about a world and a time we neither know nor care to investigate properly can amount to mere gossip or myth recitation. How much of it have we gotten wrong? How much have we embellished? A two-hundred-year debate over the Parthenon sculptures also reminds IR that international relations where it's not expected to be, in this case in the British Museum, creeps up on official international relations topics, repeating and yet complicating and broadening themes close to the eye of the field, such as war. Facing ancient art as international relations is a way of facing aspects of imperialism that usually reside, like art, at the periphery of IR. A postcolonial steering of this face-up/face-off, this needed encounter of IR with ancient art housed in Europe, would be an invaluable contribution to the field's afterlife.

Gender Marbles

We might also think about the Parthenon and IR in gender terms. The Greek word *parthenos* means "the virgin," and, of course, the city of Athens and the colossus of Athena that was constructed within the Parthenon attest to the influence of a goddess on a civilization that the West cherishes. Not just any goddess, Athena was the goddess of wisdom of a sort both cunning and practical for diverse activities of war, weaving, carpentry, and statecraft (Beard 2002, 145–46). This is not to say that classical Athens treated local women well; quite to the contrary, it seems. The point for us is that if primary rules of international relations are to be traced to ancient Greece, as realists would have us believe, mostly on faith, that we must do, then we can surely trace more carefully. Associations of "women" and the inspirational gods, women and war, and women and statecraft take their place alongside other associations IR has been able to see between states and diplomacy, states and conflict, statecraft and mancraft (see Elshtain 1987; Ashley 1989).

Gender is not as visibly close to the surface of the contemporary debate about ownership of the Parthenon sculptures, but it appears very clearly now in the story about their removal. A biography of Mary Nisbet (Nagel 2004) shows evidence in private letters, diaries, and family papers that Lord Elgin's wife was instrumental in securing the sculptures for her husband. Using tactics of the seasoned ambassador's wife and, it seems, of a seasoned flirt, she attracted the attention of Sultan Selim III and befriended his mother, who actually owned the land on which the Parthenon stood. Nisbet was the first Christian woman allowed into the court harem, where she used her privilege to persuade the ruling family to give up a good portion of the sculptures. Research and preservation are the two usual reasons given for the removal of the sculptures.

It now comes out, however, that Nisbet and her husband worked another angle with the sultan and his family, an international diplomatic angle. Both pointed out the value to the Ottomans of a recent British victory against the French in Egypt. This rendition suggests that the Parthenon sculptures were something of a payback to Elgin, and possibly to England, for the advice and the victory. It also appears that Mary Nisbet was the one most responsible for securing transport for some of the marbles to London: she persuaded a British naval captain to use his war vessel as an arts courier.

As the story goes, Elgin was also beholden to Nisbet for the money he used to remove and ship the marbles. But he quarreled with her over the number of children he wanted (they had five and Nisbet refused to have more) and over an affair that scandalized London: left alone for great periods of time, she took up with a man in their circle of friends. Lord Elgin indignantly divorced Nisbet and as a result lost access to her family fortune, which had always been larger than his own. That loss of income seems to account for the desperation with which he sought to sell the Parthenon sculptures to the British Museum, even for a price that was below actual removal costs. At his death in 1841, Elgin was in debt to the equivalent of £6 million today. As can be the case with famous men of history, van Clausewitz among them (Elshtain 1987), an interesting gender story of wives, daughters, and mothers often flies under the wings of "independent" masculine achievement. It also takes decades or longer for those stories to bubble up, and even longer for most of IR to read them.

Cosmopolitanism versus Communitarianism

IR has its own cosmopolitan/cultural property debate that bears on the discussion here. It centers on issues of moral and political community in an international system comprising both sovereign states and many other identity magnets. Should authority be properly lodged at the level of what David Held (2003, 470) calls "a world of 'overlapping communities of fate'—where the trajectories of each and every country are tightly entwined," or with identity groupings based on religious beliefs, gender, national traditions, or cultural preferences? It is an old debate that has been enlivened by the international tendencies of our time, such as the end of the cold war, the rise of globalization and singular American power, the cultural backlashes against these, mass migrations from the South to the North, the human rights agenda, and humanitarian interventions of various and sometimes questionable sorts.

The communitarian stream of the debate generally holds that individual political communities are the proper determining agents of their own rights and duties. It is a view that can be associated with multiculturalism, the insistence that distinctive communities of difference exist and must be recognized as legitimate seats of collective rights for their members. Communitarians believe that cosmopolitanism forces the culturally specific ideals or goals of powerful states on others in the name of universalism (Brown 1995). Free trade is one such idea, as is a culturally distinctive understanding of democracy. Particularly offensive for some communitarians are international human rights norms that undermine local gender relations and religious practices, as well as aspects of globalization that threaten or disallow any particularism that deviates from liberal democracy and its consumerist mores (Zolo 1997). In many ways today, communitarianism is a defensive posture toward the politics, economics, popular culture, and even certain technologies that project self-serving or ethnocentric Western values onto other cultures.

Cosmopolitanism asserts that differences between communities can be exaggerated and distinctiveness overstated. No community is entirely uninfluenced by others, historically and especially at this point in time, when products, financial arrangements, arms, people, and social problems cross identity groupings and intertwine as we move about, share technologies, and operate in global markets. Communitarian posturings can make it difficult to appreciate interconnections and can, inadvertently or, in some versions, purposively, encourage intercommunity conflict. In a connected world, it is imperative to stretch moral and even institutional boundaries to accommodate all in a normative universe that recognizes difference, draws richness from it, and also provides ample opportunities to appreciate commonalities (Beitz 1999). The moral philosopher Appiah (2006, 4), who won the 2007 American Council of Foreign Relations award for the best book published in the past two years on international affairs, suggests that European cosmopolitanism in particular shows "receptiveness to art and literature from other places, and a wider interest in lives elsewhere . . . [in] recognition that human beings are different and that we can learn from each other's differences." In other words, and picking up on a theme already developed in IR, one can be a cultural pluralist and a cosmopolitan simultaneously; it is the process of interacting that counts, more than the beliefs one brings to the conversation (see also Archibugi 2004; Shapcott 2002).

Inside museum circles, this type of debate centers more on ownership rights and the location of collections than on the recognition or not of cultural difference. At issue is who may claim or retain artworks where and on what grounds. Should a large universe of art viewers be catered to, or should the community/nation-state that makes a moral and nation-building case for heritage prevail? MacGregor maintains that the world has access to the Parthenon sculptures primarily because these are safeguarded by a secure institution, where they are properly conserved, secured, and displayed in an accessible world capital. He also argues that ethnocentrism and historical myopia can only be challenged effectively if we see our beloved civilization side by side with other impressive civilizations. The comparisons can humble us and correct any misconceptions of the other we may hold. More, great works like the Parthenon sculptures become everyone's heritage in such settings, rather than the fixed property of a nation-state or community. Indeed, while directing the National Gallery of London prior to his move to the British Museum, MacGregor (2003, 45–47) tells of receiving a letter from a visitor that influenced his views. The National Gallery, the letter writer said, "enables people to feel in one way or another that the collection is for them, and that they belong there. It's a place where ordinary people and rich patrons alike can touch base and feel they are part of a lively, learning community, a place where they can know that they are not alone."

In between the extremes of each position is the idea of democratic cosmopolitanism (Held 1995; Archibugi 2004), a form of democracy geared to complexity, interconnection, and overlapping identities, jurisdictions, and deterritorializing activities across the globe. The logic behind it is that today's world requires appropriately complex institutions of governance that connect global, international, national, and subnational communities without seeking to rule over or deny any of them. Here is where Poovey's (2004, 43) wish comes back to us: "Literature and painting can be understood as social institutions that work alongside (but sometimes counter to) other social institutions." Major international art/museums today operate as art communities and as agents involved in governing the international distribution of art, for good or for ill. They fit into larger governance arrangements for art that range from Interpol, which monitors criminal activities around art, to UNESCO committees that endeavor to establish principles to adjudicate the cosmopolitanism-communitarianism debate as it affects issues of art restitution. It is a difficult debate to reconcile. UNESCO's 1954 Hague Convention for the Protection of Cultural Property in the Event of Armed Conflict came down on the side of cosmopolitan approaches to art holdings. A communitarian preference came out in its 1970 Convention on the Means of Prohibiting and Preventing the Illicit Import, Export and Transfer of Ownership of Cultural Property (Merryman 1986b). Museums supply the information essential to monitor illegal art dealings and can shape and respond to interpretations of art cosmopolitanism/communitarianism that hold sway at any given time (Prior 2003).

Major museums are certainly squeezed hard between a number of masters: the nation, international norms and laws, and cultural interpretations of value, ownership, origin, conservation, and heritage. An artwork can be legally claimed as British, for example, even if was not created on British soil, was not produced by someone considered British, and depicts a theme unrelated to Britain. One of three conditions must be shown: it is closely associated with British history and national life; it is of outstanding aesthetic importance; and/or it is of outstanding significance for the study of some particular branch of art, learning, or history. These "Waverley criteria," named after a committee established in 1952 to bring clarity to a contentious area of policy and opinion (Maurice and Turnor 1992), help Britain reckon with its art holdings.

They do not embody the sense of absolute national heritage and ownership, which other countries in the European Union, such as Italy, maintain. If a British museum has holdings originating from countries that do not honor the British conditions of national ownership, its staff might have to answer to that discrepancy in a foreign court.

Derek Gillman (2006, 131) urges a conjoining of the problem of the loss of heritage and the problem of "how best to promote and diversify the valuable practices and forms of expression that we, as individuals with private interests, require to flourish." He stands partly in a respectful position vis-à-vis cultural property claims of nations and partly in a globalized space that respects pluralism, democratic cosmopolitanism, and changing values as components of our time. It is a stance that recognizes governance as an ongoing negotiation, rather than as rules of rights based on individuals, nations, cultures, or communities presented as clear-cut entities with unified identities and consensual interpretations of themselves. Gillman would like to see a new layer of art institutions get beyond the cosmopolitan-communitarian impasse by negotiating among diverse museum, art-producing, and visitor positions, as well as engaging UNESCO and national governments. Poovey's words hold the glimmer of that idea. So does IR work on cosmopolitan democracy, which, though not without critics who distrust juridical or bureaucratic forms of power,[9] offers institutional frameworks attuned to complexity rather than to a politics framed by rigid choices between cosmopolitanism and communitarianism.

Multicultural Displays

Now a related angle into the large question of whose art goes where. The cosmopolitan Bizot Group argues that universal encyclopedic museums like the British Museum are not about exhibiting objects from some static past but are actively working to develop international culture. Indeed, as mentioned earlier, MacGregor (2004b, 4) has it that the British Museum was set up and still exists today "to allow visitors to address through objects, both ancient and more recent, questions of contemporary politics and international relations." One can come to the museum to acquire information and, by comparing objects from all over the world, be in a position to disagree with prevailing orthodoxy about one's own self-feted culture (MacGregor 2004a, 22). By extension of this argument, if people are suspicious of each other's cultures, are racist or overly chauvinistic, they need only visit the British Museum to face a preponderance of evidence that contravenes those biases. Little wonder that the government of Gordon Brown appointed Neil MacGregor the country's first cultural ambassador. He is to increase the profile of British museums internationally, as repositories and lenders of important works, as beacons for international exhibitions, and as renowned seats of cultural knowledge and training.

At a time when religion can be used as a weapon, MacGregor's homely observation can be refreshing: "If you put together Hindu sculpture, Mayan religious sculpture and objects of Christian piety, your certainty about the role of Christianity and the exclusive nature of its truths is questioned" (MacGregor 2004a, 22). Yet that point assumes that the spectator is versed in competing interpretations of cultures and history, something a somewhat defensive British Museum does not always help viewers to acquire. Texts on museum walls and published in museum books tend to condense complex historical debates and to grant an imprimatur to certain stories of the past and present, glossing over conflictual curatorial politics. My experience in the Reading Room of the British Museum indicates that some staff still actively deflect or seek to mold spectator interpretations by limiting access to information that could cast negative light on museum claims to the Parthenon sculptures. This is a far cry from the promise to expose the "curious" to the issues. It also begs the question of what to exhibit as standard-bearers of Hindu or Mayan religious cultures and what to omit or keep in the storerooms. Cultures change. Communities change. States change. Which Hindus where? And it can obfuscate the historical question of how all these cultural objects got to the British Museum to begin with and became part of British cultural heritage.

There is also a question of how to display holdings of ancient cultural artifacts. Nearly 50 percent of the Parthenon sculptures are in Athens. Yet the display in the Duveen Gallery does not always leave adequate space between the metopole and pediment sculptures to show where the pieces in Athens would fit. Arranging the fragments and some of the frieze elements in a seamless progression at both ends of the gallery and along its walls creates the impression that all the Parthenon sculptures are there. Says one analyst, "The effect (and the intention) of the gallery design is to efface what remains in Athens" (Beard 2002, 168). We in IR are familiar with such effacing techniques. Until the 1970s, the majority of the world's states, peoples, and relations were passed over by the field in favor of studying Great Power national interests and actions. When OPEC used a valuable natural resource as a weapon, IR began to take sustained notice of other regions and actors of international relations, often in negative and fretful terms. One might be excused for thinking that the British Museum sees Greece as a country of lesser significance than Britain and with less museological sophistication. Its cosmopolitan argument can sound arrogant rather than worldly: "Only here can the worldwide significance of the Parthenon sculptures be fully grasped."

Olu Oguibe (1994, 51) reminds us that there is no "clear and shared understanding of what we mean by internationalism." Although striving to be of the world rather than entirely British-identified, the British Museum cannot escape its historical and geospatial context. Whose universal values are being preserved and shown internationally to whom? Those of us wedged into pockets of "development studies" within IR know this question well. The assumption of permanent hierarchical expertise on the part of the West informs the sense that "we" can save "you" from "yourself." Yet surely contemporary Athens is not "a kind of degeneration of God's original perfection," as one set of IR scholars puts the field's seeming contempt for the poorer parts of the world and the postcolonies (Inayatullah and Blaney 2004, viii). There is much littered ground to excavate on the communitarian side of today's art/museum issues.

IR and Culture

That is ground IR has resisted digging. The field has long had difficulty thinking about culture at all, let alone dealing with its many faces. During the cold war, when the field of IR matured, its markers of difference in the world were ideological and to some degree economic. Culture in an anthropological or religious sense, or in terms of virtuosity in arts and crafts, was not an area for IR to explore, even though the field ostensibly took the world and its diversities as its unique purview. The important distinctions the field maintained from 1950 to circa 1989 were along the lines of Western countries composing a free world, the Soviet bloc its opposite, and a clamorous and poor Third World of decolonizing countries, where the free and unfree played out their animosities. Domestic differences at home and abroad, whether ethnic, religious, racial or artistic, mattered little to IR or to its world-division models. Development studies and area studies came on strong in the 1960s but often as feeders for cold war foreign policy concerns to promote modernization, civic culture, order, and sometimes democracy in newly independent countries. As for the United Nations, well after that organization became decidedly multicultural in membership, IR was studying its aggregate voting patterns rather than emerging issues of cultural diversity.

When the USSR went belly-up, culture came onto the IR agenda in a very particular way. Francis Fukuyama (1992) treated cultural politics as a mark of arcane history, something troublesome that would be overtaken eventually by end-of-history processes tilted in favor of American or European models of political economy. Samuel Huntington (1996, 28), by contrast, identified seven or eight active cultures in the world, most of them increasingly opposed to the West, and famously declared that "the rivalry of the superpowers is replaced by the clash of civilizations." To Huntington, civilizations could be "defined both by common objective elements, such as language, history, religion, customs, institutions, and by the subjective self-identification of people" (43). His "civilizations" and Fukuyama's "cultures" emerged as totalities of power and conflict that supposedly aggregated local commonalities into "a way of life," sans internal debate and with few intercultural borrowings and migrations (Balibar 1995). Even now, when Robert Kagan (2003) discusses fissures in European and American international relations, his concern is with diverging "strategic cultures," the sense that (all) Europeans and (all) Americans hold opposing views of the world: Europe is convinced of its wise Kantian turn after World War II, and the United States, the stronger entity in international relations, is equally convinced that its Hobbesian willingness to use power is the key to safeguarding Europe's paradise. None of these sweeping treatments of "culture" explore the expressive power and meaning-making forms associated with art institutions.

Cultural communitarianism is more evident on the critical side of IR. Feminist analyses explore culture in international relations in gender terms (e.g., Chin 1998; Jabri and O'Gorman 1999; Marchand and Runyan 2000; Sylvester 1995; Tadiar 1998). Poststructuralists typically explore discourses of power and hegemony and forms of resistance to these (e.g., Masters and Dauphinee 2007; Edkins, Pin-Fat, and Shapiro 2004; Hansen 2006; Jackson 2005) Postcolonial analyses take Huntingtonian thinking, as well as neorealist and neoliberal IR, to task for missing "the way international society—as both a system of states and a world political economy—forms a competition of cultures in which the principles of sovereignty and self-help work to sanctify inequality and subjugate those outside the centers of 'the West'" (Inayatullah and Blaney 2004, 2; also Barkawi and Laffey 2002). More than in the past, scholarship from several IR camps zeroes in on processes and relations that engage, bypass, encircle, and turn to and against states and international society (e.g., Darby 1997; Doty 1996; Penttinen 2007; Apparadui 1996; Shapiro and Alker 1996). But many IR camps find it difficult to go beyond the wall that separates culture as art from culture as sociology and political economy. The persistence of that nineteenth-century art/science division in the academy might explain why the cultural politics of the Parthenon sculptures and the museum that keeps them has yet to be studied by a field that now studies cultural international relations.

THE NATIONAL/INTERNATIONAL CULTURE OF A BRITISH MUSEUM

Think of the parallels between the Parthenon, ravaged by warriors and conservationists, and the World Trade Center bombed in 1993 and then toppled in 2001 by an invasion of U.S. commercial jets flown by Middle Eastern suicide pilots. Following the destruction of pre-Parthenon buildings on the Acropolis, a thirty-year period passed before a new building program commenced under Pericles. Some Greek writings attribute that gap to a sacred oath Athenians swore immediately following the debacle at the hands of Persia. As paraphrased by Beard (2002, 46), the oath was, "I will rebuild none of the temples that have been burned and cast down, but I will leave them as a monument to men hereafter, a memorial of the impiety of the barbarians." Similar sentiments have woven through a difficult debate about what is to be done with "Ground Zero," the site on which the New York World Trade Center stood. Some families of the dead insist that any rebuilding project will defame the memory of the nearly three thousand people killed by "barbaric" assaults. Others have wanted to fill up the space with memorials for those who were "cast down," either in a new range of tall buildings forced back into the sky or on the ground. The Ground Zero project is melancholic and optimistic all at once, an undertaking with ambitions comparable to those that inspired the Acropolis plan in ancient Athens.

Invasions, removals, fallen heroes, fallen buildings, the nation assaulted, turf debates, and ambitious rebuilding schemes: while the major museums have much to answer for, the debates about their practices do highlight indisputably "big questions" that resonate with a sense Terry Eagleton (2003) expresses that taking death, poverty, pain, loss, desire and well-being seriously will deepen cultural theory. To which Mary Beard adds, with respect to the Parthenon sculptures, the themes of deracination and dismemberment, both harboring strong messages about an international relations that long took what it saw in the rest of the world and brought it home to purity. Contemporary academics should not dismiss these issues if they want to reconnect or rebuild their fields. At the same time, we must understand that "the Parthenon" is and never will be where someone says it's supposed to be. The Parthenon is always "'somewhere else'" (Beard 2002,181).

The British Museum is always artfully somewhere else, too. From an institution that initially held mostly archives for restricted access, it has grown and collected and selected and displayed more and more cultural artifacts of the world. It would not be a mistake to label it the grande dame of culture and international relations in the English-speaking world—except that debates continue about whether that museum is actually the British nation displaying its historical international relations as the world's international relations today. Nothing on the scale of the British Museum, or having its depth, exists in the United States, Canada, or the antipodes. The British Museum says to spectators: Great Britain is still great, despite stinging controversies about imperial exploits of the past and diminished power in its present incarnation. The British Museum says something to IR, too: there is no clash of civilizations; there is only international culture, which we can best caretake. The museum plays its role in engineering and reengineering consent to the British state through its exhibitionary logic historically and through its marble debates today. At the same time, the cosmopolitan drums beat: "The British Museum must now reaffirm its worldwide civic purpose. . . . Where else can the world see so clearly that it is one?" (MacGregor, 2004, 6). One or many? Managing such persistent controversies is perhaps the ultimate international relations of the British Museum.

CHAPTER 3

The International Relations of Saving Art

The politics of art, guardianship, and location have made of the Parthenon sculptures what one analyst calls "the *cause celebre* of cultural return cases" (Greenfield 1995, xiii). We might say it is the seminal case for art and international relations and the one most overlooked by the field of IR, it not being where international relations is expected to be. This chapter enlarges the concerns of chapter 2 by considering an aspect of art guardianship that receives considerable attention in museum circles of late: saving art for the nation. A rallying cry heard from Europe to the Middle East and beyond, the term refers to expert efforts to identify artworks and sites threatened by vandals, dealers, or competing museum claims and to retain or protect the threatened entities as a matter of national heritage.

At the heart of campaigns to "save art for the nation" lie questions of entitlement, identity, and ownership. The "nation" is, among other things, a treasure trove. When valued items go abroad or are destroyed by war or the ravages of time, the mythical nation can diminish, at least in the eyes of museums and heritage organizations. New artifacts cannot atone for those losses; new things are less valuable than old things. Art losses are especially problematic when items are associated with eras sacred to a nation's lore. Things are needed to provide tangible proof that the nation had a memorable past, an honorable past, a prestigious past, a past the world can mark and that the nation can protect today. Saving art for the nation is therefore about securing the stories and the material culture associated with a nation and its ways of life. This security does not come via militaries and armies but through art institutions tasked with ensuring that artworks, architectures, and landscapes survive and can be seen within the country's boundaries. One must hold on to the sainted bones, irrespective of how they got there and whether they are genuine and meaningful, in order to communicate distinctive qualities of place to people at home and those in tourist pilgrimage to your nation. Ownership turns into entitlement to own and, following the thinnest lines of logic and the densest degrees of self-idealizing publicity, the ownership-entitlement link becomes associated with the national public good.

But it is all very tricky. Large public museums have an enormous stake in ensuring that valuable artworks in their collections, wherever they are from, remain there. Highly competitive, they often calculate the worth of art, not by the role it has played in the culture of the nation, but by the value set on it in art historical narratives. Although such institutions appeal overwhelmingly to middle and upper-middle classes, they are also seen as national in title (e.g., the National Gallery, London), in accountability, in educational mission, and in the eyes of international art pundits. Their cousins, national heritage organizations, are dedicated to conserving, preserving, and restoring artifacts that embody the social and artistic elements that their members value. Heritage organizations have considerable power and everyday impact on the built environment. The British National Trust, for example, owns and administers numerous once private properties, runs regional museums, and classifies and regulates the use of architectures in entire villages and towns. Art museums determine what we associate with the term "art" and heritage organizations define which bits of prosaic life compose the national look (Graham, Ashworth, and Tunbridge 2000). Other arts institutions influence art saves (or losses) for the nation. Among these are established private galleries and auctioneers, like Christie's and Sotheby's, corporate sponsors of art and architecture, and associations of art aficionados and museum supporters. The lines between these institutions can be blurred and messy. For example, in 2005 the director of the Abbott Hall Gallery in Kendal, England, declined an artwork offered by the museum friends association. The group wanted the gallery to own and thereby protect a piece of Cumbrian history, but the professional staff of the gallery did not find the work of sufficient quality and significance to save in that way. Or consider the National Gallery of Australia, which acquired an important American abstract expressionist work in 1973 to enhance its holdings in that area, Jackson Pollock's iconic *Blue Poles*. Some hailed the acquisition as an Australian triumph in art diplomacy—a quasi-foreign-policy coup—while many others were furious that an American painting, and not an Australian work, became the pricey modernist cornerstone of the national collection (Sylvester 1996).

There are other issues implicated in saving art for the nation. Can the National Gallery of Australia say that *Blue Poles* now belongs to the Australian nation and has to be preserved there, or will it always be (really) an American painting? Which art must stay where to be considered saved for the nation? Is "home" the institutional owner, the birthplace of the artist, the place the work was executed, or the theme depicted in the work (as in an English countryside painted by a Dutch artist)? Britain's Waverley criteria notwithstanding, there is no universal consensus on the answers to these difficult questions, and many art institutions want to keep things that way. Indeed, they are good at ducking questions of whose priorities are under threat when a valued artwork is about to leave the country, those of the institution, the art-loving classes, or the nation. Yet their well-publicized campaigns to save esoteric artworks from international sale can leverage museums and heritage organizations into national debates about identity and culture. In these discussions, museums are especially adept at historicizing the nation in ways that accord with established periods of art history and nationing art that is of more art historical importance than national importance (see Bennett 1995). That is, art institutions can fight strenuously to save works that any number of logical home places could equally assert as theirs.

Saving art for the nation can be an even bigger phenomenon than this, though. It can involve urgent rescue operations to stop or reverse the destruction of art and artifacts by local vandals, ideologically driven regimes, soldiers, profiteers, or overzealous city planners. International coalitions of multilateral organizations (such as UNESCO), major museums, and noted art specialists can be dispatched to save art anywhere in the world under international cultural/humanitarian law. The rescue resources that arrive on a nation's shores can be so vast and technologically impressive as to diminish or supplant institutions in the home country, at least temporarily. Just as problematic are cases where international actors behave in ways that show exquisite sensitivity to the art they save and remarkable insensitivity to artifacts that might be in the way of those saves. Both problems emerged in Iraq in the wake of the 2003 (and onward) war.

Saving art for the nation is a brilliant political praxis and a thorny problematic that airbrushes away the difficult bits. It can be a profoundly conservative strategy that favors the past over present needs and tastes, or a progressive move that preserves things—buildings, ruins, walls, sculptures—from hasty and irrevocable removal. Against a slippery ethical template, we explore two recent cases that illustrate the international relations of saving art for the nation: the National Gallery of London's Herculean efforts to prevent an Old Master painting it displayed but did not own from being sold to an equally prominent gallery in the United States, and, as that drama was unfolding, the international effort to save art and artifacts looted or damaged during the 2003 war in Iraq.

SAVING *MADONNA OF THE PINKS* FOR BRITAIN

Throughout 2003, various British art constituencies became embroiled in a widely reported struggle over a tiny painting by the Italian Old Master Raphael. The work, *Madonna of the Pinks,* had been hanging in the National

Gallery of London for the previous ten years, on loan from the Duke of Northumberland. Now he had sold it to the Getty Museum in California for £35 million. Curators at the National Gallery were incredulous at the news, having come to consider the painting part of their collection, even though the gallery did not own it. Presumed entitlement set in motion a full-out campaign to save the *Madonna,* not for the National Gallery per se but "for the nation." To do so required that some dots be connected that did not form a cohesive picture. Raphael was not a British painter. The subject of his painting was not British, and the *Madonna of the Pinks* was not made on British soil. None of this was relevant to the National Gallery staff. In their eyes, Raphael was central to the integrity of the gallery's well-regarded Old Masters collection, one that already held eight of Raphael's paintings. The painting in question had also been in Britain for hundreds of years. Effectively, it was British and could not be lost on account of Britain's "greedy old masters" (Hunt 2005, 21).

That the painting was destined for California (of all places), and a private museum of less aristocratic mien and provenance than the National Gallery, did not help. To make matters even more bitter, in 2003 the British state was involved in an unpopular war in Iraq masterminded by the U.S. government. An art win for a major American museum would underscore Britain's position as the weaker ally all around and could cause loss of clout in the international culture wars. With an enormous endowment, said to be the largest in the art world, the Getty museum could come up with funds far surpassing those that pinched British museums could raise through donations and lotteries. In effect, the Getty had the resources to pursue private art diplomacy with individual European art owners. Yet it did not prevail in this case.

The National Gallery and Its Masters

Wealthy or aristocratic British families had a tradition of contributing their private collections to British museums, usually on long loans that turned into outright gifts or bequeathals; we remember the British Museum starting this way. Circumstances changed for much of the aristocracy in the twentieth century, however, and it was increasingly common to commercialize family property as a way of meeting mounting upkeep costs. Many estates were opened to tourists for a fee. Along the same lines, paintings and sculptures that once came to the National Gallery as a matter of course went increasingly to the highest international bidder. To one critic, this turn in the political economy of art patronage was "the death knell for any remaining aristocratic pretensions to pose as stewards of the national heritage" (Hunt 2005, 21). It certainly caused many museums to vie for limited state funding, for Heritage and Arts Council Lottery moneys, and for the largesse of heritage and arts organizations. There is, at this point, no savior of last resort for the arts sector in Britain.[1] The government can and does issue temporary export holds to stall for time while fund-raising efforts are under way to keep a piece in the United Kingdom. Not everything of merit qualifies for temporary state protection; only art that matches the Waverley criteria is eligible. That is to say, using the words of the director of the Tate Galleries, the threatened piece must be "so closely connected with our history or national life that its departure would be a misfortune; is . . . of outstanding aesthetic importance; and finally is . . . of outstanding significance for the study of some particular branch of art, learning or history" (Serota 2003, 23).

It is not unusual for pending Old Master sales to be held up on the grounds of the second requirement, outstanding aesthetic importance. For if the Parthenon sculptures embody the ideal of classical art and beauty, the "Old Master" embodies the particular beauty associated with European Renaissance painting, sculpture, and architecture. Old Master works have long been treasured in the Eurocentric world. As far back as 1602 a Florentine decree named eighteen Italian painters, Raphael among them, as masters whose oeuvre was to be protected by the state and saved in Florence. This initial effort to save art for a city-state proved illusory. The work seeped out almost as quickly as it was made, and from the mid-eighteenth century on, European intellectuals associated "the fine arts," the elegant arts, the noble arts, the polite arts, or the beaux arts with identifiable masters. The Italians remained at the pinnacle as national schools of Old Masters formed; one still sees a hierarchical logic at the National Gallery (London), the Prado (Madrid), the Metropolitan Museum of Art (New York), and the Louvre (Paris).

During the Napoleonic war years, British art connoisseurs began to use the term "Old Master" to refer to known works in France that could come to a bad end at the hands of revolutionaries (although the Louvre's collection does not seem to have been in danger during that era [Pommier 1989]). Great numbers of these began to appear in the United Kingdom—hidden, stolen, and relocated to "save" them. The leading art auctioneer in London, James Christie, purchased a large number of paintings from the heavily indebted duc d'Orléans. The Duke of Bridgewater, Lord Carlisle, and Lord Gower "selected many of the most splendid pictures for their own collections and arranged for the remainder to be offered for sale" (Haskell 2000, 24). Art was a bonus of international war, and British buyers saved it only in the sense of enabling esteemed artworks to change hands through private purchases. It was the aristocrats who soaked up the deluge of continental art, tucking pieces into their private estates for the eyes of other aristocrats. They aspired to be seen as cultured citizens of the eighteenth century and knew that by continental standards, an art collection marked one out as a member of the ruling class (Pears 1988).

The monarchy, by contrast, did not appear interested in acquiring a royal collection and showcasing it in a national museum. British royalty seemed, as the saying goes, to be more interested in horses and hunting than in the fine arts. Yet there is little doubt that Charles I was executed in the seventeenth century in part for his flamboyant continental style. Thereafter, Carol Duncan (1999) claims, the British royal family worried that it would be accused of absolutist ambitions whenever it behaved in a too European manner. As democratic revolutions swept Europe, the old royal collections opened up, giving "a liberalized face to surviving monarchies attempting to renew their waning prestige" (319). Still, the royal family of Britain remained publicly aloof from art. It was something of a surprise, then, when the Queen's Gallery opened in 2002 next to Buckingham Palace. On view were numerous pieces from a substantial and impressive royal collection of five hundred thousand prints and drawings, seven thousand paintings, and thirty thousand watercolors held in England, with more pieces at Holyroodhouse in Edinburgh. One art commentator pronounced the overall collection "of jaw-dropping quality" (Higgins 2006, 7).

The early Parliament of the country was also disinclined to support the arts, so much so that it arranged the Commonwealth Sale of 1649 for Charles I's picture collection. Art historian Nick Prior (2002, 65) has referred to that maneuver as the sale of the century, although much of the art was recouped by Charles II, often from ordinary people who had bought or temporarily kept artworks they would not otherwise have ever seen (Brotton 2006). In 1777, Sir Robert Walpole sold his well-remarked collection to Catherine the Great, after Parliament turned down a proposal to purchase it. More than twenty years after that, a prominent art dealer offered Parliament a collection of Old Masters assembled for the Polish king Stanislas Augustus before he abdicated, on condition that it be taken as a whole and provided with a suitable building. The offer elicited little enthusiasm in Parliament and was eventually turned down. With an inward-looking aristocracy, a Parliament made up mostly of the same ilk, and "a rhetoric of free trade, the British government nurtured a self-regulatory art world: it was not to provide a false stimulus but to let artists and institutions flourish unfettered" (Prior 2002, 78). Meanwhile, continental European states showed munificence toward the arts, sometimes commissioning artists to carve monarchical signs on museum doors and ceilings, much as early churches had commissioned biblical scenes for medieval cathedrals.

When the National Gallery finally did open in 1824, the British aristocracy was still hoarding art and Parliament was still trying to look the other way. It took a different class—of industrialists, merchants, bankers, and professionals outside the aristocracy—to put a national art museum on the public agenda. These gentlemen did not have titles and traditional perquisites, but they had money and know-how. To make their power known in other than traditional English class ways, some among them took aim at "aristocratic culture, contested its authority, and discredited some of its more prestigious symbols" (Duncan 1999, 320), such as private galleries of art. In a tour de force that opened the door to a public gallery, one John Julius Angerstein, a Russian-born Jew of immense self-made wealth, undermined the aristocracy by revealing its indifference to the common people. Using his own moneys, Angerstein set up a fund for dependents of British soldiers killed in the Napoleonic wars. He then published the names of all who contributed to it. The public discovered that the aristocracy contributed far less to the fund than wealthy commoners. On the back of that embarrassment, Angerstein offered his personal art collection to Parliament as the beginning of a public art gallery like those that were well established on the Continent. A shamed Parliament acceded this time and the National Gallery was decreed, with Angerstein's house on Pall Mall serving as its home until the purpose-built structure on Trafalgar Square opened in 1838.

Angerstein's holdings have been described, alternately, as "of outstanding quality" (Duncan 1999, 321) and as "narrowly confined to 'classicising' artists like Claude and Poussin, members of the Caracci family and contemporary British academicians like Reynolds and Hogarth" (Prior 2002, 79). Certainly it held few of the most valuable names in Old Masters. The first director of the National Gallery, William Seguier, reported to a select committee of Parliament several years later that the collection held, for example, no Raphaels. Instructed to build "from the era of Raphael and his predecessors" (Duncan 1999, 235), the gallery began to define a collecting strategy. The once art-recalcitrant aristocracy then morphed into national patrons of the arts, lending pieces from their sequestered art collections to the new museums, a trend that intensified as the Victorian period progressed. After World War I, when the economic and political influence of traditional aristocracies diminished, pursuit of mammon seemed to outweigh any earlier art patriotism by the well-to-do (Hunt 2005). Indeed, on learning from the curatorial staff of the National Gallery that his lent *Madonna of the Pinks* was a genuine Raphael instead of fake, as was once assumed, the Duke of Northumberland flogged it to the Getty instead of bequeathing it to the home museum as he might have done in the past. Far from being impecunious, "Ralph George Algernon Percy, the 12th Duke of Northumberland, reportedly has personal wealth estimated at £30 m[illion]" (Moss 2005, 11). In 2004 he spent £8.9 million to save the garden adjacent to his residence, Alnwick Castle, while the National Gallery scrambled to raise funds to save the Raphael Old Master for Britain.

American Museum Masters

Conventional art narratives have upheld Classical Age works and Renaissance Old Masters as the standards for Art. Other artistic traditions in the world were off the map of art history until recently, seen as primitive, naive, corrupt, local, strange, or derivative. New World art was in that large basket of denigration. Although all the colonies linked up to Europe through mercantilist, settler, and imperial practices, none possessed the basics established by art history: Old Masters and classical ruins. To Europeans, the New World also lacked artistic awareness, acceptable forms of training, and standards. Its artworks were stiff rather than fluid, and its usual subject matter pivoted between the exotic and the rustic.[2] In all cases, the work departed from the Enlightenment sense of cosmopolitan human experience. Yet forty or so years after the belated National Gallery of London started up, art museums were being established in the New World with energy, enthusiasm, and innovative standards.

In the United States, art museums arose during the Gilded Age, the forty years following the Civil War, when national industrial output surged ahead of that of Europe and "robber barons" "ostentatiously spent their wealth by living like European aristocrats" (Bjelajac 2000, 227). America's multimillionaires "combed Europe for art, bought in bulk, and shipped home as much of it as money could buy" (Duncan 1995, 53). J. Pierpont Morgan and Henry Clay Frick fancied European Old Masters. Cornelius Vanderbilt furnished his mansions with Italian Old Masters and various Japanese pieces that became popular after American business planted itself in Asia. In America, "decontextualized objects of Western and non-Western art became interchangeable and more precisely measurable in monetary terms as marketable commodities and precious investments" (Bjelajac 2000, 229). By the 1870s, private wealth and art collections were establishing the Museum of Fine Arts in Boston, the Art Institute of Chicago, the Philadelphia Museum of Art, and the Metropolitan Museum of Art in New York.

The barons had their own terms for supporting the arts, which tended to bypass established European museum practice. Aspiring to have their art largesse appreciated and widely known, some insisted, for example, that their entire collection feature as a unit, irrespective of the era or country context of individual works in it. Many wanted museum galleries and wings named after them, a gauche request at the time. Some even viewed art museums as spillover spaces for mansions stocked with garish art and furniture. The new museums became "a repository for contradictory desires and identities" (Coombes 1994, 2) that influenced other traditions of collecting and exhibition. As early as 1827 the then Boston Athenaeum began to hold annual exhibitions that mixed European Old Masters with works by living American and European artists (Haskell 2000, 88–89). When J. P. Morgan took the helm of the Metropolitan Museum of Art in 1904, the goal of emulating European museum practice gave way to collecting exceptional and spectacular fine arts pieces from all eras and places (Tomkins 1970); in 1909, it added American "masters" to its own Old Masters Exhibition.

Those who saw these exhibitions were—who, exactly? Surely not the American nation at large. In Britain, debate about who should enter museums had been resolved by the mid-nineteenth century in favor of the public. In the United States, a remarkably patrician element held sway in New York art circles in particular and became fussed about the prospect of immigrants and working people cluttering grand foyers or treating art as a mere curiosity. Meant to "serve as a magnet to draw members of America's upper class from all over the country to the city" (Conn 1998, 200–201), the Metropolitan

Museum of Art did not open its doors on Sundays until 1871; of course, Sunday was the one day available to average people for leisure pursuits. Grudgingly, and with pressure from the press, it did so as an experiment, the board of trustees said, adding that the opening "has offended some of the Museum's best friends and supporters" (204). As in the early days of the British Museum (and even the National Gallery), the fine arts in the United States were saved mostly from the people, tucked away in intimidating buildings for aristocratic or bourgeois eyes only. It would not be until the end of the Gilded Age that American art museums could be touted as "unifying, democratizing forces in society, allaying fears aroused by strikes and workers' riots, and transforming American cities by lifting the inhabitants above the material concerns of life" (Carey 2005, 100).

The Getty Center and Villa

Museum complexes associated with the name Getty do not number among the institutions that started up during the Gilded Age. The original Getty museum was the Getty Villa. It opened in 1974 after a frantic twenty-year collecting spree by its benefactor, the oil baron John Paul Getty (1892–1976). Far removed physically from the East Coast art establishment, and more than a bit tacky in its affectations, the Villa also suffered reputationally from its siting in Malibu, the beach community of movie stars. In 1997, a larger and cutting-edge Getty Center also opened, on a prime promontory nestled into Malibu Hills. With exclusive Bel Air to one side and Brentwood to the other, the complex of six Getty Center buildings, all designed by Richard Meier, now commands every view of Los Angeles imaginable: the fancy houses, the Pacific, the main business centers of the city, and a quintessential Los Angeles freeway. It is there that the Duke of Northumberland's Raphael would have been housed. If one knows nothing else about the Getty than the thin facts about its benefactor, its locations, and its architectural styles, it is possible to imagine the reactions in London when *Madonna of the Pinks* seemed destined for this institution.

Without a doubt, the Getty Center and physically separate Villa confound images of world-class art institutions. Not only is California geographically "off" the art/museum charts from a conventional British perspective, but also its origins seem as kitschy as Sunset Boulevard. Getty's original faux Roman villa housed the Renaissance works that John Paul Getty personally liked to collect, as well as sculptures and mosaics from classical Rome and Greece. It continues to concentrate in these periods. But Duncan (1995, 79) snidely described the old Getty Villa as combining "archaeological research and film industry know-how with supreme California panache. . . . [I]ts frescos, fountains, and mosaics, its porticos and patios are all Herculaneum and Pompeii—albeit polished, aggrandized and color-enhanced." Bits of populist American culture and old-fashioned museum standoffishness from the riffraff did enter the mix. When I first visited the Getty Villa in 1991, visitors with cars were turned away unless they called ahead to reserve a place in the small museum garage. The great American car was not to mar the Roman villa ambiance. Today, the car phobia extends to the newer Getty Center, where visitors park in inconspicuous buildings at ground level and board a driverless tram to move upward to a cluster of purpose-built buildings on the pinnacle. The Getty apparently wants to save the artworks from the populist mode of travel in Los Angeles, even as it thinks nothing of offering the visitor a theme-park ethos that spells "California."

The collection within the Getty Villa initially left something to be desired, too. It was valued at $200 million and included three Parthenon sculptures, numerous Roman bronzes, Persian carpets, and French tapestries and furniture. But the overall quality was said to be uneven. Getty seemed to discover fine art late in life and to approach collecting as if he were at a fire sale. He bought all he saw, good and bad, important and minor, and he bought it, said one art historian, quite suddenly, after decades of showing little interest in art, charities, or civic causes of any kind, quite "unlike his gilded-age precursors JP Morgan or Andrew Carnegie" (Duncan 1999, 81). In fact, however, Getty was interested in art from the 1930s on, so much so that he was contemptuous of those who did not share his interest, calling them barbarians (Carey 2005, 131; see also Getty 1976).[3] In the event, a reputation for culture and refinement eluded Getty and his villa museum. The latter joined the ranks of what Duncan (1995, 72) calls a "donor memorial," that is, a private art museum established by one man to honor himself. It was with similar disdain that the Duke of Northumberland was called a latter-day Getty by his British detractors, on the grounds that his "land assets alone are worth more than £800 million" and his family supposedly harbors "Machiavellian tendencies" (Melikian 2003, 7).

The Getty institutions have certainly faced accusations of Machiavellianism. An internal review of 2005 shows repeated violations of international norms of ethical acquisition over its history, as well as a flaunting of Italy's cultural patrimony laws, which save all artifacts discovered after 1902 as government property. Long after Getty's death, his institutions bought prodigiously in the face of warnings that stolen art and export-prohibited pieces were circulating in international art markets. Some say that "almost half the masterpieces in its antiquities collection are likely to have been acquired illegally" (McMahon 2005, 15), including objects from ruins near Naples, an ancient urn the Getty knew Italian police were actively seeking, and a statue of Aphrodite dating to 400 BC (the dealer could not explain how he got it). The institution's own lawyers have found an additional eighty-two suspicious items. Two Getty curators were charged by the Italian government in connection with these discoveries, and their cases were heard in Milan in 2007 and 2008. The defendants deny the charges, as does the larger institution. Yet a Getty curator who resigned in 1986 claims to have warned the museum about its "cultural avarice," saying the day would come when several foreign governments would demand the return of artifacts that the Getty looted (McMahon 2005, 15).

The Getty may be Machiavellian, but it is not as though other art museums have pristine acquisitions histories. Thomas Hoving (2005), former director of the Metropolitan Museum of Art, has called himself "a bad boy and a good boy in the antiquities game. My track record as a curator and then director . . . went from being a rabid collector, willing to grab anything even if I suspected it had been smuggled, to a reformer who helped draft the landmark 1970 UNESCO convention against the worldwide smuggling of cultural patrimony." He says it is difficult for a museum to avoid acquiring some international art illegally. "Fact is, unless an ancient Greek or Roman artifact can be proved to have been bought by Lord So-and-So on his grand tour in the mid-18th century and shipped to London, it has to have been excavated illegally and smuggled out of Italy (or Turkey or Croatia)." Of the cartload of items the Italians want back from the Getty, he thinks the museum should make a concerted effort to return the Aphrodite: the "latest evidence indicates [it] was found sometime before 1986 by *tombaroli*—looters—in what was ancient Morgantina in Sicily (near the sleepy town of Aidone). It made its way into the hands of dealer Robin Symes (whose name comes up more than once in questionable Getty purchases) and then for $18 million to the Getty" (Hoving 2005). It seems the Machiavellians in the Getty story are its latter-day curators, not J. P. Getty, whom Hoving depicts as sensitive to the legalities of art acquisition.

Despite years of art-establishment chuckles about the Getty and contemporary claims about a robber baron robbing art, the Getty reorganization into the Getty Center and a revamped Villa has earned it considerable regard. Getty Villa was closed to the public for several years so that major renovations could be undertaken. It reopened early in 2006 to throngs; it is so popular that there has been a six-month wait to get in. The Villa is the only American institution of art dedicated exclusively to exhibiting, conserving, and researching the classical arts; it now offers master's degree training with the University of California. The pre-twentieth-century European paintings, drawings, illuminated manuscripts, sculpture, and decorative arts, as well as nineteenth- and twentieth-century American and European photographs, have been shifted out of the Villa to four exhibition buildings (called the pavilions) of the Getty Center. Each pavilion is sheathed in fossilized Italian travertine stone, a departure from Meier's previous work with white-paneled walls. Stone, insists the Getty Web site, "is often associated with public architecture" and expresses qualities the Getty Center wants to celebrate, specifically "permanence, solidity, simplicity, warmth, and craftsmanship" (Getty Museum 2005). But it is also the case that the Getty Center's neighbors presented 107 conditions that had to be met before they would agree to a gigantic museum complex in their backyards. One of the conditions was that Meier not use light-reflecting materials on the exterior of the buildings. The trademark white panels are still there, but they cover what are called the functional areas of the buildings, all of which face an inner set of courtyards. Travertine, the stone of Rome, is hung mostly on the outside of the steel and cement carcasses that make up the center. The sum of $1.2 billion went into the construction of all this.[4] The entry fee to the Getty Center and Villa? There is none.

From private mausoleum to new public look, the Getty seems to be saving itself for the nation while memorializing its founder and playing in the California sunshine. It is also competing with museums internationally, though, and likes to talk about a state-of-art lighting system that enables artworks to be seen under natural light whenever possible. It boasts multiple pathways through the (history of) art instead of one route (although a related system at the Pompidou Center in Paris has disoriented viewers [Heinich 1988]). Its research centers are top-notch in the areas of Holocaust art and conservation of ancient art, and it has an extensive archive to support the permanent collection. Up-to-date, subdued, and flash simultaneously, the Getty finally specializes convincingly in art from Europe and enjoys a hard-won reputation for seriousness as well as money and toughness.

Still, a visit to the Getty Center and Villa puts an art aficionado into a large Sunday-in-the-park playground. Every inch of both Getty art spots has been planned with what Americans call the "wow factor" in mind. A garden at the south of the Getty Center complex exhibits entirely unblemished barrel cactus. To the north, indigenous oaks climb the hills. There are pools of water, fountains, grid upon grid of perfect walkways, a circular central garden. The grounds are impressive and, to this viewer, over the top in a way that dwarfs the interiors. Others disagree. David Carrier (2006, 170) comments approvingly that "Meier transforms the familiar relationship between museum interior and exterior space." Yet the four art pavilions of the center seem planned to ensure that the art viewer's patience and stamina are not taxed in any way. Patios jutting out from most floors offer both the sun and the gorgeous views that distract one from the work inside; or perhaps these are meant to be part of the art, as Carrier maintains. Museum shopettes are scattered amply around, too. It can simply be hard to come inside and get caught up in the artworks.[5] These are on offer in bits and bobs: some Italian ceramics and a bit of Courbet's landscapes, a few Degas, some illuminated manuscripts, a Renaissance cabinet. Depth is not displayed. Much of the Getty's extensive collection seems to be in storage, as though too much formal art could overshadow the artful adventure playground outside. Getty Villa retains its ersatz spirit and Getty Center has a Disney-Versailles gestalt. It is all unintentionally camp; or is everything at the Getty art staged at the end of art? It is difficult to know. It is a posthistorical museum (Carrier 2006, 175).

Little wonder the National Gallery of London put up such a fight over the small Raphael. The Getty is just too rich, too able to buy what it wants and put it in storage. It is certainly too glitzy for British tastes, too nouveau, and just hard to beat.[6] When you stand in the middle of the Getty Center and imagine a limitless budget tied to limitless ambition and limitless travertine and remember standing in the Sainsbury Wing of the National Gallery looking at seemingly limitless walls of Renaissance art, it is hard not to sympathize with the National Gallery curatorial staff. They may call it a campaign to save art for the nation, but the general idea is more along the lines of saving a few nice things in Britain as a matter of fairness in international art relations.

Saving Raphael from Getty

The announced sale of *Madonna of the Pinks* to the Getty unleashed an international battle in which the National Gallery of London fought hard and loudly, while the splashy California institution comported itself publicly in a quiet, more dignified manner. The Getty was not endeavoring to save a painting from or for a nation; as a private art institution with a public profile, it "merely" purchased a painting from its owner by offering a very good price. It was the National Gallery that defined the sale as a looming struggle of titans, a zero-sum game in which a win by the American museum would automatically constitute an unacceptable loss—not to itself, it claimed, but to Britain. The then director of the National Gallery, Charles Saumarez Smith, kicked off the campaign to save the painting by insisting that if the *Madonna* were to go to the Getty, this "would constitute the greatest loss of any work of art from Britain since the 1970s" (Brooks 2003, 7). That is a large claim to make, and it elicited considerable largesse; the National Heritage Lottery Fund stepped forward with £11.5 million, its largest-ever contribution to art acquisition. Still, that was not sufficient to match the Getty offer. The National Gallery stalled the sale by encouraging the British government to delay issuing an export license for the painting.

The gallery then launched a multipronged project to save the Raphael. Kicking up the kind of fuss that brings the media around like sharks after blood was one thing. But for the campaign to succeed, the gallery staff felt they had to prove that this old and relatively obscure painting by an Italian artist, hanging in a museum only part of the nation ever visited, was integral to British national culture. That was not going to be easy. In order to "nation" the painting, it would be necessary to raise its profile to the status of a loved work of art. People had to identify with it, see themselves there. To that end, the gallery sponsored social visits to the endangered *Madonna*. Mothers first: the gallery asked local councils to identify young single mothers, mothers from the Afro-Caribbean and Bengali communities, and mothers from London's poorest boroughs who might like to see its painting of a mother and baby of another time. Children too: the gallery transported a group with special needs to the *Madonna* and encouraged them to make drawings about the painting that would hang in the gallery café. A gallery spokesperson told the *Art Newspaper*

(2003c, 8) that she "hoped that in bringing these groups into the gallery, a greater sense of public 'ownership' will be achieved." A contributions box placed near the painting reminded the spectators of the costs of ownership, and lapel buttons imprinted with a tiny copy of *Madonna of the Pinks* were distributed while supplies lasted, giving the impression that the wearer was an eccentric Christian.

The obvious problem in all this was that the painting had not been made by a British national and did not depict a scene or event that related to the British nation. Of course, to say this is to suggest that there is something fixed and static called "the British nation." There is no such unified nation anywhere that can save art or be saved by it. In Britain that fact becomes a worry, not about how fragmentation of identity threatens art, but about how immigrants could become the chief architects of British identity in the future. Within an increasingly differentiated UK population, many British would undoubtedly place themselves outside that part of the "nation" that chooses to save an Italian Renaissance painting as a national statement, especially at a time when the transportation and health services need attention. It has been said that one of the rewards of museum work, which is a generally underpaid area that lacks job security, is the attachment that curators feel to particular works of art in their charge (Kuh 2006, 30). Perhaps this more than anything else explains the extraordinary efforts made to retain the *Madonna of the Pinks* at the National Gallery.

In any event, the battle was eventually won for Britain and the National Gallery by wealthy individuals and organizations from a variety of national locations. The contributions of art patrons, rather than of an art-loving state, saved the Raphael damsel from California Sabines. Months of international art diplomacy took place in private dining halls around England and the United States, with the Heritage Lottery gift helping out substantially, as did a £5 million contribution from American Friends of the National Gallery, which operates off an endowment that Paul Getty Jr. established for the National Gallery in 1985. A greatly relieved National Gallery insisted that its campaign won the day and saved Britain money, seeing as the price finally agreed for the painting was £22 million instead of the £35 million the Getty had offered. The gallery had argued that *Madonna of the Pinks* was badly undervalued at its last appraisal in 1991—at a mere £8,000—on the assumption that it was a copy rather than an authentic Raphael (*Art Newspaper* 2003e, 9). More than ten years of low valuation meant that the true money value of the painting in 2003 would come in less than the price the Getty was willing to pay. Under British law, if the smaller figure could be considered the true value of the painting, the National Gallery would be matching the Getty at the lower offer, in which case the painting could not be sold to the American museum. And that is what happened, with the acquiescence of the Duke of Northumberland and the rich museum in Los Angeles.

For some time after the save, visitors could see the *Madonna* in room 60 of the National Gallery if they got up very close and determinedly held off the distractions around it (plate 2). On a large gallery wall, *Madonna of the Pinks* becomes a very tiny piece of work (29 x 23cm), just larger than a miniature. It is exquisite in many respects; the composition is classic: Mary holds her son on her lap in a mood of playful love. The palette is gorgeously understated, with soft fleshy tones and bodily curves that make one weep at the beauty of Italian youth. Mary's dress sculpts to her chubby torso, draping and folding in the fussy Renaissance manner that is both modest and erotic. The baby gazes upward with one of those wise-beyond-the-years looks of greatness to come; yet he lovingly engages with his mother in a domestic scene that recalls all the prosaic intimacies of mother–preverbal child relationships. Over the infant's shoulder is a small window, and out that window a medieval castle nestles on a hillside in a quiet rural landscape. The total effect is luscious and moving.

But it is not perfect. Mary's right hand seems outsized compared to her left hand and swollen slightly near the thumb rather than merely fatty. The baby sits upright on a cushion that does not really rest on Mary's lap so much as float slightly above it, the result of trying to provide a visual means of support for a child too young to sit up with any natural ease. The baby's feet are noticeably odd. The right foot, which is in the bottom center of the painting, is too long and thin for the corpulent baby leg to which it attaches. The left leg hangs down off the cushion, foreshortened too radically for its location in the composition. As soon as the painting was declared "saved," the little thing was also squeezed by a frame of words on three of its sides. At the top was "The Raphael Saved." Running down either side, well above and below the painting, were narratives about the work and its rescue. The painting regressed farther into the wall, as if shrinking from the noise, the words, and the pawing eyes before going off triumphantly to tour the regional art galleries of the nation. This £22 million scene at the National Gallery, London, might have been called "Painting Overwhelmed by the International Relations of Its Saving."

THE *MADONNA*, THE BRITISH NATION, AND INTERNATIONAL RELATIONS

A number of issues of art, nation, and the international relations of museums enter into one little painting. The energetic campaign to retain *Madonna of the Pinks* recalls the debate around the Parthenon sculptures about where works executed centuries ago by non–British nationals should end up in today's world. It also raises questions of proportion and priorities in public funding. Whereas the British Museum acquired a large number of Acropolis sculptures for considerably less money (even at today's rate) than Elgin asked, the current art market commands massive figures for a single Old Master artwork. Artist

Jake Chapman (2003, 9) opined that "the thought of keeping around £25 million from a pretty impoverished country would require pretty extenuating circumstances." Especially in the context of a collection that already numbers hundreds of paintings from the Italian Renaissance to the nineteenth century, the priorities can seem scandalous. How many Old Masters are enough? What is the social cost of keeping them? What is it they are being saved from, exactly—the Getty, the United States? And who are such works really saved for?

Following the *Madonna of the Pinks* case, a significant Titian hanging in the National Gallery, *Portrait of a Young Man*, loomed for sale or save after its owner, the Earl of Halifax, rejected a combined national offer of £55 million (Christie's valued it at £66.4 million). The Heritage Lottery Fund had given £11.5 million to save the *Madonna of the Pinks* but balked at doing the same for the Titian (Higgins 2005, 7), seemingly letting art institutions know it would not jump every time they cried heritage. The painting would be "lost to the nation," but would that really be such a blow? Little energy goes toward saving old works done by Britons or pieces made within Britain by other nationals. Sourcen Melikian (2003, 7) tells of a British suit of armor that sold at Christie's in 1981 for £418,000. It was promptly shipped to New York by the collector. This was not just any suit of armor. Commissioned by the Prince of Wales, it had been made between 1610 and 1613 in workshops associated with the renowned Greenwich school of armor. Furthermore, its condition, with the steel even retaining an original blueing that almost always fades over the years, was excellent. Only one other Greenwich suit of armor is known to have survived in a similarly good state, and it stands in the Metropolitan Museum of Art in New York. The story is not unique; countless heritage sites across the United Kingdom have been ransacked for Roman, Saxon, Viking, Romanesque, and Gothic pieces. There are few saves for the nation in those categories of "British" art.

A parallel indifference to contemporary British art worries Michael Serota, director of the Tate. Creating a furor in late 2003, he suggested that £22 million would be far better spent purchasing twentieth- and twenty-first-century British art for the Tate and for regional British museums. In his view, Britain was working too hard to save old art and not hard enough to buy its own new art. Indeed, the main support for the arts, lottery funding, was reserved until 2003 for artworks made at least twenty years earlier. Meanwhile, pieces by living artists, such as David Hockney and Lucian Freud, were free to leave the country; indeed, they were often grabbed up by New World museums as the number of available Old Masters dwindled. Hockney's *A Bigger Grand Canyon* is now the (controversial) centerpiece of contemporary international art at the National Gallery of Australia, purchased for the comparatively low price of £1.6 million. That artwork is geospatially farther from Britain than any painting that would hang in the Getty, but this fact does not cause a ruckus in Britain. *Grand Canyon* is, after all, a work by a living British artist who has resided until recently mostly in California. An Old Master, by contrast, is an Old Master. The then director of the National Gallery of Australia, Brian Kennedy, was also criticized at the time for making another foreign painting its new lodestar rather than selecting from works by the Australian stable of artists.

Recent changes make it possible for British lottery money to be used to purchase artworks made ten or more years earlier than the sale, a move that helps the contemporary art market. Still, many of Britain's most acclaimed and controversial pieces have been made within the last ten years. The irony of not working hard to save contemporary British art for the nation is even greater when one considers that Britain emerged in the 1990s as the new art leader of the West, claiming the title from cold war America, which took it earlier from the French. Young British Artists (YBAs) regularly grabbed international headlines and often exhibited abroad and in the United Kingdom: people like Tracy Emin, Damien Hirst, Sarah Lucas, the Chapman brothers. It could seem that the British art establishment, in thrall to European Old Masters for so long, was hard-pressed to recognize the nation's enviable reputation in contemporary art.

But then there is Charles Saatchi, the one-man market, curator, and publicist for YBA art. Having filled his St. John's Wood home and Boundary Road gallery with the often enormous works produced by his favorite group of living artists, Saatchi set up a large gallery bearing his name on London's South Bank, almost directly across from the Houses of Parliament. He took tremendous flak for doing so, not least the charge that the Saatchi Gallery was just a donor memorial like the Getty, a high altar for one man's peculiar preferences in art. Like Getty, Saatchi has been accused of having "untrained" ambition and taste in collecting. Yet he is personally responsible for what the *Art Newspaper* (2005b, 1) refers to as "the rise and rise of Damien Hirst," a YBA star. In 1991, Saatchi commissioned the twenty-five-year-old Hirst to execute an artwork for him, for which he paid £50,000; it is the iconic *Physical Impossibility of Death in the Mind of Someone Living,* Hirst's sculpture of a real tiger shark suspended in a large tank of formaldehyde. Fourteen years later, Saatchi sold it for £6.5 million to an eager New York buyer. Not only did Saatchi make a profit that exceeds what most other types of investment can yield, the sale also boosted the value of contemporary British art and turned Hirst into the "the single most expensive living artist, with the exception of the American giant, Jasper Johns" (*Art Newspaper* 2005b, 1). Hirst's work has been in demand by museums and collectors from Iran to South Korea to Rome. As for Saatchi, whereas aficionados of classical music worry about an aging audience for its concerts, the Saatchi Gallery near South Bank was alive with viewers in their twenties, who clearly did not mind paying the £10 entry fee to see art of their time.

The Saatchi story would play much better in the United States, where the excesses of the Gilded Age and subsequent periods of runaway wealth-making are elements of the American dream. Americans are proud of our famous millionaires and give them a lot of credit for attaining extraordinary success in business. If they are also philanthropic and return something to the nation, such as an art collection or gallery, so much the better.[7] Architect Daniel Libeskind's (2004, 109) praise for Frederic Hamilton, chair of the board of directors and trustees for the Denver Art Museum, exemplifies that tradition: "Hamilton easily could have invested his $20 million in other ventures. Instead, because of his love of art, he chose to subsidize the museum expansion. His name will appear on the building when it is completed in 2006; he should be celebrated for his generosity." In Britain, the state is deemed the proper provider of public goods. Although the country has plenty of wealthy individuals, it has neither a strong philanthropic tradition nor straightforward admiration for self-made men; new wealth is somehow more tainted than inherited wealth cum title. The British tax system reflects these priorities and has failed until recently to offer generous incentives for Saatchi-like endeavors. All this means that when a businessman can own and shape demand for art of the contemporary British "nation," when he can afford to display that art in a gallery carved out of an old public building on the Thames, many of those most concerned about saving art for the nation reject the efforts as shocking and distasteful.

Yet like the Getty today, Saatchi is adept at updating old art stories. Renting and refurbishing disused public buildings as contemporary art galleries puts him in ideological proximity, he says, to those who worry about British heritage. As of summer 2008, he is moving his collection to another old but larger building in London, the Duke of York's HQ in Chelsea near Sloan Square, which is being fully refurbished to his orders. When the director of the Tate, Nicolas Serota, objected to British art being displayed in a private museum that charged a high admission fee, Saatchi responded that greater use should be made of available buildings rather than "spending millions on creating identical, austere Modernist palaces in every world city" (Saatchi 2003, 24); he has announced that his new gallery will have no entrance charge. Saatchi shares Serota's view that contemporary art requires support through energetic purchases (24) and claims to be in a better position than the Tate to buy——in effect, to save certain art for the nation——because he need not rely on scarce public finance. He has also rained on the rarefied parade of art history and auctions by setting up a Web site that enables artists around the world to show samples of their work without paying Saatchi a commission if they sell a piece.[8] This former marketing specialist for the Thatcher government is nothing if not clever. He almost single-handedly put contemporary art and personal art philanthropy on the agenda in Britain.[9] He is creating and reaching an international artist/arts audience too, while starkly exposing the choices facing an art-loving nation: between idolizing a classical past and celebrating the present, between spending public moneys on lifestyle art cathedrals and simply showing the art, between exhibiting art in white cube spaces or hanging it in something as "wrong" as a civil service building.

Saatchi is the quintessential art broker for the end of art. He does not even think of embedding contemporary art in distant traditions or putting it into an art historical context. What you see in his collection is mostly (but not exclusively) contemporary British art, whereas the nearby Tate Modern's contemporary art has been done by (mostly) non-British artists. Saatchi has not yet bequeathed his art treasures to the nation and currently has no need to sell them internationally in order to support himself (although he does sell the work he owns). With a good eye to match his good bank accounts, he can be where art and the museum are not meant to be every step of the way. Meanwhile, a new British campaign called "Treasures for Our Future" takes the predictably conventional tack of establishing a panel of experts from the museum community to dispense free advice on how to dispose of art holdings in ways that can be both personally lucrative and beneficial to the British nation (*Art Newspaper* 2003h, 5). Saatchi could have saved the Raphael painting for the nation; any of the top sporting, entertainment, and business millionaires in Britain could have done so. It is telling that they did not.

What Else to Save?

In November 2003, partly in reaction to the frenzy unleashed by the *Madonna of the Pinks* case, the British National Art Collections Fund (usually called the Art Fund) sponsored a conference in London called "Saving Art for the Nation: A Valid Approach to 21st-Century Collecting?" The Art Fund is a charity that was founded in 1903 to assist UK institutions in purchasing artworks of all eras and types. Relying on a membership of eighty-five thousand, and without any government or lottery funding, it has played a role in the acquisition of over 450,000 pieces; of late, many of these are contemporary artworks. The extent of the Art Fund's contributions and ties to the United Kingdom's museums and galleries became evident in its Centenary Exhibition at the Hayward Gallery (2003), where many of the items it helped save over the years went on display. Included were Constable paintings at the National Gallery, ancient Jewish wedding rings from the Victoria and Albert, and YBA Julian Opie's painting *Graham, Guitarist 2000* at the National Portrait Gallery. The Art Fund contributed to the National Gallery's efforts to retain the *Madonna of the Pinks*, although its £400,000 donation did not tip the scales in that instance. Deeply invested in saving art as a matter "vital to the health of the nation" (Allen 2003, 25), the Art Fund asked speakers from the international art establishment to address one main question at the conference: which art should a nation collect and retain today?

The program was top-heavy with associates of prominent Western art museums, whom one might have expected to rehearse conventional heritage or art history arguments about what to save. This was not the case. Many speakers put diplomatic distance between themselves and the nationalism implied by the conference title. Ronald de Leeuw (2003, 26), then of the Dutch Rijksmuseum, for example, reframed the guiding question as "Why do we want to keep things for ourselves in an increasingly global culture?" He accused rich countries of aspiring to cover all the world in their collections, leaving poorer nations to seek—and often not get—restitution as the only means of diversifying their collections. He also called for an international body to adjudicate art disputes, coordinate national laws on art exports and restitution, and equalize museum holdings internationally. Until such an institution exists, he recommended greater art sharing among museums as a way around everyone's complicated art-export laws. His points called attention to the ambiguities of international law: many European countries safeguard national art production and objects related to their histories; U.S. laws do not interfere in the export of American art; British law stipulates that all acquired items can be claimed for the nation, whether of British origin or not, if they are of "outstanding beauty." The extensive evaluations required to determine whether objects fit the various standards set forth in national legislation delay export licenses. Art thereby becomes captive to national interest politics and art museums become national "factories of identity" (de Leeuw 2003, 26).

Ali-Reza Samir-Azare, recently director of the Museum of Contemporary Art in Tehran (where a selection of British contemporary art was on exhibit in 2004), seemed more oriented toward communitarianism when he spoke about the Iranian government's "fanatical" concern with lost heritage and restitution. Yet he went on to raise sensitive questions about the fate of artworks that remain in or return to a poor country that has a weak museum-security system, using the looting of the National Museum of Iraq during the war as an example of what can happen. Valuable objects and archaeological sites are also in jeopardy, he said, whenever a local regime is indifferent to their fate, opposed to their existence, or incapable of preserving, restoring, and presenting art. Western museums, Ali-Reza pointed out, do display art skillfully and back it up with "remarkable research." So what is the answer? Mikhail Piotrovski, director of the State Hermitage Museum, St. Petersburg, also thought that sharing rather than competition should be a museum norm and illustrated his views with a discussion of the Hermitage's collaborations with British, American, and Dutch museums (*Art Newspaper* 2003j). Parallel debates have arisen in the field of IR, between those who emphasize technical aspects of national security and institutionalists who claim that cooperative norms and behaviors produce security.

Curators of two large American museums raised slightly different cosmopolitan points. They suggested that art experts should look at a "transfer of a painting from London to New York or Los Angeles, not as a local tragedy, but as an enrichment of the cultural scene" (Marandel and Goldner 2003, 25). Chief curator of the Los Angeles Country Museum of Art, Jean-Patrice Marandel, averred that there were far more important issues of conservation at stake than saving individual artworks for one nation. To pave over or otherwise destroy sites that once inspired local artistic works was, in his view, a real rather than an imagined loss. Like Dave Hickey (1997), he felt artists were being pushed out of the power loop of decision making in their own fields of expertise by "what has been allowed to be built around them" (Marandel and Goldner 2003, 25). In effect, Marandel was presenting the skeptical view of museums as institutions that can collect old objects but cannot claim to be saving works of art if original contexts are lost (Carrier 2006; see also Maleuvre 1999).

Serota was the conference headliner, and his remarks drew the most attention. Deftly, he argued against saving only old art for a nation that must live in its present as much as in its past. Serota argued that British collecting strategy was based on "pulling emotional and chauvinistic heart strings" rather than on "arguments about the value of artifacts and collections in contemporary society" (Serota 2003, 23). Along with the usual concerns about an artwork's connection with national history, its aesthetic importance, and its significance for learning or history, Serota proposed asking what the benefit is of saving an artwork for the nation compared to having it held and shown abroad. "Benefit," he argued as the practiced democratic cosmopolitan, should include the value of exposing global audiences to British art and exposing British audiences to works closely connected to contemporary British history; we should not want the British nation "to believe that great art ended sometime in the mid-19th century" (24). His address received front-page coverage in Britain and rippled through international art circles. In effect, Serota was challenging the British art establishment to wrench itself from an art historical emphasis on established styles—art where it's expected to be—to art where it is, which is often not where art history locates it. His position was postart.

Switching funding orientations away from the baroque to Britart, however, is difficult, even at the end of art. With some of the best contemporary art controlled by private collectors, Georgina Adam (2005a, 31) points out that damage can be done to a "market over the long term, because it scares off smaller buyers and ultimately makes the market both fragile and polarised." Serota is a powerful curator, but he cannot match the power of a hyper-collector-curator. As he admits (Serota 2003, 41), "we are competing for attention with other galleries. . . . It would be disingenuous to pretend that we weren't." Not surprisingly, he urges Britain to adopt the American system of tax-supported philanthropy. But he adds, "The big money for the Tate Modern came from abroad" (38), in what is the still-hidden realm of international art relations.

THE BIG SAVE? THE WAR FOR ART INSIDE THE WAR FOR IRAQ

Switch to another context, and big money from abroad can damage local art and save it too. In the days after U.S. soldiers entered Baghdad in early April

2003, the world of art and the world of international relations watched looters strip the museums and archives of Baghdad and Mosul of priceless artworks and manuscripts. American troops watched too. They were on the ground in the name of antiterrorist world order, using enormous military resources to save Iraq from Saddam Hussein's forces and save the free world from the latest evil bedeviling it. They were not there to save art; art is peripheral to or outside the more serious art of war. While troops watched for the enemy in Baghdad, big guns at the ready, smaller fry (or so it seemed) went for the art across the street. An international media caught the immobile tanks and the mobile art. The outcry was loud and immediate, directed against both the looters and the erstwhile "savers of Iraq," the U.S.-led coalition. Suddenly, a war for art had erupted within the war for Iraq. Such can happen to those trained to look out for international relations where it's expected to be: international relations where it's not expected can take the goods and run. And we can be left holding the empty bag and picking up the pieces.

One early reconstruction of events in Baghdad that ushered art into the war practices of international relations is offered by Selma Al-Radi (2003), one of the first Iraqi art experts on the ground. On April 8, she says, the staff of the National Museum (also called the Iraq Museum, the Historical Museum of Baghdad, the Baghdad Museum) vacated the premises while local militias took over the grounds and a sniper started shooting at American troops from the second floor; we now know that the Iraqi army was occupying the museum (Bogdanos 2005, 202). As the statue of Saddam Hussein was being pulled down from its public art pedestal the next day, the museum looting began. First to go were pieces of known international value, presumably the work of museum insiders, Iraqi military members, and professional thieves possibly working at the behest of overseas gallery owners. Later, mobs of locals entered the museum and removed whatever they could grab and carry. By the third day, April 10, American troops gained access to the central districts of the city and positioned tanks in locations near the museum. A museum guard appealed to an American tank crew for help. The shout back was that they had no orders to intervene. From April 11 to April 16, some looting continued intermittently without obvious intervention by American troops. Art was still outside international relations, where IR would have us believe it is meant to be.

In the event, a large number of artworks were taken or destroyed in those five days, along with everything else the looters saw, including desks, chairs, computers, safes, and cameras. Intruders smashed glass showcases and interior wooden doors, pried open filing cabinets, and scattered papers about the floor. They ground some delicate ivory carvings under foot. They defaced stone sculptures that were too heavy to move. Two months of staff salaries disappeared from the curator's reinforced safe. Meanwhile, more snipers fired out the second floor windows. The major international TV channels, including BBC and CNN, filmed all the action, the looting, the sniping, and the stationary American soldiers armed to the teeth and not moving to intervene. Having earlier watched the Taliban destroy ancient Bamiyan Buddhas, archaeologists, historians, art aficionados, and connoisseurs worldwide voiced loud and insistent demands that the attackers of Iraq save the art, on the grounds of its inherent worth and as heritage items of Western culture.

International Art Enters International War

On April 16, eight days after the looting started, the art of Iraq officially entered international relations when American tanks took up positions on the museum grounds to end the pillaging.[10] In fact, the international had been shadowing the U.S. military, mostly critically. UNESCO had already demanded that American troops protect Iraqi cultural institutions. The influential *New York Times* (April 17, 2003) had blamed American and British forces for the museum debacle. The International Council on Monuments and Sites had accused the United States of a crime against humanity in failing to protect the museum (Bogdanos 2005, 111). Eight days is not a long time for a set of activities usually considered outside the realm of war in international relations to come into clear view. But by then much of the art in the museum was gone. Rough counts put the number of stolen items at ten thousand to fifteen thousand pieces, including significant sculptures, jewels, and pottery (*Art Newspaper* 2003g, 5). Add in losses from regional museums and the number of missing pieces goes into the six digits. The world demanded an explanation and corrective action.

Matthew Bogdanos, an American Marine colonel, student of classical cultures, and assistant district attorney in Manhattan known as the Pit Bull, who prosecuted the "baby-faced butchers" of Central Park and Sean "Puff Daddy" Combs, led the team to investigate and recover the art losses. He found the museum rife with internal frictions and irregularities. The staff was uncommunicative and secretive and did not interact well among themselves. The inventories were not reliable. Some storage areas looked so chaotic when he entered that Bogdanos thought they had been looted when they had not. There were hundreds of thousands of pieces lying around, many sent before the war started, from more than thirty major excavation sites across the country or from regional museums. Much was uncataloged and scattered alongside the many fakes museum staff had confiscated over the years and used in archaeological training. Often difficult to distinguish from the real things, many fakes were looted and then counted as lost artworks. The museum was decidedly strange in other ways. It had been closed to the public from 1991, and the mostly Ba'ath Party operatives who worked on there stayed out of each other's way, to the point where no one had a complete set of keys to the rooms and vaults. Saddam Hussein and his family raided the museum regularly for treasures to fill their sixty-plus palaces around the country; the Iraqi army was said to be overseeing the early looting (Bogdanos 2005, 205). Sorting out the situation was going to be politically and professionally tricky.

Bogdanos (151) thought it would take years to inventory the missing pieces from the National Museum alone, let alone recover them. But within weeks some pieces were trickling back. He writes of a resident from the vicinity of the museum who "pulled up in his van with one of the twin copper bulls from Ninhursag (about 2500 B.C.), as well as a roughly four-foot-high statue of the Assyrian king Shalmaneser III (about 850 B.C.). He said he had taken them for safekeeping. He seemed like a nice kid, but just about everyone we met had taken it for 'safekeeping.'" The first pieces appeared on the art markets in Europe and the United States in August 2003. By September, 700 small items had been recovered in customs operations in the United States, Italy, Britain, and Jordan. About 1,700 museum objects were returned voluntarily over the course of that first year, including over 900 pieces from within Iraq (*Art Newspaper* 2003g, 5). Today the figure is closer to about 3,000 returned pieces, but thousands remain unaccounted for. Much is presumed to be in the hands of art smugglers or in legitimate galleries. The director of research at the National Museum, Donny George Youkhanna, resigned and fled to Syria in 2006, claiming the security situation was impossible; as of this writing, he is a visiting academic at the State University of New York at Stony Brook. Conservation projects had stalled and all the foreign archaeologists had left the country (Howard 2006, 17). He said there was an acute shortage of funds to save the art—the remaining collections had recently been walled up behind cement barriers as the only recourse—and radical Shia elements, interested only in early Islamic artworks, were now interfering in museum affairs.

Elsewhere in Iraq, the art situation has been no better. There are ten thousand registered, fenced, and monitored archaeological sites in the country. During the early months of the war, most of these were also overrun by illegal "diggers" toting Kalashnikovs. Another ninety thousand sites were not registered, which means they were not monitored and guarded when the war began. George (2004, 29) remarked at the time that the digging in the desert was so determined that it left marks on the ground that could be seen from the air: "In places it looks like the surface of the moon." And, quickly following the looting, new art dealerships appeared, operating out of private homes and the back of established shops. Hoping to attract off-duty soldiers and war journalists to a high class of local souvenir, the dealers often made no effort to pretend that their wares had been obtained legally. A *Guardian* reporter (Campbell 2004, 29) visited a Baghdad house and noted "ancient vases, pots and candleholders scattered about his floor from diggers in southern Iraq." The dealer told him, "People have to make a living."[11] One local driver for the BBC hauled to the museum fifty-five artifacts he had picked up at street markets.

"Making a living" has sometimes been called the greed motive for looting, even though the political economy of taking, selling, and returning art objects is obviously complex (MacGinty 2004). Some believe that Saddam Hussein encouraged looting at archaeological sites after the first Iraq war and supported a sophisticated smuggling network that was easily reactivated in 2003. More troubling is the possibility that American and British troops might have encouraged art looting as a way of erasing memories and changing culture. Cambridge historian Richard Drayton (2005, 26) warns that making logical assumptions that looting is an opportunistic behavior motivated by greed or anger at the overturned regime could put us off its military causes. In Iraq, looting could have been an element of the neoconservative war plan to shock and awe Iraqis into celebrating the coalition invasion as the liberation force of a superior culture. This was the mode of thinking that developed at American military universities from the mid-1990s onward; a demonstration of indisputable technological superiority could "terrify others into submitting to the stars and stripes" (Drayton 2005, 26) and lead to rapid dominance on the ground. Should resistance be encountered, the invading military would oversee a ruthless breakdown of society, in part by attacking its cultural icons.

The American defeat of Japan in World War II is the model for the shock-and-awe strategy. A spectacular display of might not only ended that war immediately, it also ended an empire and a way of life. To use a term coined by John Dower (1999), Japan "embraced defeat" and went on to be one of the bulwarks of the postwar international political economy. It was not just the elite who embraced the enemy's culture. Dower reminds us that people up and down the social ladder realized that "they had become prisoners of their own war rhetoric—of holy war, death before dishonor, blood debts to their war dead, the inviolability of the emperor-centered 'national polity'" and so on (22). Could not the same thing happen fifty years later in countries sworn to defeat or resist the West? A display of advanced military technology, combined with efforts to destroy social symbols used by the old regime to maintain power, could shock enemies into putting their past behind them in favor of the cutting-edge civilization.

Drayton's (2005, 26) explanation of how a strategy of shock and awe relates to art looting during the Iraq war deserves direct quotation:

> It has been usual to explain the chaos and looting in Baghdad, the destruction of infrastructure, ministries, museums and the national library and archives, as caused by a failure of Rumsfeld's [shock and awe] planning. But the evidence is this was at least in part a mask for the destruction of the collective memory and modern state of a key Arab nation, and the manufacture of disorder to create a hunger for the occupier's supervision. As the Suddeutsche Zeitung reported in May 2003, US troops broke the locks of museums, ministries and universities and told looters: "Go in Ali Baba, it's all yours!"

In this version of looting, the U.S. military's cynical encouragement of art losses as one way of destroying the collective memory of a nation was foiled—

apparently—by the also-potent technologies of international visual and print medias, which caught the looting live in their normal reportage.

Bogdanos (2005, 200) finds the "blame us" view outrageous. As a member of the invading army, he insists that the looting occurred before any international troops arrived in Baghdad and, moreover, "no U.S. Marines were stationed anywhere near the museum" in the early days. He does, however, point his finger at Washington for its slow response to the museum crisis and at the authorities on the ground. Once the Coalition Provisional Authority (CPA) was shamed into saving art as a military objective, it was difficult to respond effectively to the scale of looting and selling under way. The CPA had disbanded the army and police force of Baghdad and was itself too preoccupied with war in the streets to dispatch its limited troops to various fronts of the art war. U.S. Secretary of State Colin Powell said that the United States "understands its obligations and will be taking a leading role with respect to antiquities in general, but this [Baghdad] museum in particular" (*Art Newspaper* 2003b, 6). The rest of the country was catch-as-catch-can. Only at the end of 2003 was an international effort organized to deal with the art losses of the Iraq war. And the way it proceeded testifies to the power of militarization in international relations.

Much of the effort revolved around financing, recruiting, and training local and international art troops to patrol sites in the desert. About 1,400 strong, the Special Antiquities Protection Force donned uniforms, took up arms, and trained with Italian experts on stolen archaeology about strategies of art theft. They also trained with the New York Police Department in weapons use. Pietro Cordone (2003), the late senior adviser for the CPA, was concerned that the coalition could not inadequately safeguard art in places as far-flung as Kish, Nippur, Larsa, Isin, Ur, Babylon, Borsippa, Assur, Nimrud, Umma, Tell al-Wilaya, Um Al Aqareb, Al Ahmen City, and Hatra; indeed, it was spread too thin to safeguard itself. He was right on both counts. Looting from archaeological sites continued nonstop into 2006, spreading into areas that had not been hit earlier. By January 2004, the war for art accounted for the deaths of at least thirteen carabinieri, four Italian soldiers, two Italian civilians, two Japanese, and one Iraqi attached to the operation. A year later, Dr. Abdul Aziz Hameed (2005, 4), director of the new Iraqi State Board of Antiquities and Heritage, was asking for help "to expand the force to cover the country," saying that "vehicles, radios, and weapons are needed." He wanted the culture troops to patrol by car using "weapons and communications systems" connected "with the local police if they need back-up." UNESCO offered "45 cars as part of a three-year, $5.5-million UN Development Group programme for Iraq" (*Art Newspaper* 2005a, 4). War, art, development aid, and international relations—an emergent combination.

Somewhere within that ensemble of forces, the war circle closed in on itself and priorities blurred. As humanitarian interventions for art were under way, an American military camp in Iraq was damaging and endangering the very kind of archaeological site that art troops were fighting to save from looters. One view has it that the damage was planned. Zainab Bahrani, the former international adviser on culture to the CPA, quit in September 2004, after only three months on the job. She was incensed by "a general policy of neglect and even an active destruction of the historical and archaeological record of the land" by the occupying forces (*Art Newspaper* 2004g, 7; see also *Guardian,* 15 January 2005). It seems an American base had been established near the ancient city of Babylon, just south of Baghdad, in and amid a palace of Nebuchadnezzar, the famous basalt Lion of Babylon, and dragons of the Ishtar Gate.

A report prepared by the British Museum called the damage substantial and waxed incredulous that the military would be put "on one of the most important archaeological sites in the world." It was tantamount "to establishing a military camp around the Great Pyramid or Stonehenge in Britain" (McCarthy and Kennedy 2005, 1). Its construction destroyed ancient brick pavements and burial mounds. Antitank trenches were readied near the foundations of the ziggurat tower known as the site of the Tower of Babel, and tank fuel seeped through archaeological layers elsewhere. That warriors would save art in one part of Iraq and destroy and damage archaeological sites in other parts suggests the power of the military text to absorb and trump the subtexts on saving art.

Putting "Culture" Back Together Again

Leave aside for the moment the radical possibility that the destruction around Babylon was not accidental and that the looting was encouraged as part of the war effort. For specialists in art and archaeology, a war for art in the war for Iraq would not be an alien notion. They tend to take what Patrick Wright (1999, 137) calls an "entropic view of history," in which "it is axiomatic that 'heritage' should be in danger. To the extent that a threat defines the heritage as valuable in the first place the effort to 'save' it can only be a losing battle. The 'stewards' struggle valiantly on behalf of their trust, but a barbaric indifference is all around." In the context of the Iraq war, that "usual" struggle ratchets up a few levels. The art experts must now save always already endangered ancient art from the extraordinary dangers associated with war.

Saving endangered heritage in Iraq has had many facets. It has often meant working to repair badly damaged pieces. The British Museum has taken a key role in the repair of ivories smashed in the pillaging of the National Museum (*Art Newspaper* 2003i, 22). Three other major art institutions, prime holders of ancient Iraqi art, have also been involved in the international relations of art conservation in Iraq: the Louvre, the Berlin Museum, and the Metropolitan Museum of Art. Saving art has also meant rescuing it from the safekeeping efforts undertaken just prior to the coalition invasion. Some art was shifted to secure locations, only to be damaged after the bombardments by extensive flooding and fires. The historical archive of Iraq was one casualty. Staff moved key documents and manuscripts from the National Library building to the more secure Board of Tourism building, where the artifacts survived the initial attacks on Baghdad. Yet severe flooding and inundation by sewage four months later left a large proportion of the 1,200 saved Ottoman documents, 2,000 British colonial papers, and nearly 40,000 documents on the Iraqi royal era (1920–1958) irrecoverable (*Art Newspaper* 2004b, 10). The National Library building burned in April 2003, reducing what had remained there to ashes or charred pages. All but 5,000 of Saddam Hussein's own documents were lost along with other significant records and memories of a troubled multiethnic and multicultural "nation."

In May 2003, military personnel found a waterlogged stash of ancient Jewish books and documents while searching for weapons of mass destruction (WMD) in the headquarters of the Mukhababhrat, the Iraqi secret police. Instead of WMD, they found weapons older than rockets: written words of Judaica and administrative documents relating to the Iraqi Jewish community, itself a victim of the Hussein regime. How and why these materials were in a secret police headquarters remains a mystery, but the damage to them was instantly recognizable. CPA officials retrieved the books and tried to dry them out before packing what they could into sacks. These were loaded into metal trunks and then frozen to prevent further molding until experts could arrive to conduct conservation operations. That art rescue effort proved disastrous. The manuscripts had not properly dried before they were frozen and many pages stuck together, their ink running. The National Archives and Records Administration of Iraq (NARA) intervened and requested that everything be thawed, dried, and then shipped to the United States for mold removal, evaluation, remediation, conservation, and storage.[12]

Saving Iraqi art has also entailed an international intelligence operation. Interpol and various national intelligence networks have sought to identify and monitor potential buyers and sellers and to offer rewards for information. Some of the more spectacular recoveries have come from this type of international collaboration. The *Lady of Warka,* a sculpted alabaster mask dating to 3500 BC, was found buried near a farmhouse forty miles north of Baghdad after intelligence learned of efforts to sell it on the international art market (plate 3). Art dealerships and international museums were warned to increase surveillance of all ancient objects offered them as gifts or for purchase. The international art dragnet has also relied on nongovernmental organizations (NGOs) like Blue Shield, an umbrella organization for NGOs working in culturally complex emergencies, and the International Committee of the Red Cross.

International laws and conventions on art and cultural heritage bolster art intelligence operations. The 1907 Hague regulations require nations at war to avoid bombing national monuments and buildings that are associated with religion, art, and science. The 1954 Hague Convention on the Protection of Cultural Property in the Event of Armed Conflict disallows the export of cultural property from areas occupied by foreign armies. A more recent 1999 second protocol to that convention limits the circumstances in which an attack on cultural property can be justified as a "military necessity." As with so many international statutes, however, these have not been ratified by key states. The 1954 Hague convention has 109 signatories, one them being the United States, which never submitted the convention to the U.S. Senate for ratification. The United Kingdom announced in 2004 that it intended to ratify the convention, claiming, like the United States, that it could not do so during the cold war period, when a possible use of nuclear weapons in war made the convention's pledge to protect cultural property unrealistic (*Art Newspaper* 2004f, 4).

The war destruction in Afghanistan and Iraq, and the ease with which killers unleashed bombs in London on July 7, 2005, raises the question of which buildings and sites can be saved in times of war and terrorist attacks. Signatories to the 1954 convention must identify and list movable and immovable cultural properties that should always be saved, classifying them into categories of general, special, and enhanced protection. The British Department for Culture, Media and Sport recommends that the highest level of protection be reserved for its world heritage sites, such as Hadrian's Wall and Stonehenge; for museum collections deemed national, which would include the British Museum, the National Gallery, and the Tate; and for buildings housing records and significant libraries. Jack Pringle, a recent president of the Royal Institute of British Architects, objects to the emphasis on saving classical and neoclassical buildings. He would also save the London Eye and the South Bank festival hall (Glancey 2005, 3). If I were choosing, I would include the Victorian business district of Manchester. On it could go.

Yet if a revolution in Western military thinking matches a jihadist logic, efforts to save art and architectures everywhere could be thwarted by determined targeting of cultural institutions. Shock-and-awe warfare can erase buildings, eviscerate art, and destroy material reminders of the "old" nation. It is a strategy, after all, that takes the most extensive destruction of modern war—the bombings of Hiroshima and Nagasaki—as a template for winning over hostile hearts and minds today. Given that Al-Qaeda also targets buildings and transportation systems as symbols of Western wealth, technological know-how, and lifestyles, it is unlikely to declare Western cultural sites off-limits. International laws designed to protect art and architecture from war damage, therefore, might be increasingly in tension with assault strategies devised by Western and non-Western states and insurgent groups. This is a worrying prospect, one which art institutions and the field of IR need to monitor together.

ART INFORMING INTERNATIONAL RELATIONS

International relations shadows a variety of campaigns to save art for a "nation." The *Madonna of the Pinks* project featured international art diplomacy conducted by two major museums, numerous national art and heritage organizations, and transnational networks of art supporters. Owing to weak international norms of ownership and trade in artworks, an art institution became a political actor on behalf of the nation and itself. That particular case is beyond even the peripheral vision of IR. With the Iraqi war, the lid should have lifted on art and international relations: the war for Iraqi art within the war for Iraq features military and nonmilitary combatants, war strategies, weapons, casualties, conventions of international law, and art troops engaged in a variety of interventions. It is a war that starkly folds the intricacies of culture wars into military wars. Although it knocks at IR's core, it is not clear that the collapse of yet another wall in the post–cold war era—one that had divided the science and high politics of war from the art of nations—is being properly noted and recorded.

We might ponder the ways that saving art showcases a powerful West absorbing the world for and into itself, making all heritage ours, or ours to save and destroy. It is as though we hold a large mirror up to ourselves when we see a Raphael painting, Parthenon sculptures, or Iraqi ivories. The urge to be cosmopolitan can cross over into acts of implied curatorship of the world, disguised in grand texts of rescues, emergencies, and interventions.[13] Saving art can also indicate that the savers prefer the past to the present, perhaps because the values signified by old things can seem deeper, truer, less materialist and simpler than the values of the present. Of course, that is an illusion. Tony Bennett (1995, 130) says, "The past, while existing in a frame which separates it from the present, is entirely the product of the present practices which organize and maintain that frame." In the present we want to save our souls, the West, and our nation by saving art, which is why a war strategy that would countenance the destruction of "their" art can be seen by some as keeping "us" and our flawed present intact, secure.

Olu Oguibe (2004, xiv) casts the past-present problematic of saving art as a culture game around the meaning of contemporaneity. It is a game the West thrusts on the rest of the world:

> At the turn of the twenty-first century, the truth remains that exoticism of the most pristine kind shadows Western perspectives on non-Western contemporaneity. . . . Despite the myriad bloody and cataclysmic copulations that have taken place across cultures, especially in the twentieth century, and the numerous geographical faults that were bridged both willingly and otherwise, the idea of a shared contemporaneity remains opaque at best in the imagination of the West. Not even its ubiquitous cultural presence throughout the rest of the world is enough to convey to the paradoxically, essentially provin-

cial Western mind that the customary quest for cultural essences no longer retains the logic of previous epochs. On the broad interface of cultural response, therefore, there lies a residual yet significant translucent layer of primitivism.

It is telling that the concern with Iraqi art, as with the sculptures in the British Museum, is not at all about the present cultures of Iraq and Greece. One scours the art professional news—to say nothing of the popular press— for stories about saving the contemporary art of Iraq. The British Museum collects modern and contemporary art—it has lovely pieces from Korea and Japan, for instance, and holds periodic exhibitions of modern works (e.g., The American Scene: Prints from Hopper to Pollock, in 2008). But it has little contemporary work from Greece or Iraq. Nor does much of it hang in the Tate. Even recognizing that the ancient past and the modern past are the focus of these museums, Oguibe has a point when he says that the West is only interested in its own contemporaneity. And even then, Britain can seem somewhat uninterested in the now compared to a supposedly more glorious then.[14]

Where we do find lively contemporary art, as in the Saatchi Gallery and the private galleries around Huxton Square in London, what do we see? Saatchi's 2004 exhibition New Blood gave us young artists depicting war, death, and blood. The Chapman brothers refashioned World War II battle scenes to show the gore that war museum dioramas often excise. The "naive" painter Stella Vine showed blood trickling out of Princess Diana's mouth. Dead bodies of rats were woven together to form other art objects (David Falconer); and we know animals were killed in order to turn them into art inside tanks (Damien Hirst). Meanwhile, the official war artist of the United Kingdom, Steve McQueen, could not get to Iraq to do his job, on account of the high insurance costs involved in visiting a war with mounting casualties. Catherine Bennett (2004, 5), writing for the *Guardian*, suggested bitingly that Saatchi would be a good candidate to foot McQueen's insurance bill: given that the New Blood exhibition showed an obsession with blood and death, there was more of an affinity with war there than in the sterile surrounds of the Imperial War Museum. Part of the high entrance price for the then Saatchi Gallery, she opined, could surely be siphoned off to pay the costs of transporting McQueen to Iraq. Yet Bennett wondered whether contemporary Britartists would be quite as fascinated with blood as art if they gazed upon "a real dead person with real blood dribbling from his or her mouth." The contemporary in art, and perhaps in international relations too, is not necessarily the truer, less prejudiced place to be. And so, what to save?

CHAPTER 4

MOMA Saves the West?

Paintings by Raphael do not usually hang in the Museum of Modern Art (MOMA) in New York, nor do classical Greek friezes stalk its walls.[1] And, most of the time, one would look in vain there for ancient Iraqi sculptures, although African masks and carvings glare out from pictures that French and Spanish men painted in the late nineteenth century. At the Guggenheim flagship in New York, visitors walk around and around a central atrium looking at the abstract modernist works that dominate the collection; or they might attend special exhibitions of motorcycles and fashions by Giorgio Armani. There is not much concern in the large private art museums of the country about saving art for the nation, even though their art holdings constitute a public trust. With the Smithsonian institutions in Washington tasked specifically with showcasing art of the nation, America's private museums worry more about lingering Nazi-era restitution claims, overseas challenges to their acquisitions practices, and censorship by government agencies than about the loss of nationally significant works to overseas art institutions (see De Bolla 2000; Kelly 2000).[2]

These museums, however, cannot escape the pressures of international relations any more easily than the large public museums we considered in the previous two chapters. MOMA is always in some international spotlight by virtue of being "the" art institution known for recognizing, collecting, exhibiting, and analyzing modern and contemporary art. Its founding ties with the Rockefeller family of New York bring it political attention, too. Questions have been raised on and off for decades about MOMA's activities during World War II and in the U.S. propaganda campaigns of the early cold war. This chapter gives IR a nudge to expand the parameters of its analysis of the cold war to include issues of art/museum diplomacy. With modern and contemporary art/museums so popular as social and infotainment institutions at this moment, it makes some sense to start in the present and work back to the early days of MOMA, modern art, and the time in the 1970s when some critics claimed the art and the museum were political—and not in the right ways.

THE RISE AND RISE OF MODERN/ CONTEMPORARY ART MUSEUMS

MOMA opened in 1929 in New York City, America's haute art and haute finance capital. It was not the best of times to start a new art venture. The Great Depression loomed on one side and strictures of art history bore down heavily on the other. Modern art had to be shoehorned into a conservative canon by critics like Clement Greenberg and Harold Rosenberg, whose stature enabled them to insist on modernism's artistic merit and place in the long history of painting. Modern art did attract a stable of wealthy buyers and supporters, however, such as the Rockefeller and Guggenheim families. These did not seem to mind that the art they collected was strange, often lacking pictorial content, or prone to "spoiling" that content by applying the tawdry colors of a brothel, and with choppy strokes at that. Modernism's geometric geometric and bio-metric abstractions were unfathomable to early twentieth-century spectators. And an intellectual pedigree seemed required even to begin to appreciate it. So-called contemporary art was worse. Lying on a fuzzy line separating the mod-ernist period, roughly 1890 to the 1960s, from an ever-moving present, con-temporary art could be cartoonish, repetitive in theme, conceptual, minimal, and crazy for the ordinary or the abject. Contemporary art was initially resis-ted even more fiercely than modern art, and it was vilified by art critics, art buyers, and the press right into the mid-1990s. Yet by 2005, contemporary art had come from behind to "smash the $100 million dollar barrier for a single auction sale" (*Art Newspaper* 2005b, 29). More than $722 million in sales was reported by leading New York auction houses in November 2005 alone (Adams 2005).

With art a new cultural currency of Western nations (Millard 2001), art/museums have become growth industries. Many newer museums specialize explicitly in modern and contemporary art, because it is less expensive than the dwindling number of Old Masters and it does draw crowds. London's Tate Modern creatively recycles modern and contemporary holdings from Tate Britain. The simultaneously bolder and architecturally more staid Saatchi Gallery was filled with celebrities of the Britart renaissance, complete with a Hirsch polka-dot car perched on its steps for the opening. These museums still anchor to world cities, just as major art institutions have done since their incep-tion. Yet such is the popularity of the new cultural currency that smaller spe-cialist museums appear in ever more remote places, such as Stromness (Pier Art Center), the Orkney Islands, population 2000, and Marfa, Texas, home to Donald Judd's personal antiart art complex. There is an International Art Space in Kellerberrin, Australia, and a renovated Arts and Crafts house/museum (Blackwell House) in the Lake District of England. More, new museums are unafraid of serving multiple agendas. Guggenheim Bilbao is a vehicle for urban regeneration, a monument to contemporary architecture, and an art museum.

Several art/museum ventures in Las Vegas aim to attract a swath of the tourist population to a city mostly known for its lowbrow entertainments. At the end of art, art is all the rage and a gamut of art/museums flourishes.

Inside the new museum, viewers face as many commercial opportunities as art possibilities. On the outside, visitors often face bendy, jutting, shiny, surprising protuberances, or sleek, icy, austere lines of concrete. Quirky and eye-catching, museum architecture is a boom industry within a larger boom industry. It is Libeskind's extension to the Denver Art Museum or the Manchester England trio of Lowry, Imperial War Museum North, and Urbis. Each is an attraction in itself: a building so shouty that it dwarfs or outclasses its innards.[3] It is also the case that an art museum can have neither a strong collection nor a markedly impressive architecture, yet it can become massively popular through clever marketing. Amsterdam's popular Van Gogh Museum started up long after many of its namesake's work had been claimed for museums in Paris, New York, Los Angeles, London, and Tokyo. No matter. The blue and yellow wrappings from the museum shop are noticeable everywhere one goes in the city. They have become part of the art, rather than the souvenirs, of the Van Gogh Museum. The Georgia O'Keeffe Museum in Santa Fe claims to be the premier museum for the artist's work. It has mobs of visitors. O'Keeffe had such contempt for Santa Fe's art politics, and for the city's tireless efforts to claim her (she lived in Abiquiu, to the north), that she gave the city only two paintings while she was alive. With the best works of artists like Van Gogh, O'Keeffe, or Pablo Picasso scattered around the world, it is hardly the case that any artist-named museum can be the last word on that artist. But the art pilgrims come to worship anyway. Art museums are the new cathedrals of our time, and art spectatorship has taken on the characteristics of pilgrimage (*Art Monthly* 1999).

European cities once vied to have the best and grandest cathedral, worthy of attracting the greatest number of religious pilgrims. Entire political economies, legitimate and shady, grew up around the most famous pilgrim routes, which brimmed with the types of characters and dealings that *Canterbury Tales* depicts. The end of the journey was marked by reaching a celebrated church associated with a popular saint or imbued over the years with especially strong meaning—as has been the case for the monastery at Santiago de Compostela. The trip would invariably be hard, but the journey and its finale supposedly did the soul good. Today, trekking to out-of-the-way museums seems to replace that historical quest, and the harder it is to get to the art, the better, the more redeeming, we imagine it to be (Carey 2005). Getting to some museums certainly does require planning and possibly nerve today, if only to brave the distractions of Las Vegas en route—to say nothing about the bombs of Bilbao.

Perhaps the resurgence of art/museums has to do with the visual time it is said we inhabit. If so, that is a paradox at the end of art. Arthur Danto claims that contemporary art caused art history to fold in on itself and effectively to end, replaced by a visual culture in which high and low art, elite and mass cultural interests, and art and craft merge or form remarkable nonhierarchical art collages (see Bloom 1999). Pilgrimages to places like the Institute of Contemporary Arts in London or the Museum of Contemporary Art in Sydney—where viewers are largely left to work out on their own what they see there—pay tribute to this time when sight trumps the analytical word and contemporary sight can trump historical sight, the shouts of heritage protectors notwithstanding. Image is all—on screens, in advertising, in teaching, on the body, and, of course, in art/museums. Yet, as Thomas Crow (1996, 215) points out, much of what appears in contemporary art museums is not visual so much as conceptual. Art makers seem to distrust "the optical experience" of modernist art and can withhold visuality from beholders, giving us noisy, malodorous, wordy, audience-participatory, performative events that are everything except visual. Even painting, which is a mainstay of Western art practice, has widely and rather absurdly been declared passé. Still, it is hard to imagine that most viewers trek to famous art/museums in order to not-see what is there.

Most art-pilgrimage routes lead to predictable places, places known by IR as Great Powers. On a September Saturday afternoon in 2003, only two visitors are in the Municipal Art Gallery in Lodz, Poland, taking in the spectacular Triennial of Small Graphic Forms. Work by three hundred artists representing fifty-one countries is arranged on two renovated floors of the art nouveau building. The exhibition is lovely. The building is lovely. But art pilgrimage remains circumscribed by the sense of world space and art space we hold in our heads. Relatively few international art pilgrims journey to Lodz or to exhibitions of contemporary art at the National Gallery of Zimbabwe. Rosie Millard (2001, 211) opines that "people like to experience art in unusual places. But successful unusual art places tend to be near a branch of Starbucks." We like restaurants cozying up museum basements or in places that provide the best views in town, as the Tate Modern and the National Portrait Gallery (London) restaurants do. For the feel of a private club apart from pilgrimage hubbub, there is always a members' lounge, where viewers can contemplate what they have seen over a flute of champagne. Lodz does not have much in the way of accoutrements for art pilgrims, and Zimbabwe is rapidly dismantling everything its once vibrant city of Harare had. Museums in both locations can offer only art, not the art of the museum.

The art of the museum today is something that art critic Dave Hickey (1997, 148–49) finds appalling: "the chic building, the gaudy doctorates, and the star-studded cast . . . the normative blessing of institutions and corporations." But Danto (2002, 31) is tickled pink by its "perfect state of pluralism, in which artists are liberated to convey their thought by any means whatever." Perhaps we should be impressed by something else too: the displays of international relations we can detect in modern and contemporary art museums if we look closely. Vanguard institutions like MOMA and the Guggenheim engage with nations, people, and finances of the world; they occupy a certain cutting edge of international power. Nothing entirely new in that: MOMA was always in an edgy political place and the Guggenheim is an edge all on its own.

MOMA THEN AND NOW

To speak of the MOMA is to enter a world and its politics through a door marked "Rockefeller." This first museum of modern art was started by members of the famous East Coast dynastic family, whose wealth, influence in American politics, and contributions to the arts remain unequaled in the United States. It all started with John D. Rockefeller (1839–1937), who entered the oil business in the 1860s and founded the company that remains the basis of the family's vast fortune today, Standard Oil. John D. Rockefeller Jr. (1874–1960) showed more interest in philanthropic causes and politics than the oil business. With his wife, Abby (1874–1948), he expanded Rockefeller influence to the arts and historic preservation, areas their children have continued to embrace. So far the Rockefellers have produced men who rose to be a U.S. vice president, a mayor of New York City, and a governor of New York State. Yet it seems the family's women were the ones who put MOMA in train. Presciently, Abby Rockefeller, Mary Sullivan, and Lizzie Bliss pictured and pursued a museum that would be dedicated solely to modern art, and they did so at a time when modernism was not fully recognized in art history or popular among the viewing public.

Backed by family money, their dream museum opened nine days after the crash of the New York Stock Exchange, in a tiny venue of six rooms on the twelfth floor of the Heckscher Building, 730 Fifth Avenue. It moved three times before taking up its Midtown location in 1939. Settled there, MOMA has nonetheless been restless, expanding and renovating several times, with more plans for expansion always in the works. In the 1950s and 1960s, architect Philip Johnson was brought on board to renovate and sharpen the building. In 1984, Cesar Pelli doubled the gallery space. In 2000, Yoshio Taniguchi guided an overhaul so extensive that MOMA has since been referred to as the "new MOMA." Its 630,000 square feet of additional and redesigned space includes a new gallery building on the western side of the site, an education and research center on the eastern side, and an enlarged sculpture garden between them. Unlike the newly built Getty Center and renovated Villa, which are free to the public, the entry charge to the new MOMA, which reopened on November 20, 2004, is a stupendous $20.

Inside, a series of escalators takes the viewer increasingly higher above the din of the city, where the entire history of modern art is reenacted, top down, floor by floor. Key works of the early modern art era, mostly by male artists from Europe, occupy the topmost floor; among them are paintings by Monet, Manet, Kandinsky, Klee, Malevich, Picasso, Matisse, and Cézanne. One moves down to the Americans who put abstract expressionism on the modern art map—Pollock, de Kooning, and Rothko—as well as pop art, minimalism, and collages by Rauschenberg, Johns, Warhol, and the rest. Photography and drawing get several rooms, and design is given open floor space, where the viewer passes islands of Arts and Crafts furniture, the Vespa motor scooter, and stainless steel kitchenwares. Along the way, one can stop off at a number of eating places, one of them a chef-run restaurant. All are packed to the gills, no matter what time one gets there. A cinema shows "art" films, and a large museum shop proffers the usual books and wares, as does a separate design store. Online, the museum provides travel and hotel packages for visitors. It is all there where modern art and amenities are expected to be, up and down MOMA's cacophonous, smart, cement-gray spaces.

Not everyone is entranced by MOMA's constant reshapings. Architect Daniel Libeskind (2004, 122) finds the new MOMA all too much—too anonymous, too glassy in the skyscraper design, and actually downright anti-museum. The point, he thinks, is that MOMA must show it is the "dominant force in the world of corporate museums." Art critic Jerry Saltz (2006, 40) complains as well, about a new MOMA "so civilized, tidied up, neutralized and pruned-to-death that it's almost impossible to glean how revolutionary much of this art is." The least explicable and oft-remarked shortcoming of the new MOMA is space. The museum is still not large enough to show more than a relatively small number of works from a vast permanent collection; further extensions are already being worked out. MOMA's stash grew from an initial gift of eight prints and one drawing to more than 150,000 paintings, sculptures, drawings, prints, photographs, architectural models and drawings, and design objects today. There are also 22,000 or so films and 4 million film stills, and the library and archives contain in excess of 300,000 books, artist books, and periodicals; files on more than 70,000 artists; and primary sources on the history of the museum and of modern and contemporary art.

Much of that bounty was gathered by the museum's first and most influential director, Alfred Barr Jr. Barr was a giant in many respects (plate 4). He established the time frame for the modern art period as impressionism/postimpressionism of the late 1880s extending to the present, which at that time was the first half of the twentieth century. He created the canon of modern art styles, drawing initially on the work of European abstractionists and only belatedly incorporating most of the now celebrated American modernists. And he authorized purchase of pieces later considered seminal to modern art. Organizationally, he also gave MOMA a multidepartmental structure and for the first time included in that structure departments on architecture and design, film and video, and photography. Barr was also the first museum director to exhibit art in white cubes—those ubiquitous pale, neutral, plain, boxlike gallery spaces one sees and expects everywhere. These were a bigger innovation than meets the eye; the leading curatorial approach elsewhere put artworks in grand rooms of palatial museums and made paintings climb up ornate walls to stratospheric ceilings (as one can still see today in parts of the Louvre, British Museum, and Metropolitan Museum of Art). Nearly single-handedly, Barr stripped the museum of its faded royal pretensions and baroque spaces.

Barr was appointed at the tender age of twenty-seven and worked for the museum for nearly forty years. In curatorial circles, he remains the standard-bearer (Kantor 1999). The late Katharine Kuh (2006, 47), a well-known Chicago gallerist in the interwar years, the first curator of modern art at the Chicago Art Institute, and art commentator, said her contemporary "almost single-handedly overturned museum practices throughout the world." Besides amassing the stellar collection of early modern works, Barr made contributions in three other areas that especially impressed Kuh: his innovative, dynamic display techniques, which she describes as "a new kind of showmanship"; his interest in appealing to the intelligent art viewer as much as the art connoisseur; and his production of "literate art catalogues that were both scholarly and yet nontechnical enough to interest the more casual museum visitor" (47). Yet, in their wisdom, MOMA's board of directors fired Barr as director in 1943. It seems they disapproved of the works he was collecting and showing at the time, pieces like Picasso's famed *Demoiselles d'Avignon* (1939) that definitively broke with the naturalistic human form.

The termination of his contract must have been tremendously humiliating for Barr, but he stayed on as MOMA's chief curator, a far sight less radical one than many modern art detractors imagined. Barr was a confirmed Europeanist in taste. He maintained throughout the 1940s that American modern art was lacking the fine qualities of modern art created across the Atlantic and therefore could not be showcased. What MOMA curator Lynn Zelevansky (1996, 62) calls "resentment of the hegemony of Paris" led many American artists to protest at the museum's doors—in 1939, 1942, 1943, and 1944. Even when the country turned nationalist during the war, Barr held his somewhat anti-American-art ground. Only in the late 1950s would he embrace America's notable contribution to modern art, abstract expressionism. His assistant, Dorothy Miller, was quicker off the mark, curating several shows in the 1940s called, simply, the "Americans." Everyone knew, though, that Barr was the power man at MOMA and the one who had to be brought into appreciation of American modern art. That leap, when it started to occur more systematically around MOMA, not only had a tremendous impact on the history of modern art but also brought the museum adverse publicity years later, at the hands of a small group of leftist art historians. Against the backdrop of the tremendously unpopular and ill-conceived Vietnam War, they argued that MOMA had willingly become a culture instrument in Washington's early cold war machine.

Disruptive Abstractions at MOMA

Before going to that controversy and the intriguing international relations it suggests, it is important to recall what this controversial modern art was about. Volumes have been written on that subject. A sketch is all that is possible here.[4]

Modernism in the fine arts has been largely about the rise of abstraction as against the naturalism, illusionism and/or representational orientation that Western art history had always admired. The emphasis on abstraction came in many forms. Color could become the subject of a work rather than an aspect of a successful or unpersuasive piece. Lines could be drawn that did not outline anything recognizable. Pictorial space was often treated as flat, without depth, rather than angled through methods of perspective. Light, shadows, and space relations could appear in myriad permutations. Figures might be pulled and stretched, pinched, exaggerated, distorted, or rendered unfamiliar and eerie. Modern abstract art also broke "rules" of aesthetics by introducing degraded materials as art elements, such as house paints, shards of glass, newspapers, telephones, urinals, sand, and the like. The idea was not to make the picture look like something one sees optically as real. The aim was to communicate a concept, tap the subconscious, create an illusion, or touch the viewer's feelings; and sometimes a work would represent the strange hyyperreason of a time obsessed with precision machines of all sorts (à la Fernand Léger).

A modernist piece could be a completely stripped-down abstract offering no hint of subject matter (a drip painting by Pollock, for example) (plate 5). It could be figurative but unrealistically rendered (one of de Kooning's or Picasso's paintings of women). It could be composed of intersecting lines (Mondrian), paper cutouts (Matisse), or strange biomorphic images (Pollock, Tanguy, Dalí). It might come in small sizes (Klee) or colossal spreads requiring specially constructed display spaces (Henry Moore). Accustomed to looking at mimetic pieces and judging them in part by how well they succeeded in replicating the optical experience of object viewing, many art lovers of the time found the new styles perplexing, if not downright ugly or mystifying. The late art commentator David Sylvester somewhat disparagingly suggested that some such work offered only "one-way traffic to day-dreaming" (quoted in Wullschlager 2003, W7). The Rockefellers, Guggenheims, and Stieglitzes were not among the naysayers of modern art. They joyfully collected and showed the avant-garde. But public responses could be of a different kind: a group called Sanity in Art smashed a window of the Katharine Kuh Gallery in Chicago during a 1930s exhibition of work by Joan Miró (Kuh 2006, 5).

The abstractions that characterize much modern art came in two distinct waves and locations. A European wave emerged in the period from the 1880s to World War II, with Cézanne, Matisse, and Picasso as its grand figures. By the late 1940s, an American wave had gathered force and was reaching a crescendo in the New York school of abstract expressionism. The differences between these were not just academic. Whereas Picasso was tireless in his explorations of modernist imagery and style, applied mostly to figurative forms, Pollock eventually eliminated figuration in painting for skeins of paint roped across enormous canvases (which often covered over sketches of biomorphic figures). Some of his contemporaries connected blocks of colors through pouring and smearing techniques (Mark Rothko). Clyfford Still broke up expanses of large black canvases with yellow or red "reminders" of something else in the corners. Country-specific themes and landscapes, which had formed the backbone of art historical schools, were often abandoned or rendered unrecognizable. The Dutch minimalist abstractionist Piet Mondrian painted Dutch landscapes that reduced details to a series of intersecting straight lines of blue, white, black, and red. Instead of haystacks, sunflowers, irises, or steam-powered trains puffing in and out of Europe's central stations, American abstract expressionists set up tableaux of stroke and color repetitions that the American artist Robert Motherwell (cited in Miller 1946, 36) celebrated for going so far beyond nation that one could say, "To be merely an American or French artist is to be nothing." Artist and viewer operated outside art historical boxes and beyond the usual signposts of theme, style, and place.

Not all aspects of art making changed with the early triumph of abstract style, though, and not all figures disappeared in skeins of color. First of all, to be an abstractionist was decidedly to be a man and not a woman. As in most periods of art history, the noted achievers of abstraction, the ones we remember today, are men. And although these men could seemingly erase all other figures from their work, they rarely even tried to erase themselves as known creators. More, the early modernists were especially drawn to depicting women in ways that distorted their body parts but could not cover over or disguise an ongoing reign of "male sexual fantasy as high public culture" (Duncan 1995, 122). Sometimes the fantasy women could be fearsome and grotesque, as with de Kooning's bulbous bodies oiled into tight garish clothes and made to perch open-legged on tiny chairs, grinning maniacally through menacing, oversized teeth. These creatures could exude power of a daunting, ghoulish sort that seemed to come out of a gothic Freudian nightmare. The fantasy could take the form of a world seemingly swept clear of gender altogether and replaced with colors, lines, and spaces rather than female nudes. And there certainly were fewer "oriental" odalisques or chubby nubile bathers being spied on by old men and more colors and drips on offer than in earlier art periods.

But the women were still there, and they continued to be presented through the eye of the artist as man, which is to say with a masculine gaze (see Broude and Garrard 1992; Mulvery 1989; Kleinfelder 1993; Pollock 1992). It was not uncommon in early modernist paintings to show a naked reclining woman confronting the art viewer with a seductive look. Henri Matisse's women reclining languidly in tropical settings, their arms thrown above their heads, nothing apparently to occupy them except this posing—stand as an obvious case in point. Picasso's many dissected and rearranged women's faces and his still life portraits of lovers as pitchers and fruit are also vivid look-at-me displays of sexuality, emotion, desire, and contempt. They evoke many responses in viewers and analysts, from the critical claim that Picasso's portraits staged styles or tropes rather than people's inner lives (Kuspit 2000) to praise for his ability to portray personhood moving and dissolving into something or someone else only to re-form anew (Rubin, 1996). Feminist viewers worried that the real-life women behind the portraits, and by extension all women, were demeaned, uglified, infantilized, or made to seem psychologically disjointed and mad (Duncan 1992). Although the paintings are dispiriting at times, it is also possible to see in Picasso's work the women in his life presented with a rude honesty about love and lust enjoyed, stabilized, and lost. His women usually start off as muses and almost always end up as unattractive hysterics. And yet he was a master at inventing and reinventing "woman" in oils, a process that started to liberate "her" from the pedestals of art history—and sometimes from its lusts, his own included.

The second wave of abstraction in modern art switches continents and styles. The United States becomes its base and abstract expressionism its métier. If there were any remaining doubts that the first wave of abstraction was about strutting artist egos, the second wave brought these right to the fore. Michael Leja (1993, 256) says American abstract expressionism was "recognized from its first accounts as a male domain, ruled by a familiar social construction of 'masculine' as tough, aggressive, sweeping, bold." In part, this reputation was invented by the art critics of the time (e.g., Greenberg 1947; Goodnough 1951), who kept describing abstract expressionism as rough, violent, and virile compared to the seeming gentility of the Parisian tradition. It was an image that evoked, and also helped invent, the appealing American male of the mid-century: solitary, rugged, nicotine-stained, large, crudely spontaneous, and moving in many directions at once while seeming to stand still, smirking. "He" was rock and roll before the music fully kicked in.

Women who became involved with men of the New York school quickly learned the meaning of extreme behavior; childish tantrums, heavy drinking, and affairs were the norm of such geniuses. Yet Elaine de Kooning herself wrote articles for *Art News* that helped to anchor abstract expressionism in the image of "the prototypical American artist-as-hero" (Hall 2000, 115; Lewison 1999), and Lee Krasner, wife of Jackson Pollock, promoted the myth of her husband's masculine genius by posing in the background of his media shots. Indeed, the abstract expressionists often relied on a woman's presence somewhere nearby to ensure that they were seen as "properly" masculine, despite being artists. Claiming to despise homosexuality, they enjoyed homoerotic clubbiness at places like the Cedars Bar in New York City. Indisputably, though, women artists like Lee Krasner struggled to keep their careers from being absorbed into the swaths and swirls that earned their men notoriety (Chave 1993). They did not always succeed.

Abstractionist men of modernism were equally insouciant about the racialist content of their work. The worst offender in this regard was the postimpressionist Paul Gauguin, who left his wife and five children in France for a series of artistic escapes that eventually took him to "primitive" Tahiti in 1891. There, in a place that had turned from a French protectorate into a colony in 1881, a place mythologized by explorers like Capt. James Cook and Samuel Wallis as seductive in all respects (Thomas 2004), and a place woven over time into various orientalist themes, Gauguin painted girls. They seemed to define his sense of the primitive (Brooks 1992). Although he tried to pass himself off later as something of the anthropologist-artist expert on Polynesian culture, his own words betray him: "I saw plenty of calm-eyed women. I wanted them to be willing to be taken without a word, brutally. In a way [it was a] longing to rape" (Gauguin 1972, 23). At age fifty, he set up house with a thirteen-year-old girl named Teha'amana, who had been offered to him by an islander. Once the girl stopped resisting his insistences, Gauguin proclaimed the experience "beautiful" and "wonderful" (Solomon-Godeau 1992, 326). Today he could be jailed as a pedophile or international sex offender. At that colonial time of international relations, he was simply "going native"—and was admired for it.

Most other abstractionists were content enough to travel the primitive via art rather than going to foreign lands and to women of premodern societies. They took what inspiration they could find at a distance. Picasso and Rothko appropriated African masks, and Pollock's early work drew on Native American sand paintings and cosmological figures he knew from living in Arizona. Their interest in these "primitive" forms seemed less sexual than Gauguin's, and against the militant nationalism, fascism, and biopolitics of 1930s and 1940s modernity, less überdestructive, too. Art of "primitives" was art stripped of pretense, inhumanity, and propaganda—or so the artists thought. It was unpolluted, unchanging, and unaffected by the poisons and progress of modern civilization. Primitive art seemed to encapsulate "the basic universality of all art" (quoted in Doss 1991, 351) and the noble savage nature of all humanity; we were all primitive cosmopolites weighed down by the technologies of modernity. Returning raw human emotions, spirituality, and an unconscious to the art of artifices, like spatial perspective, was not without its own struggles: "The disruption of space, the denial of volume, the overthrow of traditional compositional schemes, the discovery of painting as an autonomous surface, the emancipation of color, line or texture, the occasional transgressions and reaffirmations of the boundaries of art (as in the adaptation of junk or non–high art materials), and so on through the liberation of painting from frame and stretcher and thence from the wall itself—all of these formal advances translate into moments of moral as well as artistic ordeal" (Duncan 1995, 109).

Simultaneously, the field of IR (in its pre-camp days) was setting about to "overthrow traditional compositional schemes" for a certain abstract primitivism of its own called realism. Realism, it was argued, was the true IR in the sense of being best able to capture the essence of international relations then and across the epochs. It was also universally attuned to the primitive nature of an international state system that had no overarching governance structure. International relations was the realm of anarchy beyond law and civilization, where states struggled for power and survival using wars, standoffs, and threats to settle many disputes. Modern artists retreated to pretechnological images, methods, and styles, while realists of IR invented a place where nation-states could operate without bringing issues of domestic morality and constitutional order to bear. IR's primitive led with guardhouses, soldiers, patrolled borders, guns, bombs, men, and, most of all, with sovereignty. Modern art's primitive charge saw male artists advancing with bottle of beer in one hand and a sand painting, African mask, or woman's savage face in the other.

The two fields presented Janus faces of masculine yearning that simplified complex histories. Native American sand paintings, for example, were lifted out of contexts of political struggle for the rights of native peoples living within sovereign states. Modern art was not too interested in such details, and IR was preoccupied for decades with interstate relations. In looking the other way, each "style" reinstantiated aspects of modernity that it sought to escape through the primitive. Similarly, the failed ideals of the Fourteen Points and the League of Nations led realists into realms of militarization that piggybacked onto a cultural mania for machines. The modern world was primitive, perhaps, but not in the ways that IR and many modernists thought.

MOMA and World War II

MOMA was at the center of every moment and phase of disruptive modernism, mapping it all onto art history. It was also an institution that learned early to meld art with international relations, largely because the Rockefellers at its helm were so immersed both in American foreign policy and in the workings of the modern art/museum.

Nelson Rockefeller is the animating spirit of the modern art–international connection. In 1939, at the age of thirty-two, he became president of MOMA. Nearly instantaneously (1940) he entered Franklin Roosevelt's administration as coordinator of the newly formed Office of the Coordinator of Inter-American Affairs (CIAA), a position that required him to leave MOMA's presidency but not its board. His leap into international relations came on the back of a trip to South America in 1937, which he made as overseer of the family oil holdings in Venezuela (the Creole Petroleum Company). Following his travels to nearly a dozen countries across the region, and in true blueblood fashion, he wrote a memorandum to the White House on "hemisphere economic policy."

It warned that poor social conditions in Latin America could easily give rise to authoritarian governments. Roosevelt formed the CIAA in response and asked Rockefeller to head it; the position led to another job as assistant secretary of state for Latin American affairs. In 1946, Nelson Rockefeller returned to the MOMA presidency, but four years later, President Harry Truman appointed him chairman of the International Development Advisory Board for the Point Four Program under the U.S. State Department; he was to recommend policies on the provision of technical aid to poor regions of the world. Rockefeller resigned that position a scant year later (1951) with the idea of pursuing his own private-sector initiatives for overseas development. In 1952 he agreed to become the special assistant to President Dwight Eisenhower on cold war strategy. Nelson Rockefeller served three American presidents and a major art institution in the span of twelve years, a remarkable achievement, albeit not one unheard of in elite circles around the world (Wu 2002; Franc 1994). Of course, he also went on to be vice president of the United States under Gerald Ford.

Rockefeller's overlapping institutional locations and loyalties gave rise to the critical view within art history circles that MOMA was sullied and compromised by political involvement in the American war effort. In 1941, MOMA and the CIAA, as well as other New York art institutions, worked together to "organize and circulate the most comprehensive exhibition of contemporary art from the United States ever seen in Latin America" (Franc 1994, 113). Approximately 159 paintings and 110 watercolors were sent to Mexico City, Santiago, Lima, Quito, Buenos Aires, Montevideo, Rio de Janeiro, Bogota, Caracas, and Havana. Allegedly, MOMA then fulfilled a total of thirty-eight wartime contracts with the Office of the Coordinator of Inter-American Affairs, the Library of Congress, and the Office of War Information, earning around a $1.5 million for its efforts (Lynes 1973, 237). Less concerning to the critics, but remarked, was MOMA's assistance to European artists like Max Ernst and Marc Chagall, who fled Germany in the 1930s. The museum also countered the Nazi confiscation of 16,000 works of modern art from German state museums and galleries, which became the infamous Munich exhibition of 1937, Entartet Kunst Ausstellung (Degenerate Art Exhibition) (see Petropoulos 1996, 52), by exhibiting work by the targeted artists in the more respectful environment of the museum, thereafter acquiring the work for the museum cheaply.

One might be inclined to laud MOMA's war efforts on the cultural front. Certain leftist critics reproached MOMA instead and accused Rockefeller of clandestinely turning the museum into a tool of capitalist American propaganda (e.g., Kozloff 1973; Cockcroft 1985; Guilbaut 1983). It is a charge that MOMA staff resist today. One former curator insists that the museum did nothing much more than put on three propagandistic exhibitions of photographs (Elderfield 1994, 9). The Road to Victory (1941), the first, used photographs from various government offices and picture agencies that would produce "a sense that the United States would win the war because of the justice of its cause and the vitality of its people" (Szarkowski 1994, 19). Power in the Pacific (1945) was put on for the U.S. Navy and emphasized military aspects of American involvement in the war. The final exhibition in the "series" focused on the American role in the Korean War (1951). Edward Steichen, MOMA's retired director of photography, claims today that he did the exhibitions with the intent of turning viewers *against* war. In his eyes, the shows must be considered failures, because audiences reacted to them in the opposite way. His antiwar approach could have been at odds with Nelson Rockefeller's government service during the war, but MOMA's many departments had their own curators and programming options. To suggest that the entire museum danced to any one fiddler or theme song would be to simplify a complex structure and falsely unify curatorial policy.

Still, John Hay Whitney, a former MOMA president who himself worked for the Office of Strategic Services during World War II, referred to MOMA as "a weapon in national defense" (quoted in Lynes 1973) and mentioned parties and other entertainment that MOMA put on for the troops (*Bulletin of the Museum of Modern Art* 1942). Others remember Steichen's supposedly antiwar Road to Victory as unmistakably pro-American. These words of poet Carl Sandburg, who was Steichen's brother-in-law, was featured on large posters mounted at the entrance to the exhibition: "In the beginning was virgin land and America was promises." A Franklin Roosevelt quotation about the four freedoms of the United State followed. Then, amid photos of buffalo, rural people, and forests, appeared pictures of soldiers and well-known American officials shaking hands with military officers. A Dorothea Lange picture of Pearl Harbor was exhibited with a photo of the Japanese ambassador and peace envoy below it, laughing. One contemporary art historian thinks the Road to Victory exhibition was organized "as if it were a national folktale. The story was linear, the message obvious, the tone both sentimental and militaristic" (Staniszewski 1998, 210). It might be noteworthy too that the "antiwar" Steichen joined the navy as head of a photography unit (see Phillips 1981).

MOMA and the Cold War

MOMA's record of involvement with the U.S. government during the early cold war is just as contradictory and full of debating points, but at least there is more information to work with. In 1952 MOMA started an international program of overseas exhibitions, using an initial Rockefeller Brothers Fund grant of $125,000. The official aim was to facilitate American representation in major international exhibitions and bring art from abroad to U.S. audiences. Cold war paranoia was rampant. The House Un-American Activities Committee, set up in 1946, went looking for Communist traitors in the arts, an endeavor that the McCarthy hearings of 1950–1953 kept up. Certain modern art styles, chiefly abstract expressionism, became despised by anticommunist contingents inside and outside government, in part because the works undermined conventional ideologies of beauty and also because some abstract expressionists dabbled in leftist politics. George Dondero, the Republican representative from Michigan, believed that the new "art" was undermining cherished Western values of order, reason, and uplifting beauty. He insisted in 1949 that cubism was about designing disorder and Dadaism was sheer ridicule of Western inventiveness. Of abstract expressionism, he had this to say: "Expressionism aims to destroy by aping the primitive and insane. Abstractionism aims to destroy by the creation of brainstorms" (quoted in Hauptman 1973, 18). The Hearst newspapers saw something "communistic" in all nonfigurative artworks. *Look* magazine, a popular middle-of-the-road publication of the period, ran a story asking whether taxpayers' money should be spent on such works (Franc 1994, 115).

MOMA came under cold war scrutiny at that point for its support of abstract works. In 1949, the House Committee on Foreign Affairs placed MOMA on the list of artists, galleries, and organizations that were traitors to the United States. MOMA, it was alleged, had supported "practitioners of 'abstractivism' or non-objectivity . . . spawned as a simon-pure, Russian Communist product" (115). In 1952, the attorney general began to publicize lists of "subversives" and banned certain artists from participating in exhibitions sponsored by U.S. agencies and institutions. The newly formed United States Information Agency (USIA) refused to allow an exhibition of twentieth-century American art to travel once it discovered that ten of the participating artists were on the "list." It also indicated that it would disallow any exhibitions of American art overseas that included works executed after 1917, the year of the Russian Revolution. It was all sheer madness. MOMA's international program was a defiant response to media mischaracterizations of modern art, as well as congressional efforts to politicize it. A liberal cadre of American politicians, among them Senators Hubert Humphrey and J. W. Fulbright, joined the art presses, MOMA, and other museums in issuing "A Statement on Modern Art," which affirmed its validity and endorsed MOMA's international program. Presumably, if there had been a Rockefeller-backed plan to use modern art as a foreign policy tool, MOMA would not have come under such intense scrutiny by Washington agencies and would not have had a reason to devise such firm responses.

Instead, Blanchette Ferry Hooker, wife of John D. Rockefeller, and Elizabeth Bliss Parkinson, Nelson Rockefeller's friend from childhood, decided that MOMA's new International Program required wider financial and political backing. To get this, they established the International Council of MOMA in 1953 as "an auxiliary organization of community leaders throughout the USA and abroad, interested in furthering the role of modern art in contemporary society, whose annual dues would support a program of cultural exchange"

(Franc 1994, 120). Hooker became the inaugural chair of the council and invited one hundred members to join at an annual cost of $1,000 (at 1953 rates). She also provided for the election of honorary members whose work for international cultural exchange was well known. In addition to this, MOMA encouraged public discussion of the arts and international relations throughout the 1950s. In 1955, it helped sponsor a symposium, "International Exchange in the Arts," keynoted by one of the darlings of realist IR, George Kennan. Recently returned from ambassadorial duties in the Soviet Union (1952–1954), Kennan talked about the need to contain Communism, a position with which he would always be closely associated in the field of IR. Intriguingly, however, he stepped across the line that usually separates politics from art by stressing that American modern art was a resource for the United States and not a liability. He called it a tool in a larger effort to change America's cultural image abroad as a "nation of vulgar, materialistic *nouveau riches* . . . contemptuous of every refinement of aesthetic feeling." Kennan urged his audience to "show the outside world both that we have a cultural life and that we care enough about it, in fact, to give it encouragement and support here at home, and to see that it is enriched by acquaintance with similar activity elsewhere" (Kennan 1956, np). MOMA circulated the address widely.

Kennan's sense of modern art's potential would eventually prevail over the paranoia of the era. Modern art would also survive the odd strands of modernist internationalism that played at the edges of totalitarian thinking. Looking back at that era with some distance now, it is tempting to mock the worries of modern art's cold war opponents. Recently reviewing an exhibition on modernism at the Victoria and Albert Museum in London, however, Bryan Appleyard (2006, 5) reminds us that modern art could have dodgy associations: "The most idealistic left-wing modernism often descends into chilling, prescriptive totalitarianism. The idea of a cult of collective health and exercise prefigured the mass gymnastic displays of which communist and fascist dictators were so fond. And the Dutch designer Mart Stam wanted to build the most minimal homes and collectivise even kitchens, private life being anathema in the new world order. Some Italian modernists, meanwhile, became handy tools of Mussolini's fascism."

Most modern artists were not menacing forces. Certainly the American abstract expressionists were not. They leaned left; some of them, like Pollock, appeared to lean far to the socialist left at certain points in their careers. But art historian Stephen Polcari (1993, 31) calls their overall political beliefs "ill-defined," saying that they tended to "hold that combination of anarchist-bohemian-conservatism typical of many modern artists." In fact, that group did not really form "the New York school" of painting with which they are associated, because egos and neuroses trumped any shared political and stylistic convictions they might have had.[5] Yet years later, in the waning days of the Vietnam War, a few leftist art commentators brought up the cold war controversies once again. They had evidence, they insisted, that MOMA remained politicized during the early cold war years, to the point where it became the cultural arm of America's struggle against the Soviet Union (see Sylvester 1996).

The Abstract Expressionist Cold War Connection Revisited

It is useful to recall that the cold war was a controversial international relations. Policymakers on both side of the so-called Iron Curtain pursued the East-West standoff with every tool available to them: propaganda, currency and trade blocs, global militarization, selective foreign aid, and cultural/sports competitions. Leftist groups in Europe and North America objected strenuously to various cold war efforts to defeat what they saw as progressive socialist movements in the world. Specific events of the time inflamed those sentiments, or created leftist sympathies where none had earlier existed. The Vietnam War was one such extended event. It devoured extraordinary resources and produced thousands of casualties on all sides, for no reason that made any sense to leftists and then to a wide range of people. That war became an economic cum political cum social debacle for the United States and for the West in general. Student movements, academic movements, women's movements, civil rights movements—conventions-challenging groups of all sorts started up during the years of that war, precipitating a legitimacy crisis for American government and for conservative social mores. All "establishment" groups and government agencies that had ever fed the cold war machinery were lumped together by militant critics and treated to the kind of harsh denunciations that the McCarthy trials had inflicted on suspected leftists in the 1950s.

Within this melee, a few leftist art historians argued that MOMA played a part in the antisocialist cold war fever of the early 1950s, thereby continuing to taint itself as an art institution. Its role in the colossal struggle of international relations was to face off with the Soviet Union in the visual arts by surreptitiously putting forward American abstract expressionism as the symbol of a big, determined, and newly creative free country, which did not have to resort to political art to get its message out to the world (Kozloff 1973; Cockcroft 1985; Guilbaut 1983). The style of that painting was stunningly fresh and vibrant, a form of "action painting" (Rosenberg 1952) that had managed to steal the thunder from war-weary Paris and replace it with dynamic motion and virile artistry; now it was about to steal attention away from the USSR's vigorously subsidized arts programs. Abstract expressionism was also associated with the vibrant city of New York, the adopted home of many European émigré artists who had escaped the earlier fascist onslaught and gone on to great things. The newly confident superpower was ready to imprint its image on the world in as many spheres possible, from moneymaking to scientific know-how to art. "As Clifton Fadiman put the thinking of the time, in a broadcast discussion about

'Art and Our Warring World,' America had passed through the childhood of the pioneer period and was 'now ready to develop as a civilization'" (quoted in Lewison 1999, 13)—with imperial ambitions, the radicals of art claimed.

Abstract expressionism would have been a breathtakingly unique choice for any American museum of modern art to showcase abroad; yet it would also have been an odd style for MOMA to push. Many a European art critic dismissed it out of hand in the 1940s, or claimed it was a continuation of the European painting tradition (Sylvester 1950; Lewison 1999, 7–8). Few spectators in the United States liked it, apart from some critics, most notably Clement Greenberg (1947), who appreciated its intellectual qualities; Harold Rosenberg (1952), who found the individual artists fascinating; and gallerists/collectors like Peggy Guggenheim and Katharine Kuh. Prior to the 1950s there was barely a market for American artworks, bona fide "art" being seen as a creature of Europe. And those who made art were often disinclined to call themselves artists: an "artist" was someone whose output "detracted from the real business of taming wilderness and industry and of accruing power and making money in the young, rich country" (Hall 2000. 107). All that abruptly changed after World War II. The prosperity of postwar/postdepression times gave people more money, more leisure time, greater access to higher education, and an optimistic curiosity about new ideas and things in general. A mere three years after the war ended, Jackson Pollock was on the cover of *Life* magazine, a popular vehicle celebrating all that was novel and glamorous. Yet America was a conservative country in the early 1950s, in its taste for visual art as in its largely Republican-led politics. For a number of years, abstract expressionism could either empty a gallery or attract an incredulous media as taken by the bohemian lifestyle of the artists as the art itself.

MOMA—or should we say Barr—was innovative in many ways but not when it came to jumping on the bandwagon for abstract expressionism. The museum bought abstract expressionist pieces, and yet it would be the late 1950s before it touted them at home or abroad, that is to say, after the period that radical art critics identified as the heyday of MOMA's cold war politics. Indeed, it was the avant-garde Institute of Contemporary Art (ICA), not MOMA, that first brought Pollock's work to London, in 1953. And it seems that keen gallerists and artist's wives (especially Elaine de Kooning) were the real promoters of abstract expressionism. It was only around 1958, after the harshest days of the early cold war had passed and antagonism toward abstract expressionism had quieted, that MOMA's International Program sponsored a traveling exhibition devoted to Pollock, the artist said to be "the" master of the new American style. Even then, there is some evidence that European museum directors pressured MOMA to put the exhibition together so they could see Pollock's work at their institutions (Franc 1994, 133). MOMA's International Council circulated a more general exhibition called Modern Art in the United States in 1956; however, against the radicals' claim that it focused on a dozen abstract expressionists, it turned out that there were 112 artists represented in that show. If international spectators wanted to see some of Pollock's work before that time, they could do so at the Greek Pavilion of the 1948 Venice Biennale and at the American Pavilion of the 1950 Biennale, which MOMA sponsored; Pollock was one of six artists in the latter show, which Michael Kimmelman (1994, 45) describes as "ancillary to a John Marin retrospective comprising eighty-one works."

In an influential piece that revisited the arguments about MOMA and the cold war twenty odd years later, Kimmelman (1994) identified numerous inaccuracies in the radical assertions of MOMA's critics. It simply was not true, he said, that MOMA had thrust the abstract expressionists forward in the international shows it sponsored between 1948 and 1958, as Eva Cockcroft (1974) had claimed. It was not true, as Serge Guilbaut (1983) had asserted, and as had been taken as gospel by a Whitney Museum study program as late as 1991, that a coordinated pro-abstract-expressionist propaganda effort was pursued by MOMA in alliance with the USIA. Kimmelman (1994, 49) writes: "Whether or not individuals at the USIA privately wanted to push Abstract Expressionism, the reality of the McCarthy era was that the agency could not co-organize an exhibition of such vanguard art, although in certain European cities the offices of the United States Information Service (USIS, a division of the USIA) could assist with local publicity and transportation costs." Kimmelman's article is also noteworthy for drawing attention not just to who was exhibited where but also to how their work was displayed and publicized. He finds that in some cases abstract expressionist works were featured in exhibition catalogs but were just part of, or even put last in, larger exhibitions, included primarily to show the diversity of U.S. modern art. Kimmelman believes that while there can be little doubt that there was a conscious cultural front to the cold war on both sides, the charges leveled at MOMA in particular do not hold up well. The museum's alleged affair with abstract expressionism seems to have actually been a tepid thing. Far hotter was the rhetoric of the antiwar days and the links the protesters of all kinds made between government institutions waging war in Southeast Asia and other powerful and privileged institutions. MOMA was clearly both; the 1950s had been the key decade when "the Museum's account of twentieth-century art took on the authority of scripture" (45). That alone would be enough to condemn it in the eyes of those who later insisted on more bottom-up accountability from all U.S. institutions.

Other figures in the art world share Kimmelman's conclusions, among them Nicholas Serota (2000) and the writer David Caute (2003), who has most recently reexamined the evidence of a cultural cold war.[6] A close reading of the historical record shows, as Caute (2003, 541) puts it, that "what the Museum of Modern Art and other sponsors exported throughout the 1950's was a mixed bag of styles and movements, the result not only of political nervousness, compromise, and continual vigilante howling, but also of a commonsensical appraisal of European taste and opinion." When the State Department art program assembled seventy-nine modernist works for display at the Metropolitan Museum of Art in 1946, the art was slammed by every group from the American Artists Professional League to the *New York Times.* When MOMA's *Modern Art in the United States* toured Europe with twenty-eight pieces by artists associated with abstract expressionism in 1956, Andrew Wyeth's realist *Christina's World* proved the most popular, and realist works in that exhibition received more favorable reviews than any of the abstractions. Wyeth's popularity extended for twenty more years; he received the Presidential Freedom Award in 1963, was elected to the Académie des Beaux-Arts in 1977, and was elected honorary member of the Soviet Academy of Arts in 1978. Caute opines that Wyeth's prominence in the era of abstract expressionism might suggest that "the cold war in the domain of painting could not be won by the rejection of human content" (554).

Caute also reviews the funding picture for overseas exhibitions in the 1950s and says that the 1970s art radicals exaggerated the museum's relationship to government agencies. Over eighty works by seventeen American artists, including some abstract expressionists, were featured in a 1959 show, New American Painting, As Shown in Eight European Countries. It was funded almost entirely from MOMA resources. A 1958 Pollock exhibition was also financed in the main through MOMA. Records show that USIA and its USIS branches abroad did help periodically with invitations, transport, and other relatively minor expenses. There is no smoking gun, however, that would suggest that the State Department or the Central Intelligence Agency (CIA) clandestinely influenced MOMA's efforts or were asked to do so by the museum (Kimmelman 1994, 49). Any CIA connection in particular remains speculative—no less intriguing for that, though. Thomas Braden, who served as executive secretary of MOMA in the late 1940s, signed on with the CIA in 1950 to direct its cultural activities. René d'Harnoncourt, who took over directorship of the MOMA after Barr in 1944, had been head of the art section of Rockefeller's Office of the Coordinator of Inter-American Affairs in 1943. Other key MOMA staff had stints with U.S. intelligence agencies as well as art careers, including Porter McCray, director of circulating exhibitions as of 1947 and of MOMA's International Program in 1952, and Nelson Rockefeller himself.

Yet the incriminating instance, the link, the "ah-haa" is still missing, and Caute (2003, 551) insists that the "CIA-MOMA collusion has been supported merely by looking at family trees showing interlocking personal connections, and not by any close examination of patterns of art patronage and exhibition policy." When an official American modernist exhibit was finally sent to Moscow in 1959, MOMA was not the main institutional force behind it, and abstract expressionist works were in the distinct minority within it. USIA asked art experts (none from MOMA) to select a large number of works for the show, and the experts chose seventy wide-ranging paintings by sixty-seven American artists. At the last minute, the House Un-American Activities Committee objected to several featured artists on the grounds that they supposedly had Communist sympathies. After the USIA was politically pressured to put more traditional paintings by nineteenth-century artists into the package, the quotient of abstract expressionist works was relatively low. The official response to them on the receiving end was more than flat; the abstract expressionist works were called antihumanist and sterile.

A Family of Man?

Discussion of the early cold war as MOMA experienced it would be incomplete if it did not mention the highly successful, if rather gauche, exhibit that also traveled under MOMA's International Program: the Family of Man. That exhibition opened at MOMA in 1955 and is still considered by the museum to be one of the most successful photography shows it ever mounted. Its 103-day run attracted more than a quarter of a million viewers, and then ten editions of the show toured thirty-seven countries for a period of ten years. Yet that Edward Steichen–curated exhibition nearly failed to come to fruition. At the moment it was being prepared, Nelson Rockefeller decided MOMA should develop a stand-alone international image and become an art institution of America rather than a Rockefeller museum. To do so, MOMA could no longer be governed by his prominent family or remain reliant on its fortune. The museum would have to diversify its resource base. The timing of his announcement caught the Family of Man in a financial vise. The museum's board of trustees suddenly had no money for this undertaking and turned to UNESCO and the Ford Foundation for assistance, without success. In the end, USIA made it happen.

Nothing about the exhibition was abstract or expressionist. It was made up of 502 black-and-white photographs (and one color shot) gathered from sixty-eight countries. What tied these together were supposedly "universal elements and emotions in the everydayness of life—as a mirror of the essential oneness of mankind throughout the world" (Steichen 1955, 3) Mostly, the photographs depicted average people doing prosaic work or experiencing emotions readily interpretable in the United States. No celebrities were included, and only unknown photographers were working the cameras. Carl Sandburg's words introduced this show, too: "There is only one man in the world and his name is All Men / There is only one woman in the world and her name is All Women." Meant "to suggest that all peoples' goals and problems were fundamentally similar, and to recapitulate in broad strokes the life cycle of the species" (Szarkowski 1994, 13), the show determinedly avoided difference, unconventionality, and religious beliefs that did not resonate easily with Christianity. All Men were heterosexual and All Women married All Men, and together had All Children, worked, cried, sang, danced, loved, voted, faced some hard times, including incidences of political oppression and war, grew old, and grieved. All of this composed a life cycle of sameness everywhere.

The most violent scene in Family of Man showed the hydrogen bomb exploding during a 1954 test; it was the one color shot in the exhibition. Viewers then moved on to a mural showing the General Assembly of the United Nations and to an upbeat concluding section called "The Magic of Childhood," a theme Steichen had also used to end The Road to Victory exhibition. Two years after the Korean War had ended, ten years after World War II, and well into the atomic era and the cold war, it seemed that "America had produced a new affirmation of the dignity of Man" (Szarkowski 1994, 23). Steichen's assistant at the time, Wayne Miller, claims that Steichen saw Family of Man as a better vehicle than Road to Victory for showing that we kill people like us when we wage war (Staniszewski 1998, 251).

Critics, on the other hand, blasted Family of Man. Many felt insulted by MOMA's bland liberal internationalism and its willful demeaning of photographic art by using it strictly for political purposes (Kramer 1955). Roland Barthes (1973, 101–102) argued in his inimitable way that the exhibition held us back from "penetrating into this ulterior zone of human behavior where historical alienation introduces some 'differences' which we shall here quite simply call 'injustices.'" The theme of the show in his view was "Adamism," which he took to be a form of wisdom and lyrical gesture that served as an alibi for immobility in the world. John Szarkowski (1994, 35), MOMA's director emeritus of the Department of Photography, later speculated that the people from around the world who flocked to see Family of Man "were sick to the teeth of contention and brinkmanship, of tortuous political arguments, of being told that half the world was their enemy; and sick also of scientific sorcerers, and perhaps of their own pompous and self-satisfied governments." Perhaps. Jacques Barzun (1959) thought at the time that the exhibition was anti-intellectual and insistent in its primitivism.

The naïveté of the exhibition has to be seen against the backdrop of international relations (Phillips 1984; Sekula 1983; Sandeen 1995). It was staged "in a country that only a decade before had imprisoned its own citizens because of their Japanese heritage and that long assigned African American and Caucasian American individuals to socially sanctioned separate and unequal rights and fates" (Staniszewski 1998, 251). It was under assembly while the McCarthy hearings were running and opened the same year Rosa Parks refused to give up her bus seat to a white man in Montgomery, Alabama. The space race was on, the weapons race was full on, the "Iron Curtain" had been drawn, and "dominoes" were falling. Family of Man defied the gloom. UN officials were so impressed that they sought to have the exhibition permanently on view at the New York headquarters. That never came to be; however, a version was installed in 1994 at the Chateau Clervaux in Luxembourg.

IR MINGLES WITH MODERN ART

Investigations of cultural aspects of the cold war reveal the many faces, forms of power, and overlapping interests of government agencies and a U.S. museum during a remarkable period of international relations. The cold war being a favorite topic of IR analysts, the field has come to know a fair bit over fifty years about cold war ideological conflict, threat, diplomacy and brinkmanship, nuclear weapons, espionage, space and arms races, divided countries, and "hot" cold wars in Third World countries. Third debate entrants to IR in the 1980s taught the field to look more expansively and critically at that fifty-year period of conflict. The feminist camp of IR deserves tremendous credit for helping us to see that the American cold war effort relied on militarized gender, which is to say on constructions of "men" and "women" that were mobilized for national security purposes (Enloe 1993). We know about "men" on the front lines and "women" cultivating a conformist conservativism at home (Elshtain 1987). We know about the sexual militarization of Korean women during and following the Korean War (Moon 1997), and we are now aware of the dangers men were in, as well as women, during the post-cold-war wars in Eastern Europe (Carpenter 2003). We can see that gender and race also kept reappearing in the connected spaces of modernist art and international relations.

Museum Gender Issues

The cultural diplomacy that brought MOMA into cold war international relations was as gendered as any other activity of the times. Names like Nelson Rockefeller, Alfred Barr, Edward Steichen, and Joseph McCarthy suggest the bodies at the front of the cultural wars within the cold war. We must look more closely to see the women at MOMA and to release them from their naturalized resting place as the men's handmaids (Sylvester 1998). Blanchette Hooker comes into view as the mastermind of MOMA's International Council. When the Rockefeller Brothers Fund grant for MOMA's International Program was ending in 1957, her council helped the International Program to execute five times more exhibitions than all the curatorial departments at MOMA put together. For her outstanding leadership of the council, MOMA named its abstract expressionist gallery in Hooker's honor, thus inadvertently causing a reversal of the usual gender dynamics of modern art and of abstract expressionism: to see the works of the featured men, one had to enter a woman's room.

Then there was Barr's assistant, Dorothy Miller, a properly gendered woman of her class and time: demure, stylish, feminine, and always already a curator but never in charge (plate 6). Although she was Barr's right arm when he directed MOMA, she was important in her own right during the thirty-four years she worked at the institution. Miller said of her career, "The idea of going any higher on the ladder at the Museum did not occur to me. I always felt it a great privilege to work with Alfred Barr and the other brilliant people there" (quoted in Zelevansky 1994, 68–69). She was not the only one to minimize her achievements. Miller directed a large number of exhibitions—ten between 1940 and 1946 alone—and is credited by some with helping Barr to see the merits of abstract expressionism. Miller's advice on collecting works of that style proved invaluable, and many of her choices later became iconic to American modern art (Rosenblum 1982). Yet the art critic who put abstract expressionism into the canon of art history, Clement Greenberg, failed to mention Miller by name when he reviewed her 1946 show called 14 Americans.

One of Miller's admirers makes the more general gender point that "historically, U.S. museums in large part have been populated by women and dominated by men. Although founded by three powerful women, the Museum of Modern Art has been no exception. Having had a male director from the beginning, the Modern's most influential curators have also been men" (Zelevansky 1994, 68). This arrangement of gender roles might have been necessary in a country that tended to invent itself as too rugged for things like art (Knight 1994, 90). Similarly, of course, for the muscular United States to take on a world beyond its shores, it had to confront men of power elsewhere, who were equally serious about their own missions. With conflict as the backbone of IR, a cadre of male analysts seemed natural there, too. Thus Ann Tickner's (1992, ix) well-known question, "Why is the subject matter of my discipline [IR] so distant from women's experiences?" Men all the way down—white men at that.

Other Cold War Pictures and Peoples

The early cold war also coincides with the last gasp of colonialism and the rise of anticolonial militancy. Some African artists challenged modernism's love affair with "primitivism," arguing that Western artists had borrowed heavily from African and indigenous "tribal" arts without letting artists from those societies into exhibitions or art historical tracts. The Nigerian painter Uzo Egonu, who trained in England and lived in Paris in the 1950s, was one artist who eluded capture by European modernism. If Soviet audiences faulted abstract expressionism for excessive antihumanism, so did African artists like Egonu, who found the style cold, unappealing, and nonuniversal. His artwork of the cold war years featured figurative remembrances of African foods, animal life, women, landscapes, and the local masks beloved of European modernists, all expressed in the romanticist tropes of negritude and dotted with fauvist expressionism. Many of us will not have heard of him, even though figures like Egonu made "the discourse of global politics, and especially of the postcolonial condition, part of the humanist imperative of late modernism" (Oguibe 2004, 68–69; see also Craven 1996). A few Westerners picked up elements of that discourse: André Breton paid tribute to poet Aimé Césaire's pathbreaking influence on surrealism, and Pablo Picasso did the illustrations for Césaire's book *Corps Perdue*. But we in IR—even those in camps that have made contributions to understanding modernity and postcoloniality—might know little about these infusions and refusals of Western cultural modernism.[7]

There is equally good reason for IR's afterlife to pay attention to the art and international relations of countries that were fought over and fought within during the cold war. Korea, a country still divided by cold war politics, offers a strong case. With a distinguished history of artistic achievement in ceramics, ink painting, and folk arts, Korea is often thought to have been the artistic conduit between Chinese and Japanese traditions. Some argue that over the centuries Korea influenced Japanese arts more than Japan influenced Korea. Twentieth-century Korean artists were certainly aware of Western classical and Renaissance works, but they first experienced Western modern art through Japanese eyes during the colonial period (1910–1945). The West too only saw examples of Korean art and artifacts as a result of Japan's interest in increasing cultural and commercial links with Western countries. Following the first exhibition of Korean art in London, held at a Korean pavilion in the Anglo-Japanese Exhibition at the White City (1910), the Japanese made a gift to the British Museum of several Korean pieces of art. For Britain, "the shared ethos of empire was, at that time, an important part of their relationship" (Portal 2000, 17).

During World War II and the Korean War, various military, diplomatic, and medical personnel built collections of Korean art—often bought for a song—that have since become the backbone of collections at Harvard, the British Museum, and museums in Copenhagen and Stockholm (Hornby 1988; Henderson 1983). Part of Korea's development strategy during the postcolonial period entailed displaying its culture in the West through overseas art exhibits, an approach paralleling America's earlier cold war concern to represent itself as a land of culture. The American, British, and French public responded enthusiastically to Korean art, perhaps more so than it did to American abstract expressionism when it finally appeared in Europe in the late 1950s. Korean galleries opened at the Metropolitan Museum of Art, the Musée Guimet, the Victoria and Albert, and the Asian Art Museum of San Francisco, often with contributions made by Korean companies (Smith 1998; McKillop 1992). In a spirit of reciprocity, abstract Western works also went to Korea throughout the second half of the last century, where it met with a less than enthusiastic reception: it was the general view that the works lacked the spiritual qualities that Korean art had long valued. Korean ink painters, such as Park Nae-hyon and Yi Ung-no, only gestured lightly to Western abstraction in their more ordered styles. A Korean Informel group of oil painters produced works seemingly derivative of the New York school of abstract expressionism, and yet their members denied the link (Portal 2000, 177). The groups' spokesperson, Park Seo-Bo, representing his colleagues at a 1961 exhibition in Paris organized by

UNESCO, declared the Parisian art scene "bourgeois" (Roe 2001, 34). It would be 1970 before a Korean artist, in this case ink abstractionist Kim Ki-chang, would feature in any MOMA exhibition. This cultural chain of international relations remains shrouded for IR, despite the field's long-standing interest in the geopolitics of cold war Korea.

And then, of course, there is the vast artistic output of the Soviet Union to reconsider. We still know relatively little about the cultural cold war from East European and Soviet perspectives, although we know more now than we did. The conspiratorial tone of radical art historical scholarship on MOMA and the cold war was ostensibly motivated, at least in part, by a reaction to America's virulent anti-Communism. Yet that scholarship placed so much emphasis on the role of American art in the early cold war that it effectively turned its back on art and cultures of similarity and difference across the Soviet empire (Richmond 2003). Caute is certain that the Soviet Union had more to show for itself during most of the cultural cold war than American culture did, even though the Soviets undercut their own vast cultural promise by constraining the avant-garde. Still, if one perseveres to the end of the cold war period, it seems, says Caute (2003, 1), that the "'stroke' which finally buried Soviet Communism was arguably moral, intellectual, and cultural as well as economic and technological." Caute has disappointed some by not analyzing the cultural productions that form the basis of his study (Kodat 2003). Kimmelman (2004, 2), reading Caute's account ten years after his own original article on MOMA and the cold war, however, is not disappointed. Describing Caute's book as "excellent," Kimmelman says that Caute has reminded us that "high art was power once, and that era has passed."

Has it? Can art be divorced from power? More likely the power-art relationship has shape-shifted with the times. The 1950s was the era of cold war international relations. Ours is said to be the era of globalization. The power forms might be different today—then again, war continues to rage around us—but a power link with art cannot be denied. We move now from MOMA to its neighboring modern art museum, the Guggenheim, an institution that travels the world with ambitious influence, architectural innovation, and the drive to forge unexpected alliances. Bigger than life, it is decried by some, embraced by others, and largely overlooked as a player in the power realms that IR associates with international relations.

Plate 1. Fight between a human Lapith and a Centaur (Centauromachy). Metope from the south side of the Parthenon, Athens. High Classical Greek, ca. 440 BCE. Marble, h. 1.72m. Inv. GR 1816,0610.11. Location: British Museum, London, Great Britain. (© British Museum / Art Resource, NY.)

Plate 2. Madonna of the Pinks, *about 1506–1507, Raphael (© The National Gallery, London.)*

Plate 3. Lady of Warka. *(PA Photos.)*

Plate 4. Alfred Barr, Director of Museum Collections. The Abby Aldrich Rockefeller Sculpture Garden, The Museum of Modern Art, New York. 1959. Location: The Museum of Modern Art, NY, USA. (Digital Image © The Museum of Modern Art / Licensed by SCALA / Art Resource, NY.)

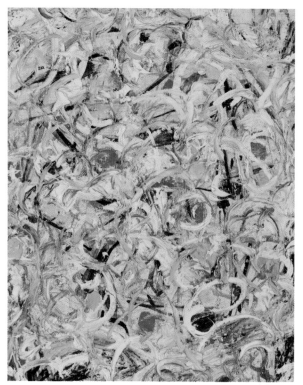

Plate 5. Shimmering Substance *from the Sounds in the Grass series, Jackson Pollock. 1946. Oil on canvas, 30 1/8 x 24 1/4". Mr. and Mrs. Albert Lewin and Mrs. Sam A. Lewisohn Funds. (6.1968) (Digital Image © 2008 The Museum of Modern Art / Licensed by SCALA / Art Resource, NY. Permission to use artwork © 2008 Pollock-Krasner Foundation / Artists Rights Society [ARS], New York.)*

Plate 6. Dorothy Miller at The New American Painting at Kunsthalle Basel, 1958. International Council / International Program Exhibition Records. ICE-F-36-57 v.38.24. The Museum of Modern Art Archives, New York. Location: The Museum of Modern Art, New York, NY, USA. (Digital Image © The Museum of Modern Art / Licensed by SCALA / Art Resource, NY.)

Plate 7. The Guggenheim Museum Bilbao along Calle de Iparraguirre, with Jeff Koons's Puppy. (© Scott Hortop.)

Plate 8. The World Trade Center pit. (PA Photos.)

Plate 9. An Allegory of Prudence, *about 1565–1570, Titian. (© The National Gallery, London.)*

Plate 10. Smile Now, Cry Later, *1998, Francesco Clemente (© Francesco Clemente. Photo courtesy of Gagosian Gallery.)*

Plate 11. Dead Troops Talk (a vision after an ambush of a Red Army patrol, near Moor, Afghanistan, winter 1986), *1992, Jeff Wall.* (© *Jeff Wall.*
Photo: Courtesy of Jeff Wall Studio, Vancouver.)

Plate 12. The Saensbury Wing, *1999–2000, Richard Hamilton. Also called* The Sainsbury Wing. *(© Richard Hamilton. All Rights Reserved, DACS 2008.)*

CHAPTER 5

The Globalizing Guggenheim Saves the Basques?

The modern art museum with the most global ambition and global presence is the Guggenheim. From a home base in New York City and a family-linked branch in Venice, it has embarked on post-cold-war expansion into Berlin, Bilbao, and Las Vegas; additional locations in Asia and South America are under negotiation, and a new Guggenheim museum has been announced for Abu Dhabi. Constant negotiations for overseas museum sites give the impression that the Guggenheim is the roving art institution of our time in international relations. That most of its art diplomatic efforts do not bear fruit, or might produce a venture that fails after opening, as a Las Vegas museum did, also creates considerable skepticism about its intentions and methods. Does the Guggenheim want art museums or global museum celebrity? Joseba Zulaika, a Basque anthropologist who has studied Guggenheim Bilbao, opines that "if you have already achieved what you really wanted, the front pages of papers and magazines showing off your next project, is building it really important?"[1] If he is right, the Guggenheim's activities might best be seen alongside other event-oriented politics of contemporary international relations, such as extravagant stadium shows and massive conferences aimed at ending poverty or publicizing women's issues or environmental problems. In this case, the Guggenheim would be publicizing itself as an empire of art.

While there is reason to query the Guggenheim phenomenon, it is important to see its museums from the perspective of societies that bring Guggenheim to their towns. Guggenheim museums can generate considerable enthusiasm and affection abroad, as well as cynicism, and it is said that the museums can contribute to local economic development and give a cosmopolitan boost to an area. The Guggenheim's energetic forays, coupled with its spectacular museum achievement in Bilbao, Spain, also bring the world of the art/museum and IR together in a web of international relations where it is not expected to be. That web encompasses big business, big politics, big money, big architecture, big development prospects, and mammoth summitry. If IR's many camps work hard to overlook all that big international relations, the art world notices every move the Guggenheim makes: its entrepreneurial director, its courting of identity and wealth for itself and for the businesses or cities it sets up in abroad, and its indifference to issues of saving art for nation or for any particular museum. Guggenheim is the museum group that the art world loves to hate and the art power IR cannot see.

Our journey around this most internationally striving of art institutions commences in New York and stops briefly in Berlin. It then lingers in Bilbao to consider the debate about the Guggenheim museum there. Many art analysts decry that venture, seeing it as akin to an imperial palace being plopped on colonized land and followed up by the announcement that the locals are copartners. Views from Basque studies are more nuanced. This region has long pursued its own international relations and continues to do so to protect itself against Spanish ambitions. Once something of that history of international involvement is understood, the salient question that emerges for us is less why the Guggenheim expanded into Bilbao than how and why the Basque regional administration wanted to coax the Guggenheim to Bilbao. Who gets what out of this international relations?

THE GLOBAL GUGGENHEIM MUSEUM

The Guggenheim art institutions carry the family name of another business dynasty of the gilded era of museum building in the United States. When the Guggenheim brothers immigrated to Philadelphia from Switzerland and Germany around 1848, they invested in mining and soon developed thriving businesses around silver in Colorado and copper and nitrate in Mexico, Alaska, and Chile. As their wealth grew, two of the brothers became associated with art collecting, Benjamin Guggenheim and Solomon Guggenheim. Benjamin's connection to art was indirect, through his daughter Peggy, who established the Art of This Century Gallery in New York to showcase modern art and supported Jackson Pollock in the early days of his career. She also amassed a significant collection of art at her Venetian villa, where she preferred to live. (Benjamin himself was a victim of the ill-fated voyage of the *Titanic*.) Solomon Guggenheim personally collected modern artworks and dabbled in museum curatorship. Working with the eccentric baroness Hilla Rebay, who was fascinated by certain expressionist streams of abstract art associated with Wassily Kandinsky, he developed the Museum of Non-Objective Painting in a New York town house near MOMA. The first exhibition opened in 1939 as the Art of Tomorrow, featuring nearly four hundred paintings from Guggenheim's personal collection. Dore Ashton (1972, 112–13) describes the ambiance of the opening:

"With thick gray carpets, silver décor, and the music of Bach, Beethoven, and Chopin piped in to facilitate the Baroness' idea that viewers should have 'cosmic contacts with art,' the strange new museum established itself importantly in New York." That museum, which was visited by the young abstract expressionists in the making, lasted for ten years.

By 1937, Solomon Guggenheim had engaged the distinguished American architect Frank Lloyd Wright to work with him to design and construct a proper modern art museum. Their collaboration produced the Solomon R. Guggenheim Museum, which opened its doors in New York City after several delays, nearly twenty years later in 1959. Rebay had been keen in the 1940s to showcase Kandinsky, Klee, and Léger, among others, as artists of "abstraction without meaning." She influenced Solomon Guggenheim's acquisitions and thought in terms of a large New York museum that would showcase mostly European abstractionists. Once the Guggenheim museum opened, however, it was the unique museum design that imprinted itself on the art world, not so much the collection inside. The flagship museum on Fifth Avenue has a circular design with a tall internal atrium at its center, around which curves a continuous narrow ramp. Visitors make their way up the ramp and stand somewhat lopsidedly as they take in artworks that can seem to march along the wall to their right. With its earlier start-up and vast modernist collection, MOMA has the reputational edge for modern art. Nonetheless, the original Guggenheim collection was significant, and its scope has broadened over time to include more-familiar European and American modernists like Cézanne, Picasso, Giacometti, Chagall, Pollock, Rauschenberg, and Warhol. And, before Peggy Guggenheim died in 1979, her own modernist holdings in Venice, numbering about three hundred, had joined the New York Guggenheim collection, her private residence in Venice, Palazzo Venier dei Leoni, following. One might say that the Guggenheim international branch approach had its start in a family arrangement.

Still, neither Solomon Guggenheim nor Peggy Guggenheim envisaged the Guggenheim as a global museum. That vision came out of the genius—or the malfeasance, if you will—of then overall director Thomas Krens. Krens took the helm of the Guggenheim in 1988, when the museum was experiencing several difficulties. One problem was overidentification with its landmark architecture and underappreciation for its collection in a city chockablock with art museums and modernist holdings. Attendance was dropping, and for a private museum, that meant revenues were declining. By the middle 1980s even the iconic building itself was looking tatty and was, moreover, limiting possibilities for showing the enlarged collection. Krens wanted to put the Guggenheim name and collection more firmly on the modern art map, refurbish the building's exterior, and open more exhibition spaces for the extensive portion of the collection kept in storage. And he wanted more visitors and more revenue overall.

The way forward, he wagered, was to develop international Guggenheim franchises while working to revitalize the New York institution. It was a novel idea that would see the Guggenheim rise, not just by attracting more viewers to the collection in New York, but also by finding new audiences and sources of revenue overseas. There would be other benefits: storage costs in New York could be virtually eliminated by sending parts of the collection abroad, and more of the collection could be put on view at any one time. The New York museum could also collect rents from franchise use of the collection, as well as for use of the Guggenheim name and the museum's management expertise. If each branch also acquired its own small collection, which would be owned by the home institution, the Guggenheim New York could even increase its total art holdings without cost to itself. The global corporate expansion model had come to the art museum.

The first step was to put the New York museum on an improved financial footing. Krens persuaded most of the museum trustees to float a $54 million bond against the value of the Guggenheim collection, a move that was controversial enough to cause several board resignations. He then stepped further onto the terrain of controversy by auctioning three important paintings from the collection in order to kick-start the renovations in New York: Chagall, Kandinsky, and Modigliani earned the Guggenheim $47 million. If we recall the National Gallery of London's strenuous campaign to save one small Raphael painting from sale by its private owner to an overseas museum, then the gravity of not-saving three works in the Guggenheim collection becomes apparent. Professional museum associations generally agree that artworks may be sold by a museum only to purchase more art for the collection, not for purposes of renovation or expansion of infrastructure. With these moves in New York alone, Krens went from being controversial to being the bête noire of the museum world.[2]

Krens had mixed success in his first forays into international art relations. Some European cities welcomed the possibility of establishing a Guggenheim branch, and many, including Barcelona, Seville, Badajoz, and Santander in Spain, rejected the idea (Zulaika 1997), some seeing it as speculative and culturally imperialist. (Bradley 1997).[3] Salzburg was especially keen for a while, and Berlin and Seoul signaled interest. First off the mark, however, was the Deutsche Bank in Berlin, which negotiated a joint venture with Guggenheim as a way of drawing attention to its own art holdings of around fifty thousand modernist works on paper. In 1997 the unusual international alliance of a major art institution and an established institution of international finance produced the tiny Deutsche Guggenheim Museum. The deal was sweet for Deutsche Bank. It already had the largest art collection amassed by a company in the world, and one that the Guggenheim coveted. It also had the means to finance its side of the partnership and space earmarked for the new museum inside the Deutsche Bank building itself, which is located on the famous Unter den Linden. The bank wanted to work with the theme "Art at Work," and the name of the new museum reflects that priority: workplace "Deutsche" comes before "Guggenheim." For the Guggenheims, a Berlin location let the family return home to its German roots. For Krens (2000a. 1), it was a "partnership in patronage" that would update a long tradition of art sponsorship by wealthy individual patrons and organizations, such as the Catholic Church and the monarchy. The alliance of banking and art is, as he put it, a case of "large-scale patronage in our culture." As for the Deutsche Bank Group, it refers to the arrangement as "1 + 1 = 3," meaning that the Deutsche Guggenheim Museum adds up to more than art and capital by "creating value added that exceeds each partner's potential were he to go it alone" (Kopper 1999, 1).

Krens openly encourages the application of profit-driven practices to the museum sector, and the language both partners have used to describe the Deutsche Guggenheim Museum is unabashedly corporate and capitalist. Indeed, in phrases heretofore unheard of in art/museum circles, Krens (2000b, 67) claims to "manage a brand and that brand is the Guggenheim." He speaks excitedly of "numerous economies of scale with international operations," of "new models of resource sharing . . . and the development of any and all opportunities" (Krens 1999, 17, 19).

He speaks of other things, too, such as curatorial diversification and showing artworks from outside a Western arc of modernism, as the Guggenheim did in 1996, when it put on Africa: The Art of a Continent; also China: 5,000 Years, Innovation and Transformation in the Arts in 1998. All for innovative conceptualizations of art at the end of art, Krens's Guggenheim also did The Art of the Motorcycle, complete with the sneering Marlon Brando photos, and a show of Giorgio Armani fashions that some say was connected to a $15 million donation to the museum (Smith 2000).

Krens knows that today's museums are idiosyncratic structures, whose spaces might also accommodate site-specific commissions rather than, or as well as, traditional collections (Bradley 1997; Serota 2000). He believes that the era of the encyclopedic museum—what the British Museum and the Bizot Group call the universal museum—is well over: we should let it go and develop a new cosmopolitanism. There is no longer a need to stock all major art styles, periods, forms, and products in one urban museum location. Today's communication and transportation opportunities enable art aficionados to do the grand art tour of Europe on cheap, no-frills flights bound for airports all over and beyond the continent. Museum design has also changed dramatically from the days when nation building and international showmanship made it de rigueur to house art in neoclassical palaces. And, as noted in previous chapters, an art museum these days is a trendy place to meet friends, drink a coffee, eat a designer meal, sip wine, read, take in a film, buy some unusual jewelry, listen to lectures, get married, or possibly engage with interactive artworks. Krens's own take on the new museum is, "great collections, great architecture, a great special exhibition, a great second exhibition, two shopping opportunities, two eating opportunities, a high-tech interface via the Internet, and economies of scale via a global network" ("Hip Versus Stately" 2000, 50).

Along with being prescient and developing a new cosmopolitanism—which might imagine a British Museum in a Greek location rather than fighting to keep Parthenon sculptures in London premises—Krens has often been the favorite whipping boy of the elite art/museum/art history world. Some critics ignore his art credentials and seize on the master's degree he received from Yale's program in public and private management to show that he is not one of them. In fact, Krens does have a master's degree in art and has taught painting at his undergraduate alma mater, Williams College, where he also directed and oversaw the expansion of its art museum. He then founded Mass MOCA in North Adams, Massachusetts, his first project with Frank Gehry, which has been billed as the largest museum of contemporary art in the world. He is hardly an art outsider except in personal and professional style. At six feet five inches tall, he shows larger-than-life energy and enthusiasm for museum unorthodoxy.

Zulaika (2003, 146) finds Krens remarkable. He describes his first meeting with the man: "Who but the exuberant Krens would invite a perfect stranger like me for a night-time interview with sushi and plenty of wine? It was almost a date for him. Only an amorous man could display such discourse of wonderment, passion, and optimism over his museums, his projects his challenges." Yet a director of one of the world's major museums, located on the posh Museum Mile of Fifth Avenue, who zips around New York on a BMW motorcycle and lights up footlong Cuban cigars, is bound to seem personally gauche. He is said to "lack the smoothness, the easy sociability that characterizes most museum directors" (Solomon 2002). One might describe him as an articulate, sober, and educated version of the Jackson Pollock man of art. His professional style, with its gleeful corporate references and language of branding, is just as provocative and has clearly rattled some elite houses of art. James Cuno's (2004b, 16) disapproval is clear and direct: "The more art museums look like multinational corporations and the more their directors sound like corporate CEOs, the more they risk being cast by the public in the same light." This is Cuno's lead-in to a discussion of the "dramatic" collapses of Enron and Worldcom in a firestorm of ethics violations.

Krens is also roundly attacked in British and some European art circles for dealing with the devil—corporations. It has been standard practice in Europe since at least World War II for the state to finance the arts, either directly or through the administration of state lotteries. Although its will to do so waxes and wanes depending on other political priorities (such as funding the London Olympics of 2012), and although the ancient regimes that sponsored the Louvre and the Prado were authoritarian and corrupt, the state is seen in Europe as the proper enabler of museums, artists, and art spectators, along with a handful of publicly minded lotteries and heritage and art charities. To use corporate money to create a museum or to shape art markets and tastes, as Saatchi has also been lambasted for doing, is to bring commercialism and the economic bottom line to art and its institutions. It opens the door to domination by pur- veyors of second-rate tastes, to rank consumerism, vulgar publicity ploys, and accountants (e.g., Gablik 2004). Karsten Schubert (2000, 115, 118), who questions whether art specialists can control headstrong leaders of industry, says the Krens approach relies on "a formidable sweatshop" of "curators, whose main job is to put together exhibitions for the New York Guggenheim and its branches." Chin-tao Wu (2002, 286) strikes out against "cultural profiteering" by a sector that would just as soon run McDonald's as the Guggenheim. Suzi Gablik (2004, 146) explicitly hits the Guggenheim for "not seeking a value sys- tem outside of the machinery of corporate commodity capitalism." Charles Jencks (2002, 19) wonders whether the Guggenheim model will "take over the world one city at a time."

Of course, Krens has his champions, too (Bradley 1997). Deborah Solomon (2002, 36), for one, describes the Guggenheim as "a model of frank- ness and American pragmatism. At times it's crass, but on the plus side, it is free of piety. It does not pretend that art is religion or that the museum is church." The fear, contempt and rage Krens inspires in some art circles, though, is star- tling. The globally aspiring museum—at least that is what it seems to be— becomes subject to the same antiglobalization rhetoric that has taken aim at the International Monetary Fund, the World Bank, and the World Trade Organi- zation. Perhaps this is a sign that the Guggenheim is an actor to be reckoned with in international relations. One wonders, though, why museum tradition- alists believe that money always already diminishes art making and art displays. In Peter Watson's (1992, xxiii) words, "there are some people for whom the mere mention of art and money in the same book, let alone the same breath, is high treason, a hanging offense." Surely we are aware of the moneyed processes by which most Old Master artworks were created and preserved, myths of artistic genius and rugged determination notwithstanding. Could it be that artistic credibility requires exhibiting in institutions that seem outside the social and economic logics of today (Thompson 2004), even though the making of art has rarely been innocent, freewheeling, wholly creative in impulse, and autonomous of money and demanding consumers/patrons?

One also wonders why the political-to-arts relationship is supposedly purer than a corporate-to-arts relationship. Those of us working in the art-wary fields of political science and IR know just how crass political regimes can be. All manner of states censor art exhibits, from the old USSR to the United States and Australia today. We know the power of special interests to influence pub- lic taste, the conservatism of legislative bodies, and the backroom deals that eventuate in compromised public policy (see Keating and de Frantz 2003). The state is not necessarily acting in the (arts) public good. If we ask what exactly, not polemically, is the serious wrong associated with art museums working with corporate capitalism rather than with the state, an answer does not emerge from critical art circles: some forms of art patronage are simply sacred and some forms simply are not. All art patronage, however, is a matter of money and power, rewards and sanctions, something one can forget when viewing Michelangelo's church-sponsored Sistine Chapel ceiling or a medieval sculpture that seems concerned only with the glory of God (Shiner 2001).[4] Power has always had its way, which is a point at which students of international political economy could very easily, and fruitfully, enter this conversation.

Another charge leveled at Krens continues to be cultural imperialism, the idea that the Guggenheim "will take over the world one city at a time" like a marauding army. Gablik (2004, 146–47) claims that "not only are these museum franchises around the world 'ultramodern showcases' for brand-name corporate trend-setters, but they are all controlled from New York and serve market-oriented mainstream art and culture, not local interests or histories." It makes it sound as though Guggenheim has as many museum franchises as Britain's High Streets have Topshops or American malls have Wal-Marts. Like a large corporation, the big museum is cast as a superpower hegemon, seducing locals into paying through their noses for the "privilege" of having its brand and its protection. Zulaika (2003, 146) appreciates Krens as a powerful seducer, intoxicated by a certain kind of challenge: "World cities had become for Krens what women were for Don Juan: useful accessories to satisfy his fantasies of power and conquest." But the metaphor of seduction suggests that the powerful American museum would not want a partner it had to compel, one that buys into whatever the seducer wants rather than what it also wants. The issue then is whether the Guggenheim is an art Enron that carves out unequal relationships by controlling the rules, costs, architects, and collection standards for receiving partners, or more of a Don Juan. Zulaika thinks that in his relationship with the city of Bilbao, "Krens was doing nothing more than "letting the tiger be a tiger" (146): that is, he was letting the tiger grab him.

In October 2005, Krens became director of the Guggenheim Foundation, a position he relinquished in early 2008, while remaining senior adviser for international affairs. He is overseeing a number of overseas expansion projects, including the new museum in Dubai.[5] Krens has required quite a bit of overseas partners, at least on paper. They must absorb the costs of building a museum, if that is called for, which locals may not have designed. Based on the Bilbao case, the franchise fees can also be steep, ranging between $20 million and $30 million.[6] The franchisee must set aside approximately $50 million to acquire works for a collection that will conform to standards set in New York. These costs of partnering with Guggenheim are enormous. At the same time, Guggenheim makes no secret of the costs and works only with partners that wish to consider them. It is unlikely that the Guggenheim intimidated Deutsche Bank into doing its bidding or dazzled it with a museum brand; the bank has its own name, its own exhibition space, and its own collection.[7] Something more complicated is at play than cold war or neoliberal politics crudely inscribed onto the globalizing museum, more complicated than installing U.S. values, tastes, and institutions abroad. Such models of contemporary international relations are always short on appreciating local agency.

Timothy Luke (2002, 226) tells us that "one must be extremely cautious about . . . becoming coopted too fully by any museum's power plays." We must be equally cautious, I think, about proclaiming a new mega-enemy of art for each era of international relations; yesterday, fascism and communism compromised artistic values, then American cold war foreign policy was a problem, and today the devil is neoliberal globalization. Power begets power, say Foucauldians, which means that it is impossible to erase agency or subsume it within a grand global problematic of false consciousness. Seemingly weaker partners are not hapless and without resources or options in international relations. It just might be the case that the global museum is one consequence of an art history narrative that has been shorn of its power to command art/museums to be the way they are traditionally expected to be. And within that new space, it might also be possible that local forces gain as much or more than they lose by partnering with a museum. The origin stories of the Guggenheim Bilbao help us appreciate the possibilities. We start with the New York side of the story and then consider the way the picture looks when sketched from Bilbao.

A Guggenheim *in Bilbao*

Krens (1999) likes to suggest that the Guggenheim expansion into Bilbao came about largely by accident rather than by any plan to take over the art world. The two existing Guggenheims at the time, in New York and in Venice, were short on space. Krens wanted to renovate the exhibition spaces at the Fifth Avenue location and also expand the gallery in Venice. The New York side of the plan came to fruition as a result of the controversial sale of the three modernist paintings. The plan for the Venice gallery fell victim to Italian bureaucracy, but it did catapult the Guggenheim board into thinking about the museum in new ways. As Krens puts it, the board began by considering how to use the Venice collection better and quickly moved on to economies of scale that would come about through international museum operations: "It doesn't take a rocket scientist to determine that we are living in a world that is becoming increasingly international or transnational. There are more and more projects that benefit from audiences in different locations" (17). In the event, the Guggenheim's "international program" would far exceed the prototype that MOMA established in the 1950s. The idea now was to grow a museum's finances, collection, and reputation through international expansion.

Once word got out about the new thinking at Guggenheim, Salzburg made inquiries. Krens (1999, 14) claims that he was wary; Salzburg was relatively close to Venice, which made it a potential competitor destination, and it had a locked-in international reputation for music rather than fine art. He nevertheless commissioned a feasibility study and seemed to change his mind about the prospects for a Salzburg Guggenheim as the study evolved. Everything moved along well until late 1989, when, Krens says, Austria became distracted by a collapsing cold war order that was spilling over into its borders. In other words, the international relations of regime change might have upset a key moment of international art diplomacy. Some commentators think the talks faltered on other issues too, including a scheme endorsed by the Austrian government to partner a Guggenheim with its Kunsthistorisches Museum in Vienna rather than fund a Guggenheim museum in Salzburg (Schubert 2000, 116). The view from Salzburg looks rather different. Zulaika's (1997) research there indicates that Krens made a series of personal and professional errors that hurt the project; he was less than transparent in his interests and politicking, made people wait for him when he came to the city, and then appeared there with his girlfriend from rival Vienna.[8]

The next, most unexpected and improbable, candidate made itself known: Bilbao, Spain. Krens was initially even less interested in that locality than he had been in the early Salzburg bid. Bilbao was a provincial European city with minor standing in art and a very big reputation for terrorist bombings and assassinations conducted by a Basque separatist movement. It was a depressed and rundown city. At the turn of the twentieth century, "the ten-mile corridor from Bilbao to the Atlantic was producing almost 20 per cent of the world's steel" (Zulaika 2003, 147–48); in the 1990s, its unemployment rate was running close to 25 percent of the workforce (de Ros 2002, 283). The very idea of siting a Guggenheim museum in Bilbao seemed wild, an art-is-good-for-you dream of surreal proportions. Yet the Basque administration persisted.

Disinclined to pursue the matter at all, Krens admits to setting terms that most prospective partners would have seen as highway robbery. He rejected the site for the museum that local authorities had chosen, "a turn-of-the-century wine warehouse. It was a terrible location" (Krens 1999, 20). A decrepit industrial area on the banks of the Nervion River, adjacent to the train tracks, proved more intriguing. Krens set the price for a Guggenheim Bilbao there at roughly $150 million and stipulated that 95 percent of that cost would be financed locally, in return for which the New York museum would make no ownership claims on the building.[9] The Bilbao side would raise $50 million to acquire a core collection of international value, approved and owned by the Guggenheim, plus examples of local and regional art. It would pay "an initial $20 million rental fee for use of the [Guggenheim] collection [and] participation in New York-originated exhibitions" (Holo 1999, 154). As with the art acquisitions for the museum, all decisions on exhibitions at the Guggenheim Bilbao would be made in New York.

Clearly "not really determined to encourage them," Krens (1999, 20) also stipulated that the museum had to be on a grand scale, "a structure of spectacular architectural character. . . . I told them to think in terms of Chartres Cathedral" (22). And for such a building, he was "not interested in doing an architectural competition in the sense where you throw open the project and waste time. We would participate if there were three architects in a competition that lasted three weeks" (22). Krens wanted to invite Frank Gehry, Arata Siozaki, and Coop Himmelbau to bid—a North American, an Asian, and a European. Each would be given $10,000 to prepare preliminary models from just one site visit, with no restrictions placed on the nature of the designs they could render. Krens writes: "I didn't really expect that they would do all of this. It was just conversation, but they did everything they said they were going to" (22).

What won him over, he later claimed, was really the attitude of the Basque government. It was already "making a substantial investment in the infrastructure of their city" (22) and in regional regeneration in general through the unusual route of cultural branding. The British architect Sir Norman Foster had been commissioned to design a new subway system for Bilbao, which he had executed in the style of great billowing glass worms sweeping up from the depths and discharging people onto city streets. Santiago Calatrava, a Spanish architect of world-class reputation, was designing a new air terminal. The city was also constructing a concert and convention center and undertaking to renovate its train station for high-speed travel to Paris and Madrid. Now the government wanted a cultural lodestar to crown resurgent Bilbao and Basque identity for the twenty-first century. This big vision was in step with Krens's own view that art and culture can be "a cheap investment with incredible returns for any ambitious city, when comparing, for example, the cost of building a museum to the cost of adding a single mile of highway" (Holo 1999, 156). The seducer was seduced by the tigers of Bilbao.

Krens signed a twenty-year agreement with the Basque administration in 1991, the Development and Programming Services Agreement for the Guggenheim Museum Bilbao, which offered an option to extend for a total of seventy-five years. Frank Gehry's gigantic mass of cylinders and towers went up, and the museum opened its doors in 1997. Like the Wright building in New York, the Gehry building in Bilbao has become one of the most striking architectures of our time. Its monumentality, virtuosity, design, and materials laser the eye and miniaturize the body; the entrance atrium alone measures 55 meters, and the main exhibition space at 130 by 30 meters can accommodate the enormity of virtually any contemporary sculpture. The exterior lifts upward and around, catching and throwing light off the Australian titanium exterior. Titanium has become trendy in public architecture today, but it is an unconventional building material historically; Danto might see it as one of those new materials in art that challenge us to make sense of it all for ourselves. The design and engineering relied on state-of-the-art computer technology, particularly the CATIA program developed by the French firm Dassault Aviation to aid in fighter-plane design. CATIA enables a designer to rotate the components of a structure until an optimal moment of structural integrity and design emerges. Krens "had promised that Bilbao would get the best museum in the world: one and a half times taller than the original Guggenheim, 50 percent taller than the Pompidou" (Holo 1999, 156). He describes it now as "a combination of Egypt's Pyramids, China's Forbidden City, and the Taj Mahal" (Zulaika 2003, 146). The British novelist J. G. Ballard (2007, np), known for turning car metal into the ultimate turn-on in *Crash,* sees the Guggenheim Bilbao as "part train crash and part explosion in a bullion vault." It is, he says, "Disneyland for the media PhD."

Insiders say that it was obvious from the beginning that Gehry would get the commission, having worked earlier with Krens on the Mass MOCA project. Rather like Bilbao, though, Gehry is a relatively recent success story in celebrity architecture, despite being on in years. For decades he endeavored in his work to get away from cold, boxy modernist design without lapsing into the nostalgia suggested by postmodernist styles, with their chaotic gestures to various pasts all in one go. He found, however, that "there simply wasn't much of a support system for anyone trying to do something different . . . in LA. I've long been considered strange and odd, a maverick" (*Connaissance des Arts* 1999, 32). Gehry's position in architectural circles has certainly changed over the past two decades: outside the box is now good, especially in museum design these days. Still, Gehry has his critics. Hal Foster (Rappolt 2003), for one, describes the Guggenheim Bilbao as a stylized ready-made that infuses aesthetic pleasure with commercial consumption. Gehry claims it is a building that fits the hard and gritty realism—what many refer to as the toughness—of the city without imparting to it a hard-edged aesthetic. That it is also an investment in urban regeneration pleases him: "I think artistic expression is the juice that fuels our collective souls, that innovation and responding to desperate social needs are not exclusive imperatives" (34).[10] But is this sense shared in Bilbao? Is any of this a Basque view of the global museum? Judging by the vehement objections some art world commentators raise about Krens and his "imperial" obsessions, one might think the answer would be no. On the ground in Bilbao, though, a different and more independent set of stories prevails.

A *Guggenheim* in Bilbao

"Few people know the Basques." So contends Mark Kurlansky (2000, 3), who wants us to know and appreciate a relatively small group that consistently punches above its weight. The Basque nation is simultaneously old and new, nationalistic and worldly, uniquely local and attuned to the international, self-protective and secure enough to be open. Known for one of the oldest languages in Europe, Euskera, Basques should also be known as some of the longest-standing practitioners of international political economy. A Basque in the pay of Spain, Portugal, or Italy often navigated the seas in the Age of Exploration. Basques were among the first Europeans to practice tariff-free international trade—with the colonial city of Boston, for example—and were known to use competitive pricing to break the monopolies of their competitors. In the years of the Industrial Revolution, Basques were leading shipbuilders, steelmakers, and manufacturers in Europe; "'Bilbo' was the name of a sword made of Bizkaia's famed steel" (Zulaika 1999, 262). They were also reluctant warriors and frequent practitioners of diplomacy throughout their history, whose location straddling France and Spain put them in the way of numerous threatening forces, whether of Carthage, Swabia, Rome, or France. "Today," writes Kurlansky (2000, 5), "in the global age, even while clinging to their ancient tribal identity, they are ready for a borderless world." In that case, the Bilbao Guggenheim extends a long, long tradition of alert local identity keeping company with others.

It is worth considering a few more historical examples of Basque international relations in light of the contemporary decision to bring a New York–based museum to Bilbao. In 1728, a group of wealthy Basques formed the Royal Guipuzcoan Company of Caracas with the intention of breaking into a Venezuelan cocoa trade that was monopolized by the Dutch. The company attracted backing by a large coalition of forces, including private investors, authorities in the city of San Sebastian, their counterparts in the Guipuzcoa province, and the Spanish royal family. Within five years, and after a very shaky start, the company had greatly increased its share of world cocoa trade and had grown the international market significantly by reducing cocoa prices. As the tide turned against the Dutch West India Company monopoly, the Basque company diversified its South American interests to include tobacco, leather, and coffee as well as trade in Basque iron commodities, chemicals, fish, wood, and then wine and textiles. While Spain squandered its national capacity by extracting precious minerals from South American locations, the Basques were building national wealth through vigorous trade; they exemplified the Adam Smith tradition of international political economy.

As well, though, their entire recorded history provides object lessons in national exceptionalism. In medieval times, the Basques developed their own legal code and laws (*fueros*). In the period of exploration and mercantile trade, they were able to negotiate exemption from Spanish customs taxes. They fought two "Carlist" wars (which they lost) to preserve their autonomy from the centralizing Spanish nation-state and repeatedly resisted forced military service to any leader, royal family, or state (Mari-Molinero and Smith 1996; Medhurst 1982; Payne 1975). In the mid-nineteenth century, while much of Spain fell further behind northern Europe in industrial development, the four autonomous Basque provinces thrived, having made a timely shift from shipbuilding to iron exports, steel production, and banking. "From 1885 until the early twentieth century, Vizcaya [including Bilbao] produced 77 percent of Spain's cast iron and 87 percent of its steel" (Kurlansky 2000, 135). Indeed, the region was a leading economic force within Spain: "Basque capital represented 25 percent of Spanish banking resources, 38 percent of the investment in ship-yards, 40 percent of the ownership of engineering and electrical power firms, 68 percent of the funds dedicated to shipping companies, and 62 percent of the monies invested in steel manufacturing" (Zulaika 1999, 265). It also produced for Europe: "consider that Great Britain, the world's imperial power, imported two-thirds of her iron from Bilbao (65–75% of Bilbao's annual exports)" (265). And it usually made and controlled the profits. Even when about 40 percent of Basque ironworks was in the hands of foreign investors in 1880–1890, approximately 60 to 75 percent of all profits stayed at home.

Basque prosperity always depended on an exceptionalism that was also symbiotic with international capital and European technology (Glas 1997). Despite constituting only 3 percent of Spain's population in 1929, leading Basques never believed that their difference in identity and cultural traditions would be compromised by economic engagements with Europe and other centers of capital. They were less certain that this would be the case closer to home. Successive royalist, republican, and Francoist governments pressured the region to incorporate with an entity emerging as Spain. The Basques continuously resisted what they interpreted as efforts to assimilate them out of existence, finally forming the Basque Nationalist Party (PNV) in 1895, which put out an anti-Spanish and anti-Communist (and fanatically pro-Catholic) line. By 1931 the party was strong enough to negotiate an autonomous Basque government within Spain, which is what the area around Bilbao strongly supported while other Basque provinces supported Francoists (Aguilar 1998). The rise of Franco to power in 1939 ended the special status for Basqueland. Franco wanted to incorporate the splintered ethnicities and political loyalties throughout the country (Conversi 1997) and took the hardest line on the recalcitrant Basques, banning literary works written in Euskera and all cultural activities that referenced Basque ethnicity. The entire population living within Spanish borders was to consolidate politically and culturally around a Spanish identity that harkened back to the golden era of Ferdinand and Isabella.

Basqueland united against Franco's dream of Spanish unity, and Madrid considered punishing it by razing the city of Bilbao. Franco was aware, however, that in destroying Bilbao he would be razing a good proportion of Spain's industries. He selected the market town of Guernica (population 7,000) to the east of Bilbao as his target instead. On April 26, 1937, German Heinkel 111 bombers and other advanced aircraft pounded Guernica for three hours, leaving approximately 1,600 people dead. The sudden and pitiless devastation was difficult for most people to comprehend. Desperate to ward off the thunderous backlash that came immediately from within and outside the country,

Franco insisted, ludicrously, that the Basques had dynamited and set fire to their own city; he maintained that position for years (Kurlansky 2000, 200–201). Anyone familiar with modern art can imagine the ferocious attack on Guernica from the powerful gray-black mural Picasso painted for the Spanish pavilion of the 1937 World's Fair in Paris. Its abstract scene is full of anguished falling people and terrified animals. Spanish authorities allowed the mural *Guernica* to be exhibited, it has been claimed, because Franco was relatively blasé about the power of art. He would later remark that Picasso's works of the Civil War years had poked fun at "us" in a way that was "very interesting" (De La Puente 2002, 106).

Bilbao eventually fell to Franco's forces, but not in the Guernican way. The guerrilla-based Basque army chose to withdraw from the city rather than face the prospect of military assault by Franco's forces. The relentless and brutal military attacks on the region forced the Basques to surrender their regional autonomy in August 1937. A Basque government in exile retreated to the French town of Biarritz and then decamped to New York City, where it was officially recognized by the United States, Britain, and France. Various international relief agencies delivered food and medical aid to Basque regions of Spain and France, with Britain alone taking four thousand Basque children to safety in England, an effort that other states—mainly Belgium, Denmark, Switzerland, Mexico, and the Soviet Union—assisted. Throughout the Spanish civil war years, France maintained an open-door policy for Basque refugees crossing the border—until, that is, France came under German occupation. Then, during World War II, the Basque underground helped downed Allied pilots, Jews, and refugees escape from France and Germany to the safer zones of "neutral" Spain.

When the Second World War ended, Franco was still in power in Spain, and the Basques were still targets of surveillance and state terrorism. During the 1950s a new Basque underground movement formed known by the acronym ETA (Euskadi Ta Askatasuna, Basque Homeland and Liberty). Its members took a far harder, more militant line on Basque independence than the more conservative Basque Nationalist Party had done; indeed, ETA was frustrated with the PNV's inefficacy. Operating from the French side as a small decentralized organization, ETA proclaimed the goal of liberating Basques from Franco's Spain, using violence if necessary. Its banners waved Marxist and Maoist themes of the time, but its actions were relatively moderate until 1973 (although the organization allegedly killed six people in the intervening years), when ETA assassinated Franco's designated heir, Luis Carrero Blanco, "the Ogre." It was generally assumed that ETA would fade into history once Franco died.

Franco's rule did eventually end, but the government of King Juan Carlos did not bring an easier life for the Basques. Their flag and language remained banned in Spain, and the Basques themselves continued to be targets of politically inspired violence, in large part because the state security force was riddled with Franco holdovers. Perhaps out of sheer frustration, ETA upped the ante by restructuring itself to form a military wing and a political wing. Both arms of the movement became increasingly embroiled in antistate violence, the military wing through assassinations and the politicos through extortionist actions that included kidnapping leading Basque businessmen for ransom money. ETA's most violent period was between 1978 and 1980, when up to 80 people were killed through terrorist activities. These assaults continued, with peaks and troughs, through the 1990s. In 1998, the U.S. State Department added ETA to its list of thirty terrorist organizations that American citizens were prohibited from supporting financially. The European Union also branded ETA a terrorist organization, accusing it of 850 deaths since 1968.[11]

The Spanish government itself estimated, however, that of the nearly 2.4 million Basques living in Spain, only around seventy people had ever been active commandos in ETA, a figure that Zulaika says is unrealistically low (personal correspondence 2007). Whatever the true figure, because ETA was very active until approximately 2003, and intermittently since then, the Spanish government has kept up pressure on the Basque regions. It banned the Batasuna Party, alleged to be the political wing of ETA. Judging by international human rights reports, the government also routinely detained and tortured individual Basques suspected of ETA sympathies. When Al-Qaeda bombs struck the commuter rail in Madrid, the government was quick to attribute the attack to ETA. Despite government excesses in Basque areas, the Spanish government and its allied press in Madrid have often prevailed in the battle for international sympathy. ETA has become known as a desperate but outdated terrorist organization seeking to undermine a country that has shifted from fascism to democracy and is now a popular location for European beach vacations and culture tourists.

Nonstop rounds of nationalist-separatist violence turned many Basques themselves against ETA. The older Basque Nationalist Party, the PNV, revived during the last days of the republic and became the leading political force in Bilbao thereafter. The PNV is still the unchallenged legitimate party and the driving force to revitalize the area by combining international input with local steering, a tried-and-true Basque strategy. For several decades, the PNV had been particularly concerned about Bilbao's downturn and responded by developing five major goals to improve the city. These included cleaning up the river Nervion, which runs through it; clearing away the debris of closed industrial plants; expanding and updating the local transportation system; building new industries and locating them outside the city; and enhancing the region's cultural base and unique identity. One might say that the PNV was determined that Bilbao could and would fight "against its own death," as Nerea Arruti (2003, 167) puts it, or build on the ruins late capitalism wrought, as Zulaika (1999) prefers to say. Certainly the party's thinking was millennial, focusing on endings as much as on new beginnings (Zulaika 1999, 265).

Against this complex background—an outward-looking history combined with inward-looking politics amid violence—we turn to the remarkable Guggenheim museum in Bilbao. The PNV grand scheme for Bilbao served notice that the party was going for regeneration through urban entrepreneurism. Sara Gonzalez Ceballos (2003, 178) tells us that entrepreneurism is a distinctive approach to urban governance for a time when cities are "losing the structure imposed on them by nation states and becoming nodes and hubs for transnational relations." It involves a deliberate shift of policy away from conventional concerns to improve the distribution of goods and services in the city toward policies that aim to change an area's image, attractiveness to the world, and location in the global pecking order. By changing the built landscape, a city can attract new businesses and moneyed populations. The use of public funds for leisure amenities is especially important; leisure and cultural enhancements help reshape the landscape and can rebrand an area as a vibrant spot with a regenerating economy. Museums, theaters, waterfront developments, stadiums, and sleek transportation networks especially appeal to people, including investors, who want to be part of environments that are urbane as well as urban. The PNV was so keen on this approach that it could even imagine "creating a European headquarters of the [Guggenheim] Foundation" (Vidarte 1999, 6) as part of its urban regeneration plan. With a new subway system designed by a British architect of international standing in place and a revitalized airport embellished by a renowned Spanish architect, a flagship project of urban entrepreneurial regeneration loomed: a world-class art museum.

Again, though, there are critics of the development-through-culture-and-architecture approach. Urban entrepreneurial regeneration is innovative and has become trendy in the last decade, but detractors warn that it has an anti-democratic bias. Decisions on the new urban landscape are taken at high levels and often result in projects that pole-vault over the interests of local citizens in order to go for the gold of the global market (Evans 2003; Hubbard 1996; Moulaert, Rodriquez, and Swyngedouw 2003). That this has largely been the case in Bilbao cannot be denied. PNV projects for Bilbao unfolded under the aegis of a group of bureaucrats, lawyers, and accountants operating in a broader alliance with local city managers, the Guggenheim Foundation in New York, and a celebrity architect. These groups closeted themselves from public scrutiny in Bilbao and surrounding areas, like so many diplomats hunkered down at Camp David. As one critic puts it (Ceballos 2003, 181), "the project was negotiated in a top-down fashion, without the active promotion of public participation mechanisms, at the highest level of the ruling party, PNV, in an atmosphere of secrecy." Allegedly, they chose Bilbao as the major site for regeneration, for example, mainly because PNV headquarters were located there. This meant that the capital of Basqueland, Vitoria, was summarily passed over, as was the region's colorful, popular, and internationally better-known city, San Sebastian.

In addition, although art and design feature prominently in the regeneration scheme, the PNV may have been guided by "almost every imaginable calculation other than art" (Kurlansky 2002, 335). Cultural entrepreneurism was to prime the pump of business rather than enable art to become the business of Bilbao. This order of priorities can be read off the two arts projects PNV rejected before settling on the splashy Guggenheim. The more hard-fought of the two was a proposal for an arts center in the old winery that Krens would later reject as a site for his new museum. The elderly, well-regarded Basque artist and nationalist behind the idea, Jorge Oteiza, wanted an art institution designed, financed, and constructed entirely by Basques, saying it would regenerate Basque spirit after the dark Franco years. A long cycle of approvals, objections, changes, and delays ensued, culminating in cancellation of the project in 1989. Apparently, the PNV determined that the Oteiza plan was too inward-looking to capture the worldly Basque spirit and too local to generate the international visibility that urban entrepreneurism required. One analyst suggests that "while most Basque citizens do enjoy being grounded in their own uniqueness, especially in their own autonomy of Madrid, they also like to visualize themselves as operating in a wider sphere" (Holo 1999, 147). An earlier arts-led proposal would have beefed up Bilbao's local art museum, the Bilbao Museum of Fine Arts. That institution had been open since 1914 and was considered innovative in its collecting until the Franco dictatorship forced it into an artistic straitjacket. Despite acquiring bold contemporary art from Europe, the United States, and the immediate region in the 1980s, that cultural institution was not "sexy" enough for PNV. Local arts organizations and artists had to fall in line behind the PNV "curators" of managerialism, the very trend Dave Hickey (1997) has decried in the United States.

Urban cultural entrepreneurism certainly accentuates a neoliberal political economy in which profit-seeking replaces concerns with justice and equity. The strategy involves a great deal of concentrated project money chasing the hope of a broader spillover of economic benefits. For it to work, partnerships between leading political forces and leading businesses, local and international, are required and are avidly sought. The Guggenheim Bilbao's Web site alone lists over thirty-five corporate "trustees," among them the multinationals Iberia, Price Waterhouse Cooper, Unilever, Deutsche Bank, Vodafone, Renault, and Lexus, as well as numerous local and regional businesses. Public participation in the management of the museum is thereby marginalized even more. And, of course, to many artists and art commentators, a strong infusion of the corporate into any museum results in a false economy. The museum's director general, Juan Ignacio Vidarte (1999, 10), asserts that "support from the private sector is particularly significant if one considers the innovative way the sector operates in museum management." He says he wants to ensure, however, that the economic and political aspects of the museum do not overshadow its cultural significance. The museum deserves support "in its own right as a stimulus for creativity, artistic expression, and the promotion of a cultural identity" (6).

In the event, the Basque government minister for culture, the chief executive of the provincial council of Bizkaia, and a representative from the board of trustees of the Guggenheim Foundation signed the Development and Programming Services Agreement for the Guggenheim Museum Bilbao—significantly, in New York—in December 1991. Vidarte (1999, 6) admits that the Basque administration had to overcome considerable skepticism and suspicion to get to that point. For example, Krens (1999) likes to suggest that he wanted a three-architect contest when it was the Basque administration that demanded it of him on the grounds that buildings paid for by public moneys require public competitions (Zulaika, personal correspondence, 2007). The local artistic community was up in arms about the city's pandering to foreign art and architecture. Nationalists warned that Basque history and culture would be purged to make way for a toady globalism (see Jones 2003). And the price tag was enough to make everyone faint, even though PNV foresaw that the museum could end up a bargain at $100-plus million if it could draw new industry, investment, and tourism to the diminished industrial city.

It seems that the optimistic view has prevailed in and around Bilbao. Instead of the 400,000 visitors the museum projected for 1997, the year it opened, the actual total was in the order of 1.3 million visitors (Vidarte 1999, 6). Vidarte claims that "the popularity enjoyed by the Guggenheim Museum Bilbao in its first year has shown that culture can be an effective instrument to promote development and urban renewal" (6). His words could be called hasty, except it has been reported that a total of 9 million people visited the museum between its opening in 1997 and 2006. Moreover, the museum contributed 212 million euros to the Spanish gross domestic product and 29 million euros to the Basque treasury in 2006 (*Art Newspaper* 2007a, 32). This is the latest good news. A 2002 consultant's report found that the economic impact of the museum in only five years was ten times the total cost of the investment (Jones 2003, 163). A Guggenheim Bilbao official report of 2004 claims that the initial investments had been fully recovered by 2004. Others put the full recovery date as 2006 (Plaza 2006). All this is a far cry from the $14 million the Basque administration had projected as annual museum income from the entrance fees, shop sales, and private and corporate donations.

Still, some have their doubts. Zulaika (personal correspondence, 2007) claims that the big success for the museum is not in earned income for itself or the city but really in its ability to reduce various museum subsidies from 50 percent in the early years to 25–30 percent now. Although he has become a museum supporter after initially resisting the idea of a Guggenheim Bilbao—happily if also ironically saying that "yes, love is back in Bilbao" (Zulaika 2003, 146—Zulaika is skeptical about the shining economic statistics relative to the gloomier picture some in the city's tourist industry paint of declining profits in recent years. He is not alone in this pessimism (see, e.g., McNeill 2000). Graeme Evans (2003, 43) indicates that the museum generated "growth of only 0.47% to the Basque GNP in 1997," and that base was in decline within three years of opening. Using a return on investment and net present value technique of quantitative analysis, Beatriz Plaza (2006), of the Economics Faculty of the University of the Basque Country (Bilbao), finds that although the overall initial investment, plus the operative deficit of the museum, would be recuperated by 2006, the real figures have to include the museum's continual investments in its permanent collection. That would extend the investment recovery period to 2015. Her findings do indicate, though, that there was an increase of 61,742 in monthly overnight stays in Bilbao from January 1976 to December 2004, as well as an increase of nearly 1,000 jobs in the hotel and tourism sector for that period. The *Art Newspaper* (2007a) mentions 4,200 jobs related to the existence of the museum in 2006 (whether these are new jobs or not is unclear). The overall picture for the museum and for its city, however, does look stronger than critics claim. The museum itself is crowing through its Web site, which thrusts the museum front and center as "revitalizing the Basque Country's recession-plagued economic structure" and moving the city forward as a "major reference point for European regions on the Atlantic seaboard" (www.guggen heim-bilbao.es/ingles/informacion/informationo.htm).

As for the PNV, Bilbao hit the global big time and breathed new life and energy into Basque identity and exceptionalism. The regeneration initiatives boosted party insistence on special recognition for Basque rights within Spain and within Europe. Madrid was reluctant to grant the Basques the status of a historic nationality of Spain, which meant that Basque rights remained ambiguous (Medrano 1995; Heywood 1995). Yet where the Basques "have not found multinationalism in Spain, they have found it, to some extent, in the 'Europe of the Regions'" (Keating, 1995). EU members interact at three levels of institutions: regional, state, and all-European. Basqueland has been able to join the European Union as a member of the Assembly of European Regions and the Consultative Council of Regional and Local Authorities. This gives it access to the European Regional and Development Fund, which assists in infrastructural development within Europe's poorer regions. Europe of the Regions also puts Basqueland into a space it often seeks to embrace, the realm of international relations, where it can work around a recalcitrant Madrid to achieve cherished aims. In its efforts to overcome the "meddling" nation-state (Jesse and Williams 2004), Basqueland has succeeded in working within Europe to end border controls between French and Spanish Basque country. Basques can now travel unfettered in their own historical region for the first time since the 1930s.

And they and we can all wander into and out of the Guggenheim Bilbao museum, where an extraordinary spaciousness also invites open movement. Richard Serra's korten steel sculpture *Snake,* which is installed on the ground floor, provides an apt metaphor for the latest Basque experience. It is a site-specific commission made of six winding steel plates that together measure 31 by 4 meters. Set freestanding in an architectural space designed for large sculptures and unobstructed movement around them, a spectator negotiates the long narrow corridors of *Snake* as though meandering the winding streets of Bilbao's medieval quarter or walking through a labyrinth of laws that once limited Basque aspirations and no longer can. That the building is similarly sited free of any claustrophobic hemmings-in suggests that spectators and city dwellers can readily see the art of the museum and participate in the art of urban regeneration. On my first trip in 2000, a Basque taxi driver and I were unable to carry on anything resembling a conversation until the museum appeared ahead of us. "Gure Guggie" (our Guggie); he pointed at the crazy quilted structure in the middle of the old rail yard, at the top of a road called Iparraguirre (for the Basque author of *Tree of Guernica*), lined with sooty nineteenth-century city residences (plate 7). There was an understated tenderness and pride in his expression as well as confidence and sincere pleasure. That museum was "his" and "ours" in a city that was not to be disparaged or painted as "terrorist," as the Madrid press had once been freer to do. That the Guggenheim Bilbao sits just across the river from the Cuartel de la Salve, a station of Guardia police forces long associated with the worst offenses against the Basques, is icing on the cake.

It is said that apart from the Serra—and now there is an entire "fish gallery" for his torqued ellipses—the art inside the Guggenheim Bilbao consists of minor pieces from the New York collection and recent purchases that merely fill in gaps in that collection: a Mark Rothko here, a Clyfford Still there, and a room of Anselm Kiefer's grim collage paintings. It is certainly the Spanish and Basque art that beckons me. The late Juan Muñoz's "men" might be sitting around talking but not looking at each other quite. Sculptural pieces by the Basque artist Antoni Tapies dialogue with works by Eduardo Chillida. Txomin Badiola and Cristina Iglesias, two younger artists, are there, as are other would-be YBA (young Basque artists). The feel is Euro-American-regional set in a temple to international relations and to urban regeneration/development. I am regularly astonished that most of IR, and all of its international development wing, is unable to see this phenomenon as something operating on its turf. It is as though we are blinded rather than enabled by the titanium; we just can't see something so big.

THE GUGGENHEIM AND IR

Many art critics and museum directors look at the Guggenheim Bilbao and see a venture impelled by a superpower institution bent on showcasing itself at Bilbao's cost. The Guggenheim Bilbao might be seen instead as a powerful case of glocalization. A Basque-led collaboration with a key institution of global art yields a local-international collage, a hybrid, a mermaid, a minotaur, a cultural hyphenation, perhaps a double disseminNation (Bhabha 1994). That much of the art/museum world does not value this particular form of hybridity, while often lauding the hybrid forms that make up contemporary art, points to an underlying elitist view denying the "margins" power, agency, and acumen. To art critics unschooled in political analysis, or perhaps ill at ease with concepts like "power," the whole thing can seem a rotten setup, an example yet again of artists "become increasingly dependent on the complicated bureaucratic machinery which now organizes and administers the consumption of art in our culture" (Gablik 2004, 66). The art world of northern Europe especially fixes negatively on corporate aspects of the new museum model, so much so that it cannot recognize the stereotypes and regional inequalities that its own discourse perpetuates (e.g., Cuno 2004b). It is a view that is decidedly not based on research undertaken from local angles; and in that sense perhaps Kurlansky is right to say that few people know the Basques.

At the same time it is unwise to glorify or romanticize "the Basques" as Kurlansky tends to do. The economic regeneration process in and around Bilbao has not been a democratic project, and the verdict is still out on the long-term success of the urban entrepreneurial model embraced by the Basque authority. If a game of seduction entangled the Guggenheim with Bilbao, a region unheard of in global art circles before, one effect beyond romance has been a customizing of the art museum, if not always the art inside it, in local-international circumstances undreamed of in the age of art. A new institutional form has emerged for a new era, and it has development qualities that could expand the reach and spillover effects of art for governments, corporate boardrooms, ateliers, museums, foundations, spectators, participants, and academic fields. This is something big within, not something parenthetical to, globalization. It is also one afterlife of IR and of art that raises questions about whether the Guggenheim Bilbao project is akin to the types of infrastructural projects the World Bank funds in Third World and transitional societies, complete with its own conditionalities. Are we looking at a misguided urban/regional structural adjustment program that will eventually drain the city of Bilbao of resources, or is the Guggenheim indicative of new pathways to power in the international political economy? To catchy concepts like the "global city" or "Pacific Rim cities" should we now add "global art cities" or "global museum cities"? Superstar architect of the moment Daniel Libeskind (2002) regards the Guggenheim Bilbao as a brilliant way to represent a city through a museum. When are we who study international relations going to study this power collage?

And how many others will there be? The city of Seoul failed to pursue interest in a Guggenheim Korea when it got caught up in the Asian economic crisis of 1997–1998. Talks on a Guggenheim Rio got as far as agreeing on a site on the Guanabara Bay, an architectural design by Jean Nouvel, and the main outlines of cost sharing before stalling over an internal Brazilian dispute about whether the deal was properly authorized. Even while the Guggenheim expansion periodically shows some signs of weakness, such as layoffs in New York and the closing of branches in Soho and Las Vegas, other prospects emerge for it in Singapore and Hong Kong. Moreover, cities that could never afford a global museum pick up on the Guggenheim regeneration idea. The grim English seaside town of Folkestone, for example, aspires to rebuild itself around an arts theme and is actively recruiting artists to live, work, and display their art in the town (Baggini 2004). Once depressed cities of the northeast of England now boast Antony Gormley's large public sculpture *Angel of the North,* the Gateshead Arts Centre, the Millennium Bridge, and the Sage Music Centre. Manchester is in the midst of redeveloping its grubby canal area via the Lowry Centre of theaters, shops, and restaurants and the Imperial War Museum North. This is the "Bilbao effect." It is the idea that "culture, very broadly defined, can be used to revive declining places and the idea of urban living in general" (Beckett 2003, 2). The notion is spreading that culture-driven regeneration is not just a newfangled form of urban renewal, with connotations of sprucing up inner-city areas, but a synonym for "creativity" in public policy. It is one way of saving the nation, or parts of "it."

Gehry (2000) himself insists, however, that "you can't just go to a town and do what they call 'the Bilbao effect.'" It is a tricky business that requires a clear vision of social transformation, strong and unified leadership, a museum that generates new knowledge as well as new and exciting architecture, exhaustive planning locally and for global impact, and civil society institutions liaising with the cultural center—the Poovey institutional linkup referred to earlier (*Art Newspaper* 2007b). Beatriz Garcia (cited in Beckett 2003, 4), of the Centre for Cultural Policy Research at Glasgow University, cautions that "what is important is to look at the sort of jobs, the sort of visitors, whether people are just passing through, or moving to the city being promoted to live." Employment in new cultural quarters may amount to little more than waitressing jobs, which could perpetuate uneven development within the city (Keating and de Frantz 2003). And with cultural regeneration the rage, there is a very real risk that another city will rapidly steal your city's creative thunder simply by garnering more media attention for its latest, bigger, bolder venture into culture. In this regard, one remembers London's hyped Millennium Dome, built at an inflated budget, used a few times, and then left bankrupt, unloved, and subject to a succession of disastrous schemes until morphing into the O2 stadium/performance center (as compared with the London Eye, a bolder millennium project that quickly became an integral part of the city). Even the Guggenheim Bilbao, whose appeal at the moment seems secure, may simply reap the benefit of being one of the first, and surely the most impressive, large-scale venture of its kind.

All this is relatively new territory for regeneration studies, let alone for IR and development studies, where it would be useful to raise questions about whether the cultural-entrepreneurial strategy of regeneration would make sense for certain cities or regions of the Third World. To relegate such issues to art disciplines could be to watch them disappear, owing to a lack of attention to the politics, power, and agency involved in putting together solid international collaborations of political, social, and art institutions. A potentially solid local plan for cultural regeneration could also falter around an art-world suspicion that art/museums should not be corporate in model, sponsorship, or taste. At the end of art, art/museums are both popular, and they are assuming roles that give them new responsibilities—regeneration—attached to older values of nation building or saving. The Bilbao Guggenheim deserves considerable attention, not least for symbolizing international relations where it is not expected to be but where international relations indisputably is.

CHAPTER 6

Twin Towers of International Relations: The Museum

Art museums reflect, frame, and shape complex and often hidden aspects of international relations. As we have seen, they do so in a variety of ways. Some endeavor to save the cultural power or reputation of a particular nation by keeping the artworks they hold from museums and collectors in other countries (the British Museum, the National Gallery London). Sometimes the save is from direr threats, like war or international looters (the Iraq Museum). Some art institutions shape international cultural relations through art diplomatic practices (MOMA) or globalizing ventures (Guggenheim). Others are thrust before international audiences as symbols of nations or regions coming of age, even when the nation is otherwise preoccupied: Sydney's Opera House is in a country that loves the beach and bush far more than opera, and the powerful Getty is located in movieland United States. Arts institutions are not fixed entities, though; they shape-shift in architectural features, collection priorities, and the places they hold in memories. What starts as a royal palace, a commercial building, a church, or a factory can later become a powerful art center. Think of Tate Modern's reworked energy plant as a triumph of changing taste over tradition.

In this chapter, we consider the complex situation that arises when acts of international relations instantly transform a space known for one thing into a living memory museum of something else. The World Trade Center site in New York City is undoubtedly a place where architectures of commercial and national "persuasion," to adapt a term Robert Venturi and his colleagues coined in *Learning from Las Vegas* (1972), must re-form after a calamitous experience (plate 8). What had been there was big and jutting, defiant of air and space, demanding of attention, and belittling of everything around. The twin towers once persuaded all gazes upward, to linger, to be impressed, to be awed, and to be more than a little scared, too. Now, negative and traumatized shapes dominate a diminished skyline, and several years later we still cannot avert our eyes or agree politically and aesthetically on the shapes and meanings the replacement architectures should have. The World Trade Center had artworks on its walls and around its grounds, but it never held a museum or other specified arts institution. Today Ground Zero itself is a museum, with an enormous collection of precious objects produced by two violent acts of international relations conducted during peacetime.

Specific commemorative museums have been designated as part of the larger rebuild project, negotiations over which have been fierce. Heritage has a piercing urgency at a wounded site. Everything in and around Ground Zero is artifactual. Everything has been carefully excavated. All that could be saved has been saved for what will be, is already, the key museum of early twenty-first-century international relations. Guggenheim Bilbao renews city spaces that were subject to terrorist attacks over many years, but Ground Zero is something else again. Ghostly architectures and bodies stand in injured space, assaulted space, sepulchral space, wealthy space, pivotal urban space. As the British sculptor Rachel Whiteread knows, spaces that are hidden from the eye underneath the things we can see are heavy, solid, and airless. Ground Zero is acutely heavy, ponderous. The interests surrounding it are myriad. The architects trying to rebuild it are several. The people of Lower Manhattan and the people who lost loved ones on a September day are clamorous, insistent, politicized, and tough. Interests separate and overlap in a sometimes careful and sometimes chaotic politics. All the while, warrior America, failing to secure its own twin towers, tries to secure tower Afghanistan and tower Iraq using the violent means of the attackers. The life-and-death questions that some social theorists wanted to be put ahead of the usual preoccupations of theory in cultural studies suddenly connect, as Mary Poovey (2004) thinks they should, to institutions of art and governance, war and peace. How this memory museum collage is shaping up and who is vying to curate its exhibitionary spaces is the question of the hour.

TOWERS OF INTERNATIONAL RELATIONS

The twin towers were always architectures of international relations. They were created by a cold war reading of international political economy, and their original tenants engaged mostly in international trade, finance, or maritime pursuits. The World Trade Center of which they were a part was meant to be international trade central where it would be expected to be, projecting the commanding economic heights of a superpower. Yet when the towers were there, neither the steel, glass, and concrete, nor the people doing mundane jobs inside cubicles on the 103rd floor, to say nothing of janitors removing heel marks left by thousands daily, were seen as part of those international power buildings. Death to average tower people and to their workspaces above New York made the everydayness of international relations visible in the end, throwing a nation and a city into a spin, spawning international wars, and ushering in a fierce case of "stranger danger" to the United States and abroad. Those towers were always agentic, though, whether we saw them that way or only see it in their death and labored afterlife.

Cold War Towers

The idea of a world trade center in New York originated early in the second decade of the cold war of international relations. It was a time when the United States was worrying about a missile gap with the Soviet Union, about the meaning of the Sino-Soviet split, and about missiles in Cuba. Those insecurities heaped themselves on top of the considerations discussed in chapter 4 about projecting power, confidence, culture, and "free world" ambition. By the late 1950s, the postwar reconstruction of Europe was nearly accomplished. The currencies of most Allied countries had stabilized against gold via the U.S. dollar. Gross domestic products were rising steadily alongside postwar production. At that moment of ambition, projection, posturing, confidence, and fear, the Rockefeller family was prescient. David Rockefeller commissioned the New York City architectural firm of Skidmore, Owens and Merrill to plan an international business center for Lower Manhattan. The foresight in this thinking was remarkable. In 1958, American international trade accounted for less than 3.8 percent of its gross national product. Moreover, 80 percent of that trade was handled by multinational corporations that had no interest then in joining a world trade center that bundled them together with competitor companies.[1] By the year of John Kennedy's inauguration, a scion of art and international politics had assembled a Downtown–Lower Manhattan Association promising that "the world stands on the brink of a boom in international trade. . . . [T]his country must marshal its resources . . . establish a single center, planned and equipped to serve that vital purpose" (quoted in Glanz and Lipton 2003, 7).

David Rockefeller's original idea was to facilitate American import and export operations in the maritime trades, commodities brokerages, foreign banks, stockbrokerages, and insurance companies by housing them all under one roof of about seventy stories. Brother Nelson Rockefeller, then governor of New York, liked the novel world trade center scenario and devised a plan to finance the project by siting it on land owned by the Port Authority of New York and New Jersey. Only Port Authority could float the bonds needed to raise up a monumental venture like this. Old New York port without the water would be dedicated to international commerce and built as a semipublic American enterprise by the first American government agency dedicated to channeling private moneys into public works. The accountability of the World Trade

Center to New York City would be minimal, its office space maximum, and its command from on high of world trading activities stunning.

Port Authority was clearly in the cold war superpower league. Angus Gillespie (1999, 20), author of one of several biographies of the World Trade Center, describes it in a way that would be very familiar to students of feminist IR:

> [Port Authority] unabashedly took a masculine outlook on the world . . . Its bridges and tunnels were all business. . . . It favored male recruits with backgrounds in engineering or law. Though it was never made explicit, a tour of duty in the military—especially the US Navy—helped to place a newcomer on the fast track to promotion. Engineers especially found the Port Authority to be a place that was a manly environment rewarding the brave and the courageous . . . who could turn in not only engineering successes but financial successes as well. . . . Pride ultimately fueled the ambition to build the world's tallest building.

Construction began in 1966 on the project, which chief architect Minoru Yamasaki was told would be New York's counterpart to Kennedy's plan to put a man on the moon in a few years (48). Port Authority was expected to spend $200 million paying wages to about eight thousand construction workers. The architectural plan required 200,000 tons of structural steel, 6 million square feet of masonry walls, and 5 million square feet of painted surfaces. It would eat up 1,500 miles of wire, 200,000 lighting fixtures, and 7 million square feet of acoustical tile. Construction of the upper stories would be powered by Australian kangaroo cranes, and the steelwork would be put in place mostly by Mohawk Native Americans, whose fearlessness at great heights was part of New York skyscraper lore. Each tower would be fitted with ninety-seven regular elevators and six freight elevators, which, along with the air conditioning units and the utility ducts used for water and sewage, would be at the center core of each building. It was a design that maximized floor space (the tubular principle). The towers—there were now two instead of the one originally envisaged—were designed to withstand prolonged winds of 150 miles per hour, the kind of wind that would give each tower a 13-million-pound push, equivalent to being smashed by a large ocean freighter. The architect claimed that the towers could also "withstand the force of a 747 shearing into them" (Darton 1999, 117).

When completed, the twin-set statuary was impressive in the extreme at the same time that it was ponderous, blocky, and inelegant. To climb over one hundred stories while maximizing interior space, the external walls bore the weight of the twin towers, with half of each building's weight supported by two outer sheets of steel. This affected the appearance, as did the architect's plan for the comfort and security of people working within the buildings. A sufferer of vertigo, Yamasaki did not want broad expanses of glass at high elevations, even though these were common in international style skyscrapers of the time. His design provided for narrow glass windows spaced between reassuring weight-bearing concrete barriers. Such humanizing concerns were cast aside in reviews of the finished towers. To Joseph Rykwert (2000, 128), the towers were so unattractive that either one of them could have been the shipping box in which the far more graceful Empire State building came wrapped. Anchoring Lower Manhattan to upper political economy ambitions internationally, those twin towers were respected, one might say, but not especially loved. It was no help that they were dedicated in 1973, a time of increasing American shame in Vietnam, when their gigantism struck some as inappropriately gung-ho. Urban symbols of wealth and international power were also about to be overtaken by low-rise exurbias, exemplified by Microsoft's later three-story headquarters set among taller fir trees in the American Northwest. One might say that both the timing and the scale of New York's twin towers were off.

International Relations in Pre-Tower Spaces

The new World Trade Center took up most of the old natural harbor of Nieuw Amsterdam. In 1626, Peter Minuit had directed the Dutch company colony of New Netherland to negotiate with local Algonquins for rights to fourteen thousand acres of what we now call Lower Manhattan. The acreage would provide company settlers with fresh water and pasturage and an excellent location for trade at the confluence of the Hudson River and the Atlantic Ocean. Gabled houses, a windmill, and a fort sprouted on Lower Manhattan, and Dutch merchants and fur traders swarmed its early trading post. By 1640 the New Netherland colony was a free-trade zone, which boosted Nieuw Amsterdam's harbor business and attracted boisterous, colorful, bigger-than-life settlers from a variety of backgrounds—Germans, Swedes, Jews, Italians, Norwegians, Africans, and indigenous people that the Puritan English colonies to the north kept out. All were "characters playing parts in a drama of global sweep, a struggle for empire that would range across the seventeenth century and around the globe" (Shorto 2005, 27).

In 1664, the legendary leader Peter Stuyvesant, then the governor of the colony, faced the prospect of war with the encroaching and stronger British forces. Reluctantly but diplomatically, he surrendered Nieuw Amsterdam. By cooperating with the British, he was able to negotiate unprecedented terms that would imprint the city's personality well into the future: freedom of movement, trade, and religion plus rights to representation in all political affairs. Multicultural Dutch Manhattan carried on with no shot fired, mingling fitfully with English settlers and their traditions.[2] In constructing foundations for the twin towers, an anchor dated 1785 was happened upon (Gillespie 1999, 73). Further digging revealed so many artifacts of the Dutch and British eras of Manhattan that one Port Authority staff member was assigned to collect everything that seemed of archaeological interest. He kept numerous early Dutch clay pipes and hand-blown drinking glasses, bottles with British markings, and a leather shoe dating from around 1865. The World Trade Center would fill in a worldly place, a place, claims one of the city's biographers, where the America we recognize today really began (Shorto 2005, 21).

The World Trade Center filled up not only the old Nieuw Amsterdam port but also its later New York City counterpart. New York's port had been as amazing in its way as its Dutch predecessor. When the agricultural heartland of America connected up to the region via the completed Erie Canal in 1825, New York's port brimmed with domestic commerce and with ships traveling between the United States, Europe, and South America. Financial businesses flocked to the area to be near the new business center.[3] By mid-1914, the port of New York was handling over a billion dollars of foreign trade, an amount that surpassed London, Hamburg, and Liverpool. In 1913 alone, according to *King's Views of New York* (1915), "175,000,000 tons of freight were carried, the value exceeding $12,500,000.00" (Darton 1999, 19). With almost four hundred miles of developed waterfront, more if one measured around the piers on the Hudson, it was the home of 3,637 large American shipping vessels and saw more than 4,223 large foreign vessels come into port each year around 1915. Between the late nineteenth century and World War I, the port was also the entry point for thousands of Europeans, many of them from Italy and Ireland, who took employment in the shipping industries and lived in Lower Manhattan tenement buildings with the characteristic metal fire escapes trailing down their fronts. Lower New York had produced the greatest port in the world and a tough, dirty, claustrophobic warp of living space.

By the 1920s, shipping activities were already dispersing to other ports in the region, mainly because there was no freight rail linking the end of the Erie Canal routes with the port of New York City itself. It was easier and cheaper to ship from the side that did connect to the canal—New Jersey—than from Manhattan Island. Urban reformers of the time welcomed the creeping shift of port activity to New Jersey. They hoped it would free up space in crowded Lower Manhattan and improve living conditions. Financiers too reveled in the new profits they could make around the dwindling New York port by the "capitalization of its real estate . . . the core article of faith around which New York's financiers, developers, politicians, and planners have repeatedly organized their efforts" (Darton 1999, 21). Architects saw an opportunity to rebuild Lower Manhattan, perhaps with Corbusier-style towers placed in straight lines surrounded by parks.

New neighborhoods eat up money; yet when the time came to build the World Trade Center, it seemed to take shape precisely because it required big money to build. Darton explains:

> In the postwar United States, popular mythology abounded in examples of
> the healing power of big money, especially when linked to big plans. Had

not the millions spent on public works lifted the country out of the Great Depression—modernized, electrified, and fused it into a vast network of suburban utopias? Was not the largesse of the Marshall Plan responsible for raising from ashes a free and prosperous new Europe to stand against the tide of communism? Weren't even the world's most intractably backward nations racing into the modern era fueled by hundreds of millions of foreign aid? (64)

It was not the aura of money alone that did the trick. At the middle of the century, New Yorkers were enthralled by Rockefeller Center, the Chrysler and Empire State buildings, and the Rockefeller-backed United Nations building at the former site of an East River slaughterhouse. Technology, architectural monumentalism, and money together promised solutions to dingy city areas. "Renewal" rang out as loudly in the United States as "modernization" did in early development studies and "regeneration" does today. Tear down and build back up: between 1948 and 1960 around one hundred thousand New York residents, nearly half of them nonwhite, were displaced by demolitions of "undervalued," eyesore properties to make way for spectacular business and leisure architectures.[4] Ten years later the slash-and-burn approach to urban renewal would be dropped as too destructive of historical neighborhoods and community ties. The new cry would be "preservation." Had "the proposal to build the World Trade Center come only a few years later than it did, the twin towers might have been either shelved or rescaled" (37).

Towers at the End

Instead, they were built. Instead, neighborhoods were cleared of people and secondary businesses and streets rejiggered to give pride of place to the new colossi of Lower Manhattan. Instead, the old port of New York got the debris. The building plans were challenged time and again in the courts, not least by merchants of the Radio Row area earmarked to be "cleared" for the towers. Citizen groups were simply no match for the combined power of the Port Authority, the Rockefellers, and the city government. In 1964, the Downtown West Businessmen's Association was so disappointed in the response to their protests that they wrote to eleven European heads of state warning of "a scheme which is shortly to be perpetrated upon you, your government, and your people under the thinly veiled lie of a 'World Trade Center.'... This is sponsored by financiers who have no honest interest in world trade, but who believe they have found a way to create the issuance of almost a billion dollars of tax-free bonds which they are in a favorable position to exploit" (quoted in Darton 1999, 136). Real estate developers balked too, not relishing competition with government-backed office buildings that could accommodate a hundred firms in one fell swoop. Architects decried demolition of historic buildings to make way for tower blocks. Even eager urban planners wondered about the wisdom of siting a pace-setting international trade center in Lower Manhattan at a time when the center of commerce had moved north to Midtown.

A late change of site caused additional controversy. For most of the 1960s, the plan was to build the World Trade Center on 13.5 acres near the Fulton Fish Market on the East River. The State of New Jersey, which was party to the Port Authority, balked when it realized that that location did not link up well with its international ports across the Hudson River to the west of Manhattan. A specially crafted 16-plus-acre "plot" suddenly became available closer to Manhattan's lower western edge, adjacent to outmoded underwater tubes linking Manhattan with New Jersey. The attraction of the new plan to some was that all rubble and building debris would be used to fill in swamp and marshlands around the nearby Battery area. Narrow Lower Manhattan would thereby end up with more space than it previously had, the much-loved fish market area could remain, and New Jersey would be appeased. The big loser would be the historical ports, which literally disappeared under the World Trade Center. The long process of clearing, contracting, financing, and negotiating also left many human victims of slum clearance and power politicking at higher levels. As an indication of just how polarizing the battles over the twin towers were, on April 4, 1973, the day the towers were dedicated, the official from Port Authority who had pushed the hardest to make the trade center a reality, Austin Tobin, was not there. He had been forced to resign the previous year during the political dispute over benefits of a World Trade Center for both New York and New Jersey. President Richard Nixon was there, though, in the form of a message from the White House praising the towers of international trade.

While the center was new, most tenants were indeed associated with international trade. Some of them stayed on over the years: Mutual International Forwarding, an original tenant, was still there in 2001. When city real estate boomed in the early 1980s, however, rents went up and many maritime firms left for cheaper offices in less flashy buildings. "Stockbrokers in dark suits and button-down shirts replaced shipping agents wearing jeans" (*Der Spiegel* 2001, 80–81). The World Trade Center was no longer a magnet for firms engaged in international trade so much as a gathering of banking and other financial services. Cantor Fitzgerald took up five floors of the North Tower; Morgan Stanley and Fuji Banking also had multiple floors. At the other end of the size spectrum were small insurance companies like Metlife, public relations companies like Cosmos and Strategic Communications, and business property agencies like Julien J. Studley Inc. The prestige international businesses were on the top floors, the smaller businesses below, as though the farther one traveled vertically in the towers, the more one could be "above it all"—above the scruffy, noisy, distracting urbanity below, above the weaknesses of human institutions or poverty or war. Like the dioramas of toy warriors gouging out intestines, decapitating their enemies, and mercilessly knifing everyone in the back, which the

Chapman brothers created in 2003, floor 110 of the World Trade Center miniaturized all horrors below it.

But that was all illusion. The cold war beacons of persuasion crumpled in the end, themselves victims of a macabre, horrifying, urban "clearance" and human-miniaturizing operation from above. Even before September 11, 2001, the Al-Qaeda-linked basement bombing of 1993 had sent a number of high-end firms fleeing towers that were now seen as "jinxed" or too tall for their own good. It was difficult to replace those tenants. Vacancy rates increased; in 2001 a quarter of the total office space on the eighty-ninth floor of the North Tower, for example, was empty. The lower tenancy rate translated into less-than-fastidious building maintenance. A survivor of the September 11 attacks remembers thinking that very morning that "the World Trade Center was pretty run down. Considering the millions of dollars traders around here earned, it looked kind of pitiful. It smelled of dust, stale coffee, and old food—probably because nearly no one went out for lunch. . . . The millionaires sat at their desks and ate Big Macs and french fries out of boxes. . . . And why did one of the richest banks in the world choose mud green for the color of the wall-to-wall carpet? Maybe because you couldn't see the dirt on it" (*Der Spiegel* 2001, 65).

It was already the end of glamour at the architectural heights. Within the smelly onion skin of the twin towers that morning, however, the daily routines of international relations must have initially unfolded in the usual ways. Calls were put in to European firms. E-mails from Asia flashed on computer screens. Scores of *New York Times* newspapers poked out of attaché cases. And then the shock of elevators spewing flames. Tips of airline wings appeared to employees in the South Tower. Clogged staircases went on and on without end as firefighters fought their way up and employees fought their way down (see, e.g., Langewiesche 2003; Glanz and Lipton 2003). "You know how it ends: everybody dies," writes novelist Frederic Beigbeder (2005, 1) in his tale of a wayward father guiltily making up for weeks of self-obsession by treating his boys to breakfast that morning in Windows on the World. Against all that transpires and all that has been said about it, a description of life in the twin towers in the late 1990s, after the first bombing but before the fatal second one, rings especially eerie.

> Around 7, as people continue coming into the complex with folded newspapers under their arms, there is a large number of office workers who have forgotten their identification cards. Large lines start to form at the visitor desks. But by 8 some are already ensconced in large offices, sipping coffee and reading the Wall Street Journal. Other workers slip into their windowless cubicles and turn on their computer screens. There is much work to be done in importing, exporting, freight forwarding, international banking, publishing, steamship line, engineering, commodities trading. . . . [At World Trade Center 4] a number of exchanges share a joint trading floor for such goods as coffee, cotton, sugar, potatoes, lumber, and beef. The vast trading floor, about

the size of two football fields, placed side by side, is all under one unsupported ceiling, not broken by any columns. On my first visit there, I asked one of the floor traders why there were no windows. He said . . . "That's so nobody can jump out on a bad day"(Gillespie 1999, 212–13).

TOWERS AND STRANGE ACTS

On the ultimate bad day, of course, people were desperate to escape the buildings, even if it meant finding ways to get out of narrow windows engineered to safeguard them within the twin towers. Quite a few did jump or blow out from elevations too far up possibly to fathom. When they hit the ground, their bodies made a sound like a small explosion, disintegrating or discharging their insides like ripe figs. Ground Zero: body and architectural dust—the ultimate warped and wounded space of a city, of global ambition, and of an era.

Those who plotted the attack used the code word "architecture" to refer to the World Trade Center and called the Pentagon "arts." No one reading their e-mails or listening in on their international phone conversations was supposed to make the connection between "architecture" and "international business," "art" and "military affairs." The attackers knew their audience in that regard: despite globalization jargon referring to economic "architectures," despite the common term "art of war," the code words for the attack landed on clueless intelligence networks.[5] The attacks themselves were intelligence-aware and conducted as luridly as possible by men of the postcolonial "East," who, having lived Western lives (for the most part) for several years, had imbibed secrets about a society that could treat flights as nonchalantly as other countries think of bus travel.

Those men had eaten from America's material temples, had seen the decadence of its life, the nakedness of its men and women. They had noted the dewy and feminine touches of democracy, where women could vote too, as well as the shallowness of a nation's summer interest in a senator and his missing female aide. They cast apple-y Emerald City as the Decadent West, the Heartless West, the Anti-Islamic West, and as a soft emasculated city of the West. That city, that architecture, that space—it was all a blasphemy to men whose global reach sent shivers out of cave strongholds in a country that IR's development studies camp had nearly forgotten after the fall of the Soviet Union, Afghanistan. Full of grisly imagination and fiery passions, men with numb-looking expressions instigated deeds that are now well known and chewed over by committees and commissions and students of IR. On videos, and through interviews and remembrances, the events of September 11, 2001, are re-represented, mourned, made national, and made international on a regularly repeating basis. They compose a big afterlife of IR called "war on terror."

We could be forgiven for thinking that the whole nasty, inhuman affair is a thing of crude masculinist competition, rage, and revenge. On one side is a cunning mastermind, described by a sage of cloak-and-dagger fiction as "self-adoring" in his radiating "narcissism" and "male vanity" (Le Carré 2001, 17). On the other side is a U.S. president who, by many accounts, had stolen an election seven months earlier. He radiates smug vanity through an arrogant, bullying, superior international relations of neoconservatism. He pushes America's luck at the end of the cold war by trying to stamp "our" norms, institutions, protocols, and diplomatic priorities on the world as an activist insurance policy for the United States. In the future, things will go "our" neoconservative way rather than some wishy-washy multilateral, Communist way, or terrorist way. If the World Trade Center had been originally construed as trade central, then striding forward from its footprints was to be an international relations of liberty central.[6]

Towers and Strangers

"Our way" has had its problems, and it certainly is not a golden rulebook for a multicultural world. Intriguingly, though, that way has harnessed the talents and work habits of immigrants to a powerful saga of "America" from sea to shining sea. Very much unlike Europe, and unlike Australia until the 1970s, America's foreign roots have in the past rendered it difficult to be a bona fide stranger in America. America is the home of strangers; even Native Americans are said to have traveled across the Bering Strait to reach their home places. There are no alien Americans, only alienated Americans and aliens in America who, if they play their cards right, often get to stay anyway. America is the final urban and rural homestead writ large (Sylvester 1994a). So when the plotters of death walked through security checks at various American airports on September 11, no one recognized them as the enemy. They could just as easily have been waved through similar security posts at the twin towers themselves, where it was said that "scrutiny diminishes to the point that a person bearing a reasonably accurate [identity] facsimile stands a good chance of gaining entrance unchallenged" (Darton 1999, 148). No, the attackers in Timberland garb seemed to be where they would be expected to be rather than at the verge of their end. Initially, we try to imagine the psychological and cultural processes that produce ordinary men as monsters of international relations, but we can have difficulty doing so. Fig leaves covering innocence do not drop at the sight of their faces, because those who will topple buildings, incinerate workers, and burn themselves into our memories do not look like strangers. They look like us.

If we are in any doubt, American law tells us that this must be so. In a fascinating story of "strangers" in the skies, journalist Annie Jacobsen (2004) recounts what happened on a flight she took with her family from Detroit, Michigan, to Los Angeles, California, on June 29, 2004. Fourteen Middle Eastern men between the ages of around twenty and fifty were among the passengers boarding the plane. Two wore track suits with Arabic writing on the backs, two carried musical instrument cases, one sported a yellow tee-shirt and McDonald's bag, and yet another limped in what appeared to be an orthopedic shoe. One man in a dark suit and sunglasses took a seat very close to the cockpit door in the first-class section, and the other men scattered through the economy section. Each one proceeded to make countless visits to the toilet carrying a bag or other object, took a fair amount of time in that cramped space, and returned to his seat with what appeared to be a near-empty bag or an object gone missing. A group of these men congregated in the back of the plane, with the man in first class standing and watching them. Nods and thumbs-up signs, finger-across-throat hand signals, all passed among them up and down the narrow plane corridor. Jacobsen's husband became alarmed enough to speak to a flight attendant, who informed him that the behavior was being closely watched and monitored by the attendants, the pilot, and the federal air marshals on the flight.

As the plane descended for the landing in Los Angeles, she writes, "seven of the men stood up—in unison—and walked to the front and back lavatories. One by one they went into the lavatories, each spending about four minutes inside. Right in front of us, two men stood up against the emergency exit door, waiting for the lavatory to become available" (1). After the plane landed and passengers started to disembark, her family noticed scores of police agents heading for the gate; she learned later that in addition to these, FBI agents, federal air marshals, and Transportation Security Administration agents were there.

Jacobsen decided to look into laws about "strangers" suspected of planning terrorist activities on aircraft. She found that airlines were not legally allowed to question more than two Arab males on any flight or they would face a heavy fine. Discriminating against passengers based on their race, color, national or ethnic origin, or religion was forbidden under U.S. law. Both United Airlines and American Airlines, whose planes were involved in the September 11 crashes, found this out the hard way, settling cases with the Transportation Department with fines of $1.5 million. Federal marshals were increasingly assigned to flights, but they could act only if an "event" actually occurred. A spokesperson for the Federal Air Marshal Service told Jacobsen that the marshals on her flight had been carefully inspecting the lavatories at regular intervals, finding nothing incriminating in them. That was all they could do.[7]

The frightening men claimed to be Syrian musicians traveling to the Los Angeles area to play at a casino. And that turned out to be the case, notwithstanding their suspicious behavior. The men might have looked like strangers in light of the events of September 11, but according to U.S. law they were not to be treated as such unless they did something more than they did. Jacobsen's recounting of events suggests that what Sara Ahmed (2000) refers to as "stranger fetishism" had started to invade the American traveling public, urged on by the politics of fear associated with the "war against terror." Jacobsen and her flight compatriots were hyperaware of post–September 11 dangers to commercial flights and associated these not with, say, the older couple sitting nearby or the flight attendants serving them. They associated the dangers with men of a race, nationality, language, and/or clothing style that seemed to signal dangerous cultural difference. That these men also carried "suspicious" items on board and used the spaces of the aircraft in ways that triggered memories of past threats in the air turned them into "strangers." In other words, as a result of a violent act of international relations that used planes against towering architectures, average Americans could draw the terrorist "stranger" vividly into American landscapes for the first time since the McCarthy era of the 1950s, which took aim at Communist strangers masquerading as loyal Americans. Airport security has similarly been fetishized, contributing to a 17 percent drop in visitors to the United States since 2001 (Discover America Advocacy Campaign 2007).

Stranger fetishism means that people we judge to be like ourselves are automatically above suspicion while certain unfamiliar others are put under a cloud of wariness. One might say that the average American now looks at people and artifacts with the eyes of museum curators. We examine portraits of men and scrutinize textiles and costuming. Still-life compositions at the rear of planes draw our attention, as does the art of movement in confined spaces. In the always already claustrophobic places of commercial flights, faces, bags, shoes, reading material, and fidgeting become the materials for building installations of death, or so it can be feared.

Towers and Trauma

Jacobsen's suspicions turned out to be unwarranted, but she offered no remorse or ironic turn to her account. That those particular men did nothing wrong was certainly a relief to her, but it was also beside the very serious point. For Jacobsen, fear about personal safety has a privileged place in the skies. We were baptized into an anxious way of knowing international relations and its mobilities at the dawn of the twenty-first century. We wish it were not so. We do not like the way anxious knowing feels. In the remainder of her article, Jacobsen suggests various mechanisms of scrutiny and surveillance that could keep the usual anxieties associated with flying—fears of mechanical problems, turbulence, and late arrival—from expanding into fear of everyone on the flight.[8]

For Americans, the destruction of the twin towers was a traumatic event that made heightened fear reasonable in certain circumstances; the scene on Jacobsen's flight would have frightened me silly, too. Trauma blurs the usual distinctions between victimhood and protest (Edkins 2003). As part of a national group that has experienced traumatic victimhood around terrorist penetration of borders, Jacobsen becomes a traumatized protester against saving the rights of some individuals whose physical features, languages, and cultural styles recall the characteristics of the perpetrators. Subsequent Homeland Security measures have encouraged this dual response—worry that one's own body will fall next and wariness about the person sitting near one. We also see retaliatory military action in countries that had nothing to do with the twin towers trauma. And then there is the media response to September 11: highly visible architectures turn invisible before our eyes, over and over. Planes disappear into solid buildings, carefully engineered architectures fall into heaps, and national trauma is memorized.

Jenny Edkins (59) says that trauma "is that which refuses to take its place in history as done and finished with." Something happens out of sequence that puts us out of order and continues to do so. It is the unthinkable thought, or a thought located where it's not really expected. And being where it's not expected or supposed to be, it repeats in our minds, interrupts the present, and has nowhere to go or be put. Other potentially trauma-inducing events of international relations, such as involvement in war, do not seem to trigger a generalized fear like this in average people, not until the wars are at the point of pathetic pointlessness. The twin towers difference is enabled in part by the entitlements it has brought to an executive branch of the American government already bent on interventionist war in (certain) countries. As the violence carries on, Steve Smith (2003) finds the field of IR complicit with the tragedies of September 11, owing to its stubborn disinterest in the South and poverty. So too, many Americans burqa ourselves against thoughts of how violent and presumptuous we have become because we are traumatized.

Architectural historian Anthony Vidler (2000, vii), however, claims that trauma can also inhere in architectural spaces. A building and its interiors stand as "a projection of the subject, and thus as a harbinger and repository of all the neuroses and phobias of that subject." The warped space of a skyscraper or a plane is full of disturbing objects and forms that threaten to damage, distort, or magnify our usual realities. We have put them there, and now we watch them take shape. Community crime "watches" form in the air. Passengers who once sat tapping on laptops or dozing in front of film miniatures make snap judgments about who is trustworthy and who is not (Anderson 1990). A country that has had little reason to fear immigration suddenly tunes in to stranger danger. Darton (1999, 119) says that spaces anticipate these outcomes through their very design. He thinks the creators of the World Trade Center and the 1993 bombers of it shared "a radical distancing of themselves from the flesh-and-blood experience of mundane existence 'on the ground.'" One group went higher and higher with steel beams and another went higher in the aspiration to destroy those beams and the people walking, as in an airplane, in high spaces sharply defined by them. The ambition to build such colossi and the ambition to destroy them similarly transcend the earth, the mundane, and the prosaic.

Yet after direct hits by planes smaller than 747s, and on a calm and windless day in 2001, the ground and sociality were all there was in Lower Manhattan: eyes of survivors and victims, sounds of firefighters and screaming office workers, the mayor of New York, one presidential adviser after another, platoons of hard-hatted construction workers and troops of CNN staff. We realized then, through a diabolical change in architectural design, that the towers really had teemed with lives as much as with formal design relationships, stocks, and international trade. The warped space of two gigantic twin towers warped even more in their absence. We became trapped in layers of trauma. Even those of us who never entered the towers, never engaged in the trade for which they were originally built, never worked for Cantor Fitzgerald, and never approved of the brash tower intrusion on the old New York skyline, sketch in those tall cylinders as we wind along the New Jersey Turnpike, cross the Whitestone Bridge, or watch a movie filmed in New York City before September 11, 2001. How long will this last? Will new buildings snuff out the obsessive memories and their aftermaths? Unlikely, but some responses will alter, one thinks, depending on how the many damaged spaces of the twin towers are curated.

CURATING THE TWIN TOWERS "MUSEUM"

How to quiet the anxiety surrounding a pair of monumental buildings that were here then and are gone now? How to mark the bones and ashes of the dead? How to do business again in a graveyard? How to cast an architectural cum social resurrection in a complex political setting? How, in effect, to make Lazarus more handsome and memorable than the unloved original? Who is dealing with all this? Where are the curators of the museum?

The Winning Architect

Ask Daniel Libeskind, the architect whose design study for the World Trade Center site, called "Memory Foundations," bested four hundred others submitted from thirty-four countries. It was the second competition run by the Lower Manhattan Development Corporation (LMDC). The first had produced six sterile models of commercial development, all devised by one local architectural firm (Beyer, Blinder Belle). The more open second competition yielded seven finalists, including firms associated with Norman Foster and with

Richard Meier working in collaboration with Steven Holl. That Libeskind's ideas and possibilities outdid them all did not earn him the right to have a building he designed constructed at the site or to decide where anything would be situated. The final outcome would reflect pooled ideas, possibilities, and politics on an order few could anticipate. The winner would be pushed back and forth and around by politicos, citizen groups, landlords, and other architects in a complex political economy of layered aspirations. Everyone, it turns out, has wanted to curate the Ground Zero rebuild.

Libeskind is a globalized man, which means he is always where he is expected to be when he is out in the world. His buildings dot urban landscapes from Milan to Seoul, Hong Kong to Tel Aviv, Denver to Copenhagen. Until recently, he has been best known for designing the remarkable Jewish Museum in Berlin. Other Libeskind designs, such as the Imperial War Museum North in Manchester and a newly opened postgraduate center for London Metropolitan University, have put him neck and neck with Frank Gehry, Norman Foster, Zaha Hadid, and Rem Koolhaas as one of the most celebrated architects of our time. In 2001 he also became the first architect to receive the Hiroshima Art Prize, awarded to an artist whose work promotes international understanding and peace. In 1999 he received the Deutsche Architekturpreis for the Jewish Museum design and then the Goethe Medaillon for Cultural Contribution in 2000. The American Academy of Arts and Letters had already recognized him in 1996 for architectural achievement.

Libeskind is part of the post–World War II Jewish diaspora. Born in 1946 in a hospital for refugees in Lodz, Poland, he lived his early life there in an atmosphere he remembers as "all gray . . . the angry gray of the cold northern European winter sky, the dusty gray of industrial Lodz, overlaid with the grayness of communism" (Libeskind 2004, 56–57). As a little boy, he was warned to be careful; there were only 5,000 Jews in a city that less than ten years earlier had been home to 220,000 Jews. His parents had met during the war. Each had fled Poland for the Soviet Union when the Nazis invaded in 1939, and both were captured by the Red Army and sent to labor camps. Released in 1942, they met in a refugee camp in Kyrgyzstan. As a couple, they returned to Lodz, the city of his father, and lived an anxious existence. In 1957, they finally received visas to leave the country and initially embarked for Israel. The eleven-year-old Daniel was smitten with cosmopolitan Israel: "The country was not even ten years old when we arrived, and everything was brand-new: crisp, white, modern" (64). Two years later, the thirteen-year-old sailed with his family to yet another life in New York City.

Libeskind had been an accomplished and award-winning child musician, an accordionist, and many expected him to continue with music. Instead, he enrolled in New York's Cooper Union program in architecture. He was there when the twin towers were going up and thought them "exciting in terms of their sheer scale and daring, but . . . pretty frightening" (quoted in Glancey

2004, 8–9). Libeskind became a U.S. citizen in 1965 and married Nina Lewis, a Canadian he met at a Yiddish camp in upstate New York. With their three children, they have been itinerant by design, moving between Berlin, Milan, and New York, with stints in Michigan and California. Their stay in Berlin was longer than they originally anticipated and somewhat fraught.

Rehearsing for the World Trade Center: The Berlin Jewish Museum

The Jewish Museum was the first commission Daniel Libeskind won. He was invited to enter the international competition by the West Berlin senate in 1988. He won in the summer of the fateful German year, 1989. He was forty-three years old then and fifty-five when the museum opened its doors at another fateful moment: three days before September 11, 2001. The intervening twelve years became a rehearsal for the complex politics of international relations that would swirl around the rebuild at Ground Zero.

It was not clear, first of all, that the Jewish Museum would really be built once the wall was breached and reunification exuberance was in the air. The original idea had been to expand the existing Berlin Museum to "architecturally integrate Jewish history into Berlin's rich, multi-textured history and enable people, even encourage them, to feel what had happened" (Libeskind 2004, 82). No funds had actually been committed to the project at the time of the competition, however, and within two years the enormous reunification costs, coupled with Berlin's bid for an Olympics, eliminated much of the public money that museum supporters had hoped to tap. The project was controversial from the start, and the German senate summarily voted in 1991 to cancel it.

Even before the seeming endgame had begun, Libeskind found the process trying. Under normal conditions, he knew that only around 1 percent of winning designs ever went on to be built. In Berlin, strong forces had sought to stall or cancel the very idea of a Jewish Museum and now used the collapse of the cold war to insist on new agendas for a new Germany. Libeskind was stubbornly determined to bring the museum to fruition and had countless meetings with influential bureaucrats. One was Hans Stimmann, the building director for Berlin appointed in 1992, who was relentless in his opposition to Libeskind and the project:

> Stimmann summoned me to his office to present the museum project once again (once again!). When I finished the presentation, he turned to the people in the room—his administrative aides and members of my staff. "This building is an architectural fart," he said. . . . "I'm sick and tired of all this Jewish history. We've got too much Jewish history in Berlin as it is. We don't need any more." . . . Stimmann's antagonism toward me and my architecture

was relentless. . . . It was soon evident that Stimmann was determined to keep us from building anything in Berlin, even a phone booth. We'd won commissions for many projects in the city. Stimmann intervened, and blocked them all. (134)

Stimmann and his ilk did not prevail. The museum was built.

Libeskind puts it all down to his wife and her successful international relations of pressure and influence. Nina Libeskind is from the Russian-Jewish family that founded the New Democratic Party in Canada and that sent family members to the Canadian parliament and provincial legislatures. Her brother has been Canadian ambassador to the United Nations and special UN envoy for HIV/AIDS in Africa. Nina herself managed political campaigns and served as a trade union negotiator. Through her efforts, the winning design for a Jewish Museum got off the drawing board and onto the ground. First she alerted the international press that the project was being canceled. That news precipitated serious debates in the German media about how a Holocaust-guilty state and society should best remember those it had grievously wronged. Nina Libeskind then enjoined influential political and cultural figures to make their views about the project known to the German people and the government. She marshaled the support of leading Israeli politicians, the French minister of culture, several prominent rabbis in the United States, and—the prize of them all—Willy Brandt, former mayor of West Berlin and former chancellor of Germany.

The international pressure was symphonic. The then mayor of Berlin, Eberhard Diepgen, tried the duck-and-dive ploy of buying off the Libeskinds with an offer of other important and highly remunerative commissions throughout the city in place of the Jewish Museum. But the architect turned diplomatic spouse of Nina Libeskind refused. Frustrated when a BBC reporter demanded to know what he was going to do about the museum, the mayor instructed an aide with him at that moment to do whatever it takes to "'get that Libeskind woman off my back'" (146). The comment ended up on the reporter's tape and was broadcast on British television. A month later, in October 1991, the parliament of Berlin unanimously overruled the senate and voted for the Jewish Museum.

Like most diplomats, Nina Libeskind operated in high elite circles, made judicious use of the international media, and knew how to call in favors due her or her family. In the campaign to get the Jewish Museum of Berlin built, she was where she could be most effective, but she was outside the IR box labeled international diplomacy, which is about the bargaining moves of state leaders, foreign policy appointees, and international organizations. Mainstay IR could not see architecture and "her" at the end of IR. The big Guggenheim has gone virtually unnoticed in IR's globalization studies, and the building of the Jewish Museum Berlin must rank as the great underresearched case of international cultural-art diplomacy led by a woman.

The World Trade Center Rebuild

Redesigning and rebuilding the World Trade Center site thrust Daniel Libeskind into the diplomatic batter's box this time, wearing his New York immigrant Yankee colors on his sleeve and undoubtedly coached by his wife. The challenge was to persuade the parties selecting the architect to take the one design that was "odd." Libeskind (47) tells us that the finalist designs all "aimed to create an impressive high point, and ultimately to replace the Twin Towers." His design, by contrast, featured one tall building, Freedom Tower, and four other buildings around a semicircle at the outside of the site. The tower would twist up to a height of 1,776 feet, a number to pluck at the heartstrings of Americans' patriotic remembrance. On its top would be a spire locked in a wave with the sweet lady on Liberty Island. Much of the upper level of the tower would be left transparently empty of business, graced only with communication cables or internal gardens "up there," where hundreds had walked, worked, flown, and perished. The additional buildings would ascend gradually in height from south to north, forming a pattern that would hug and shelter the footprints of the old twin towers. Libeskind envisioned a real neighborhood emerging around the buildings, too, something the original World Trade Center had destroyed. It would have a new park, scores of offices in the five buildings, seven stories of infrastructure below ground, a new transportation and road network, and a cultural/museum complex, all enveloped in an intricate security and safety system.

The heart of his design, though, was in the earth below rather than in vacated spaces in the sky: "I focused down—into the bedrock, into the pit, because I felt that was where the memory of the site also resided, and not only in the development of high-rise buildings" (46). Libeskind became mesmerized by the slurry wall that stands seventy feet down into Ground Zero. The foundation dam for the area, it holds back the water surrounding Lower Manhattan as effectively as any Dutch polder. Without that wall, the site would be engulfed—could have been engulfed, in fact, had the collapse of the twin towers led to its disintegration. Libeskind maintains that a potential wall of sorrows in the depths of Ground Zero says something in its refusal to yield. He has referred to it as "an engineering marvel, a metaphoric and literal stay against chaos and destruction" (43).

His interest in keeping the slurry wall and the footprints of the twin towers to a depth of seventy feet does not overshadow the places Libeskind designed for business and leisure. He wanted a pair of glass-structured museums cantilevered over the sunken memorial area. He wanted historic Fulton and Greenwich streets up and operating again (they had been cut off by the twin towers) and a new performing arts center created where none had previously existed. Features conjuring passionate mourning could stand side by side with elements recalling the city's historic strength, vital business centers, and lively neighborhoods. And there would be wedges of light, too, calculated to fall in two lines on the plaza of the new World Trade Center site every September 11 at 8:46 a.m., the exact time the first jet slammed into the twin towers, and at 10:28 a.m., when the second tower fell. For Libeskind, and for those who supported his plans, it was all where it could be. Saying modestly that it would be great if he could actually get to design and build one of the architectures in the complex, in an echo of the earlier Rockefellers he also messianically called the design "the rebirth, effectively, of Lower Manhattan" (Glancey 2004, 8).

Still, getting something significant built in New York City today is as much a question of money and politics as design. After judging Libeskind's designs best suited for the twin towers site, the city reverted to its usual haggling between established power brokers, each with a particularistic sense of how Libeskind's winning design study should be interpreted. The Port Authority, which still owns the land at Ground Zero, felt Libeskind lacked the experience required to design and oversee a central transit station at the site. It was agreed that Santiago Calatrava, the acclaimed Spanish architect of bridges and terminals, would join the architectural team to design the station. The company that had leased and operated the World Trade Center's retail spaces, Westfield, lobbied for a replacement underground mall at the site, something Libeskind had purposely tried to avoid in the interest of enlivening the aboveground neighborhood. The leaseholder and insurance collector on the twin tower buildings, Larry Silverstein, insisted that the new buildings had to contain 10 million square feet of office space, even if that would leave less area for memorials. Silverstein also wanted the Freedom Tower relocated from the position Libeskind painstakingly designed to a spot close to the new mass-transit center. There were even objections to the sunken memorial Libeskind designed, on the grounds that Lower Manhattanites would have to maneuver around it in order to reach the subway from Battery Park City. Various commentators also argued that the wedge of light Libeskind wanted to channel would not really fall on the designated plaza each year at the appointed times.

Myriad power centers outshouted the architect's moral, political, and design angularities. After ferocious negotiations, the final working design for the most eye-catching of Libeskind's proposed buildings, Freedom Tower, was under the control of Silverstein, the leaseholder. He awarded it to his own favorite architect, David Childs of Skidmore, Owings and Merrill (SOM), the earliest firm involved in planning the original World Trade Center. Refinements on Libeskind's twin towers footprints memorial went to Michael Arad and Peter Walker of Handel Architects, who designed a 4.6-acre memorial called "Reflecting Absence." Other contracts brought in Norman Foster of

England, Fumihiko Maki of Japan, and Jean Nouvel of France. Only a few Libeskind marks appeared to be slated to survive the power struggle: the revealed slurry wall, the footprints of the twin towers, and aspects of the design study that had evoked the Statue of Liberty.

Ground was symbolically broken and work was meant to get under way in 2004, but everything stalled time and again. Libeskind sued Silverstein for $843,750 in unpaid fees to himself, his wife, and his design studio. Ever upbeat, though, he claimed that "there have been fewer compromises than people imagine, and . . . compromise is an integral part of the architectural process" (Libeskind 2004, 270). Positive spin, however, could not disguise the hijackings that had pushed Libeskind to the margins of the project.

The Leaseholder

The main action around the World Trade Center site shifted to Larry Silverstein. He held the insurance policy on the downed buildings and kept reminding everyone that he thereby controlled what went in. Hoping for double insurance compensation of $7 billion, because two buildings and not one collapsed, he ended up with a bit more than half of that and a bill of $100 million for court costs. With less insurance money to work with, Silverstein said he had no choice but to insist on a higher ratio of commercial space to memorial space. It was the only way to recoup his financial losses on the twin towers and the other destroyed buildings the Port Authority had leased to him at the site on ninety-nine-year terms. Determined to show that he was in charge, Silverstein moved quickly to rebuild, starting with World Trade Center 7, just off the Ground Zero site. It rose in 2006 as an architecturally underwhelming Childs (SOM) design.[9]

Silverstein could be all business and seemingly no heart. As he became adamant about subordinating most design considerations to the priority of rental income from the resurrected area, the city balked. Survivors balked, too. Politicos waffled. Everything was held up time and time again. Silverstein simply did not have the resources to rebuild on the scale required, but he would not yield, either. Stalling for time, he tried to raise the $4.4 billion or so the city estimated he needed to rebuild his lost properties at Ground Zero. Some wanted Port Authority to buy out all of Silverstein's interests in the area, and others thought he should cede several proposed buildings to another authority. He was not the only one stalling, though. Governor George Pataki's appointees dominated the Port Authority and the Lower Manhattan Development Committee. They tended also to slow progress when the architectural choices of the day threatened Pataki's 2002 reelection prospects and then threatened the success of the 2004 Republican Party convention.

By early 2006 it was Silverstein, however, who had become immensely unpopular. Charles Gargano, vice chairman of the Port Authority, publicly dubbed him "greedy," and Councilman Alan Gerson, chair of the Lower Manhattan Redevelopment Committee, insisted "enough is enough." Ground Zero was still nearly at zero more than four years after the day of the attack, and people in the United States and abroad wanted to know why (*City Broadsheet* 2006, 1). The city was embarrassed. Instead of buildings and memorials, visitors to the area could see only a cleaned-up- and fenced-in urban building lot, somewhat like any other except for the lingering photos, impromptu memorials, and official museum-style information narratives and photos tacked to the fences. The effect was of the immediacy of everyday life lost and yet still there through the fog of violent international relations. It was not unlike the impromptu offerings affixed to the fences at Greenham Common peace camp twenty years earlier (see Sylvester 1994a)—although peace was not the overall sense that Ground Zero fence exhibitions projected.

Pataki set March 14, 2006, as the final deadline for movement forward. That date came and went. On April 26, Silverstein was ultimately persuaded to reduce his role at Ground Zero and surrender Freedom Tower and one-third of the Ground Zero building area to the Port Authority. The next day, the land movers arrived. It seemed like the 1960s all over again; the original twin towers had abruptly gotten the go-ahead at the highest levels of a city determined to save face after years of delays. And now, once again, some opinion had it that the "erratic rhythm resulted in inferior design and planning solutions that might not have been accepted had there been more time for thoughtful deliberation" (Filler 2005, 7). One group of lobbyists had been giving rebuilding matters considerable thought and determined deliberation: the survivors of September 11. Their views would carry much more weight than the concerns expressed by those whose homes and shops were destined to be obliterated by the first World Trade Center build.

Survivor Groups

Survivor groups at Ground Zero have been numerous and powerful. They represent direct survivors of the attacks on the twin towers and the Pentagon, the workers in or near one of the buildings, and the emergency workers called to the scene; relatives of the dead, including those killed on the planes; and even members of the public who reside or have a business in Lower Manhattan and are affected by decisions made about Ground Zero. As the years pass, the groups and their concerns proliferated, leading to disagreements among them over priorities, designs, compensation, and the types of museums and leisure activities that should be allowed at the site. Their interests have run the gamut from earmarking a sacred burial ground (Take Back the Memorial) to campaigning for stricter building codes (the Skyscraper Safety Campaign group), equitable distribution of survivor funds (the Lower East Side–Chinatown Consortium), and gender equity in the economic revitalization activities of the area (which has resulted in the Coordinated Construction Act for Lower Manhattan).

Most survivor groups deal with local, even neighborhood, issues, but a few have become involved in the international relations of the twin tower attack. A Committee of 9/11 Families United to Bankrupt Terrorism filed a fourteen-point lawsuit in the U.S. District Court for the District of Columbia against Arab and Islamic organizations they claimed were funding terrorist activities. A subcommittee of that group looked into the process by which visas were issued to suspicious aliens, and they lobbied the U.S. Senate against the appointment of an assistant secretary of state for consular affairs whom they found lax in vetting visa applications. The Port Authority has also emerged as a survivor group itself, seeking damages from Saudi Arabia for support provided to Al-Qaeda in the lead-up to September 11. International firms are involved: Cantor Fitzgerald lost 658 employees on September 11 and has brought its own legal case against Saudi Arabia. A different survivor politics emerges from Peaceful Tomorrows, which seeks "effective, nonviolent solutions to terrorism, and to acknowledge our common experience with all people similarly affected by violence throughout the world" (Peaceful Tomorrows 2004); that group denounced George W. Bush's reelection efforts to use September 11 tower images for political gain. A Family Steering Committee for the 9/11 Independent Commission (2002) monitors actions taken on the 9/11 Commission recommendations, and has sought to learn what plans the Energy Advisory Council, headed by Vice President Dick Cheney, had for pipeline development and gas and oil exploration in Afghanistan, Iraq, and other Middle Eastern countries in 2001.

A handful of survivor groups have achieved enormous power and visibility. The tiny group of widows called "Just Four Moms from New Jersey," or simply "Jersey Girls," is one of them. These self-designated housewives claim to have paid little attention to the workings of the federal government until the day their husbands died in the twin towers. A rapid learning curve took them to the point of questioning the Bush administration about its resistance to transparent inquiry into national security failings on September 11. The Jersey Girls get credit for embarrassing a recalcitrant George Bush into appointing a transparent 9/11 Commission. They have also been severely criticized for expressing unpatriotic and self-serving views (e.g., Robinowitz 2004; Coulter 2006). Indeed, the key small survivor group to emerge after them has called itself "Take Back the Memorial," its original eleven or so members at odds with the Jersey Girls' early concerns about government failings. That ensemble of self-styled patriots has lobbied for Ground Zero to be dedicated nearly exclusively to remembering "the heroes" of September 11. Oozing righteousness and death-privileged entitlement, the group became so powerful for a while that it could practically veto any Ground Zero plans it deemed "dishonoring." And veto it did, its biggest victim so far being the International Freedom Center, a museum cum education center planned from the beginning of rebuild discussions to portray the concept of "freedom as a constantly-evolving world movement in which America has played a leading role" (International Freedom Center 2005, 2). It is a death worth noting on the road to a museumified Ground Zero.

Survivors Kill the International Freedom Center. The idea behind the International Freedom Center was to find a way to insert hope into the pain and mourning that had warped the spaces of the World Trade Center site. Its mainstream pedigree seemed unquestionable. Shortly after September 11, President Bush declared that freedom was under attack. In an address to a joint session of Congress, he said that the terrorists "hate our freedoms—our freedom of religion, our freedom of speech, our freedom to vote and assemble and disagree with each other." His narration of 9/11 as an assault on classically American values and rights echoed around the world. British prime minister Tony Blair spoke of a battle "between the free and democratic world and terrorism." German Chancellor Gerhard Schroeder said the attacks were aimed against "our own freedom." Prime Minister Junichiro Koizumi of Japan added his agreement to the international freedom chorus, as did the Canadian prime minister, Jean Chrétien (International Freedom Center 2005, 3). The International Freedom Center was to embody this resonant theme by putting a tragedy of international relations that occurred in one country into a global context. Visitors would contemplate freedom and the ways various people across the world struggled historically and in the present time to achieve "it." Complementing two other planned memorials at the site—the World Trade Center Memorial and the Memorial Center Museum, both to focus on remembrance, mourning, and healing—the International Freedom Center was meant to exhibit living hope.

The center amplified an aspect of Libeskind's original sense that the site needed "a dramatic, unexpected, spiritual insight into vulnerability, tragedy, and our loss. And we need something that is hopeful. . . . Glossy, contemporary, ironic, self-satisfied architecture isn't the answer." One needs a more "profound indication of memory" (Libeskind 2004, 30–31). When Libeskind lost control of the overall design, Michael Arad picked up Libeskind's idea of adding hopeful elements to the site. The footprints of the twin towers would be turned into landscape architecture, with waterfalls dropping into pools of water set into the footprint "bathtubs." Around the sides would appear the names of all the victims who died as a result of the attacks of September 11. This would be the World Trade Center Memorial. Nearer to bedrock, the cemetery bottom in the view of some survivors, a World Trade Center Museum would tell the story of the bombings of 1993 and 2001 through artifacts, images, and testimonials. A cultural center would to be the third memorial element in the site. Close to the old north tower, at the corner of Fulton and Greenwich streets, it would be an aboveground glass building (designed by the Snohetta architectural firm) that divided an ample 250,000 square feet of space between an International Freedom Center and a Soho-based arts group tasked with organizing a Drawing Center. At the entrance of the large building would be Fritz Koenig's iconic sculpture, *The Sphere,* the only artwork that survived the collapse of the twin towers, albeit with a large and meaning-laden gash on one side. To the north of the cultural center and across the newly restored Fulton Street, a performing arts center designed by Frank Gehry would sit next to the new Freedom Tower. Hope and sorrows, work and leisure, memory and insight were to share Ground Zero.

The International Freedom Center, the only one of these cultural elements specifically created for the site, was quick to establish a board of directors. Included were prominent people associated with the promotion of world peace—people like Stephen Heintz, fourth president of the Rockefeller Brothers Fund; Sara Bloomfield, director of the U.S. Holocaust Memorial Museum; Nathan Sharansky, a former Soviet dissident and political prisoner; and Fareed Zakaria, editor of *Newsweek International* and author of *The Future of Freedom.* A Family Advisory Group would give voice to four survivors of September 11, and a Committee of Scholars and Advisors counted among its members Timothy Garton Ash (Oxford), Jagdish Bhagwati (Columbia), Michael Posner (Human Rights First), Xu Wenli (exiled founder of the Chinese Democratic Party), Kwame Anthony Appiah (Princeton), Henry Louis Gates (Harvard), and Pauline Maier (MIT).

The center planned to open in 2009 with a multipart exhibit called The World and September 11. Visitors would initially walk among pictures showing the world responding to the news of the hits on the twin towers, from the silence observed in Tehran to the declaration by the Italian paper *Corriere della Sera* that "we are all Americans." Each of the ninety-two countries that lost citizens in the September 11 attacks would be represented. A film called "To Be Free" would then situate Lower Manhattan as a worldly place, where commerce and dreams of freedom crafted a unique environment of twisting Dutch streets, fish markets, stock markets, international port activity, and small electronics shops. The main exhibition was to unfold through a Freedom Walk reminiscent of MOMA's Family of Man exhibit of the 1950s. Visitors would walk past an evolving international history of freedom punctuated by high points like Martin Luther King's letter from a Birmingham jail, the standoff in Tiananmen Square, and the fall of the Berlin Wall. As in Family of Man, visitors were expected to become more aware of "how circles of freedom have expanded. And they [would] see a wide range of people—from celebrated statesmen and revolutionaries to anonymous slaves and tram drivers—treated more or less equally, so that the Walk [would] become a celebration of the individual—an embodiment of the concept that there is no ordinary life, that everyone has the potential to change the world" (International Freedom Center 2005, 9).

There would be side galleries off the walk to present historical facets of freedom as it emerged around the world, encompassing examples of Athenian democracy and Roman law as well as religions of India, China, and the Near

East. Important freedom documents like the Magna Carta and the Declaration of Independence would be on display. The American Civil War and Franklin Roosevelt's Four Freedoms would be highlighted. In the interest of communicating a sense that freedom relies on an active and engaged citizenry, the walk was to end in a room of volunteer organizations, whose representatives could sign up visitors who wanted to participate in freedom activities of all sorts, from voluntary fire departments to human rights organizations. Here was one institution in the making that would purposely meld visual art (photography and drawing) with social and political governance concerns, and do so with international awareness. In many ways, the center aimed to be a quintessential American display, combining sentiment, patriotism, and information. But it was not to be.

Empowered Survivors. Commemoration of heroism, death, mourning, grief, and collapse bested the International Freedom Center and the Drawing Center. Few doubt that the demise of the two elements least focused on the people and events of September 11 per se reflect the priorities and (dirty-tricks) lobbying of Take Back the Memorial. Some of its stated objections to the center were petty: the aboveground location would attract more visitors than the World Trade Center Museum; the center would be larger than the museum; the center had already been more successful in fund-raising than the planned museums. The big concern, however, was that an International Freedom Center would deflect attention from the dead, from America, and from New York to focus instead on the peculiar, distorted notions of freedom that animated some regimes, particularly those that routinely criticized America. Warning New York that it was about to get a left-intellectual, blame-America museum of September 11, Take Back the Memorial grabbed everyone's attention. Nearly overnight, the center's chief political backers —Governor Pataki, Hillary Clinton, and then mayor Rudy Guliani, all presidential aspirants—withdrew support, and the project abruptly ended. As for the Drawing Center, its demise came about in a similar way: its overseers were accused of taking artistic license to the point of gross insensitivity by displaying a caricature of George W. Bush as Osama Bin Laden in its temporary gallery.

Take Back the Memorial also used the U.S. courts in an effort to save every inch of the remaining twin tower foundations out of respect to those who died there, even if that would mean halting the construction of Calatrava's transportation hub. A few consistently objected to any performing arts center being located at Ground Zero at all, on the grounds that it would be inappropriate to stage entertainment over the graves of loved ones. Some even sought to control the types of shops and tenants allowed in the commercial spaces of Ground Zero. For a while, it seemed that anything the group determined had the effect of trivializing the heroes of 9/11 became politically impossible.[10] As recently as the sixth anniversary of September 11, Take Back the Memorial and other survivor groups were wrestling with New York mayor Michael Bloomberg over the commemoration services. Each previous anniversary had been marked by a gathering of families in the pit to hear victims' names read, lay flowers in the pit, and touch the bare bedrock. In 2007, construction at Ground Zero was sufficiently advanced that the mayor initially disallowed a gathering at bedrock for safety reasons. A storm of protest led Bloomberg to pull back a bit and approve a proposal by the families that they descend into the pit in single file and briefly touch the bedrock. Their lawyer indicated that despite the need to close the pit in order to construct the World Trade Center Memorial, some families wanted arrangements to be made for special access privileges into the future. A wearied Bloomberg reminded everyone that there would soon be no pit to access.

Once the militant survivor groups tried to expand their influence beyond the specific memorials planned for the site, their political power diminished. As buildings began to go up, Lower Manhattan came to life in a way that it had not during the lifetime of the twin towers. It was clearly time to move on and to choose life over death. Yet by equating all efforts to broaden the meanings and uses of Ground Zero with left-wing politics or political insensitivity, the survivor groups positioned themselves for several years as curators of cultural spaces in an American and global location. Writing for *New York* magazine, a chagrined Robert Kolker (2005, 4) boldly asked in 2005, "How did a group of 9/11 families go from being seen as the entirely sympathetic victims of perhaps America's greatest tragedy to being viewed as a self-interested obstructionist force that could hold up ground zero's progress for years, banishing any sign of cultural life downtown—except, perhaps, for the culture of mourning?" Put a bit differently, when is an effort to save architectural ruins for the nation a selfish curatorial power play?[11]

In February 2006, Alice Greenwald became director of the World Trade Center Museum. This was less than six months after the Freedom Center and Drawing Center projects were derailed, with controversy still roiling about larger priorities and purposes at Ground Zero. Her appointment seemed to comfort Take Back the Memorial and other militant survivor groups, largely because she had spent much of her career in the area of traumatic history, mainly Jewish history; indeed, she was associated for nineteen years with the Holocaust Museum in Washington. Greenwald immediately made it clear that she saw parallels between that museum, and the tragedies it memorialized, and the World Trade Center memorial museum she hoped to shape. A city with a strong and powerful Jewish presence took the analogy to heart. She said that what links the two historical tragedies are memorialization and loss, exactly the themes that Take Back the Memorial (and a related survivor group called September's Mission) could readily support. According to Greenwald, "the 9/11 narrative [is like] the ritual retelling of the story of Passover each year. 'You are not telling it just to tell the story. . . . You tell it so you remember you were slaves in Egypt, to be kind to the stranger in your midst, to be a better human being. You remember for a reason" (Pogrebin 2006, nytimes.com). That Greenwald links 9/11 with murderous moments of modern and ancient Jewish international history gives the survivor cause worldly gravitas and context. That a specific ethnic-religious history can be so easily accepted as the framework for understanding a very different time, place, and one-off catastrophe, though, is a bit troubling.

Greenwald is generous to survivor groups and declares that their "authentic voices" must be recorded. "The question," she says, "is how do we get it right and who makes final decisions about it. We're not going to please everybody" (Pogrebin 2006, nytimes.com). The voices are certainly many, and some have shouted louder than others all along. A clamor has been heard from town-meeting-style gatherings in the early aftermath days, where thousands debated design and memorial issues for the site; to the wrangling of developers and the Port Authority as in the 1960s; to survivor groups of all persuasions that use the courts, the media, the State Department, and the U.S. Congress to bull-horn their demands. There are international interests in the melee—Cantor Fitzgerald, for example—but even though five hundred citizens of other countries also died on September 11, much of the movement around the 9/11 memorial is in the realm of American politics. With the International Freedom Center out of the picture, the war in Iraq dragging on humiliatingly for the United States and punishingly for Iraqis, and family survivor groups pushing for more space to contain narrower agendas, the world that experienced September 11 is pushed to the margins of the Ground Zero picture. It can seem that the twin towers of international relations have been reduced to towering politics of grief, memory, commerce, and art manqué.

As director of the museum, Greenwald is also executive vice president for programs for the National September 11 Memorial and Museum at the World Trade Center. This is a not-for-profit foundation-corporation responsible for raising the funds, overseeing the design for the project, and operating both the World Trade Center Memorial and the museum (that is, eight of the sixteen acres of Ground Zero). The organization's Web site explains that the museum will "communicate key messages that embrace both the specificity and the universal implications of the events of 9/11; document the impact of those events on individual lives, as well as on local, national, and international communities; and explore the legacy of 9/11 for a world increasingly defined by global interdependency" (Build the Memorial.org 2007). Curatorial scope may yet expand from the narrow concerns of Take Back the Memorial and other American survivor groups to larger issues of 9/11 and the world. Still, the organization changed its name in 2007 from the more encompassing World Trade Center Memorial Foundation to a more restricting National September 11 Memorial and Museum, "in order to reflect more fully the Memorial and Museum's commemoration of the September 11, 2001 attacks as a national tragedy that changed the course of history" (Build the Memorial.org 2007).[12] The messages of empowered survivors continue to be varied but influential at Ground Zero.

ARTLESS ENDS?

> With architecture, alas, the jig is already up. Architectonics has become an *audio-visual art*, the only question now being whether it will shortly go on to become a VIRTUAL ART.
>
> —Paul Virilio, *Art and Fear*

In the international relations that are the afterlife, the particular aftermath, of September 11, 2001, stakes are high. Because so much is important to so many, the World Trade Center site entered a state of suspended animation, frozen in cleanup time, and stalled in a certain audiovisual virtual architectonics. With the exception of World Trade Center 7, which is technically not on the official site, almost everything else remains "under construction" as I write this, amid babble, histrionics, power plays. Even as earthmovers prepared the foundations for the Freedom Tower, which now boasts six steel beams towering up from the seventy-foot-deep bathtub, and started on the World Trade Center Transportation Hub, controversy raged. Some were dead set against another tall tower that could throw down a gauntlet to transgressors. Some maintained that all the emphasis on commercial areas at Ground Zero would reproduce the twin towers' glut of speculative office space chasing vanishing tenants. Then there are the ongoing concerns that family survivors still command a moral-cultural high ground that sometimes cannot be questioned, which means that aspects of the rebuild and its programming could be an exercise in mausoleum museology . . . or else. Which "jig is up already" is open to debate.

In the midst of the pulling and hauling around the famous "space," it is instructive to consider the audiovisuals of the Coalition of 9/11 Families. Now part of the umbrella organization called World Trade Center United Families Group, it was working to ensure that "the future memorial at the World Trade Center site is America's Memorial and must be treated with the same historical reverence as comparable sites in American history (e.g. Shanksville Pennsylvania, Pearl Harbor, Gettysburg, and the Oklahoma City National Memorial)" (Coalition of 9/11 Families 2002). Through a series of online polls conducted in 2004, which still command the pages of Take Back the Memorial's Web page, the coalition sought to determine how survivor families wished to see the names of "September 11's heroes" listed on the memorial walls. These were the options they gave: random placement of names; names listed by the company worked for; names accompanied by a picture and date of birth; names with an insignia; an alphabetical listing; individual markers within the memorial; or no preference. The most popular answer among 3,198 people who responded to the survey was that the dead should be grouped under the name of the company they worked for and placed on the relevant twin tower footprint; for example, Cantor Fitzgerald casualties would be listed together on the footprint of One World Trade Center. A full 33 percent of family members and 23 percent of concerned citizens supported this option.

The preferences of 2004 startle because they suggest that the "authentic survivor voice" at that time wanted to memorialize companies and employees and not individuals, the opposite of the priorities today. A person who happened to have a part-time job at a burger joint in the north tower would always be associated with that firm, while the millionaire burger-eaters on the hundredth floor would be mostly remembered for being high fliers. Passengers in the planes, people visiting the twin towers that day, hotel guests at the nearby Marriott, and the hijackers themselves would not be listed, having no World Trade Center company list to join. Some among them—surely not the hijackers—would be listed elsewhere on the footprints, perhaps under "other," or at another spot on the memorial.

The type of survivor Greenwald thinks of as "authentic" had other concerns, such as whether putting the museum seventy feet below ground would make sense (Rogers 2006) and whether the now emptied cultural building planned for the International Freedom Center could be commandeered for a World Trade Center museum about four times larger than the Holocaust Museum in Washington (Kolker 2005). Some are still interested in the corporations that will take up tenancy in the new towers, but another contemporary issue is whether some countries and firms should be entirely denied commercial space at Ground Zero, either because they are associated with terrorist areas of the world or because they sell commodities that are not sacred enough for sacred spaces.

Through this melee, the virtual winners of the politics reshaping the World Trade Center site are the hijackers of 2001. It is their deeds that leave negative, warped, and traumatized spaces, footprints without bodies, and a slurry wall supporting ruins. Their destructiveness establishes the very need to museumify violent international relations as perpetual tears. That there are buildings to quarrel about suggests the difficulty of replacing towers for towers and new buildings for lost buildings as long as the mental video of planes crashing into structures keeps running and reminding us of terrorist power. The more abstract approach used in the main Vietnam War Memorial in Washington works differently. It enables viewers to reflect on a war by seeing themselves in the black reflecting marble that etches the names of America's war dead. We have to be looking at the memorial in order to complete it, and that means we see ourselves in violent international relations rather than strictly as mourners of it, victims of it, or survivors of it only. We become part of an art/IR juxtaposition. Without seeing ourselves in September 11, the trauma of what happened to us, and the accompanying fetishism of strangers, could persist and intensify rather than diminish. If a twin tower casualty is not American and her family does not find the all-consuming memorializing strategy adequate or consonant with their memories or beliefs—if they find it artless—then what? Does that dead person become a stranger to her moments in the World Trade Center? Is her story inauthentic or irrelevant?

Possibly so. The twin towers always overshadowed the people who worked in them; people were not really expected to be there any more than "strangers" were expected to hijack international relations. It was all to be kept separate, the everyday and the bloody business of international relations. Instead, high towers turned into a high politics. Architectures became causes and effects of international events. Now there is "ambient murmuring" (Virilio 2003, 81) at Ground Zero. One would like to think that many voices of regeneration ensure representativeness as well as quality and appropriateness. Yet the prospect still looms of a disaster theme park as the final rebuild, full of assorted cabinets of curiosities, cameo structures by a lineup of celebrity architects, and mausoleums crafted by survivor groups. Or could it be that we are facing the prospect of a ghost? Lower Manhattan's financial services industries now are scattered around the city and are unlikely to cluster ever again in one or two towers.[13]

IR also struggles in its murmuring camps to apprehend the noise reverberating out of Lower Manhattan. We might wish to be more involved in curating the international relations of our time but get caught up in our own World Trade Center–like politics of suspicion. That there is no overall design for IR any longer can signal democratization of a field built around a survival politics of the camp. Or, we who babble to ourselves only might remain unable to hear certain ambient murmurs within our locked-in circles. And with that in mind, the art/museums of international relations—our own temples and those of the art world that we have never claimed as our own—become the issue for the next and final chapter.

CHAPTER 7

Art/Museums/International Relations: Collaging Afterlife

> To be inside and outside a position at the same time—to occupy a territory while loitering sceptically on the boundary—is often where the most intensely creative ideas stem from.
> —Terry Eagleton, *After Theory*

Art/museums/international relations compose an inside and an outside to one another. Throughout the preceding discussions, several facets of boundary mutuality have come to light. We have seen that everyday competition can involve art/museums in political economies of international diplomacy and law, even foreign policy, to say nothing (more) about the efforts art institutions can make to save works from museums "over there." Art/museums can fit well with the international boundary loiterings of globalization; in times of international war they can suddenly be inside dangerous spaces peopled by outside militaries and inside thieves; and they can be saved in part by foreign art institutions and international organizations that safeguard, find, and repair art, artifacts, and buildings threatened with destruction or loss. Should significant architectures be razed through international terrorist assaults, a museum of international relations just might take their place.

Although IR is keenly aware of a multilocated international, and relations of varying kinds, art/museums have largely been extraneous to the field at large, confined to individual researchers and small groups that barely qualify yet as camps. Other types of institutions, regimes, and movements have far greater visibility and legitimacy in IR as bona fide international organizations (Gordenker and Weiss 1996; Finnemore and Sikkink 1998; Fuchs 2005). Art/museum specialists cannot afford that level of myopia, which is why it is largely in those circles, and in cultural studies, that one finds research about museum foreign policies and wartime actions, debates about international cultural laws, and concerns over international business culture seeping into temples of art. Some would leave behind the old boundaries between art/museums and other kinds of political institutions and recognize, as Neil MacGregor puts it, that "museums can reach very large numbers and the contacts go on despite political ups and downs" (quoted in Woolf 2007, 4). He has taken a lead in helping museum visitors appreciate knotty relationships between ancient artifacts and contemporary international relations. Yet even in proactive realms of art/museum scholarship and practice, museum mutualities with international relations can be thinly presented. The problem is not lack of interest or awareness of salience but rather disciplinary distance from the specialist knowledges of international relations that IR has as a field. Thus, to return to the question that opened this book, can we talk about art/museums and international relations in the same breath, or is the relationship too fugitive—or trivial? Trivial it is not, but how to work creatively across the boundaries?

One way might be through the art of collage. Collage places odd and seemingly incommensurable materials, images, objects, and themes in proximity to one another. Borders between the elements can seem intact and possibly even impermeable, yet the unexpected juxtapositions alter meanings and enable new relationships to be imagined or invented. Without supplying a narrative road map, collage art invites the viewer to contemplate mutual relations loitering skeptically on the boundaries of the oddly joined-up pieces. It is up to us to interpret those mutualities and invent the afterlife of their elements.

Boundaries in collage are not necessarily places of cooperation, though. All boundaries harbor dangers, as IR knows (but as Eagleton does not consistently emphasize).[1] Zimbabweans today live with collaged elements of political economy from the country's precolonial, colonial, and early postcolonial past and its fascist present. The borderlands of each overlapping era are increasingly rough, filled with ever-harsher raids on opposition parties, raging inflation, profound levels of unemployment, agriculture turned into a battlefield, and conditions of rapidly advancing bare life (Sylvester 2006a). It takes creativity to occupy that collage and live at those borders, but no one wishes that type on anyone. Or consider a group of people drifting on the boundaries of international and national waters as they seek to leave one place and find homes in another place. The creativity required to get on a boat and away can be instantly stripped or restricted by an intervening state that scoops up the watery traveler and puts her into a camp for people who lack proper documents (Sylvester 2003). And then what? Deportation lands her at home, in a place that lacks the kind of creativity she sought by going out from its borders to begin with (Sylvester 2004).

Borderlands are badlands and borderlands are goodlands. Collage can put them together to visualize, create, and map new logics and mutualities, with results that can be powerful and risky or exhilarating for institutions and individuals.

THINKING ABOUT POWER, IR, AND ART/MUSEUMS

In thinking about art/museums/international relations as mutualities under discovery, we might begin by acknowledging all three components as instances of power. Whether construed as agents and subjects of art diplomacy, as pieces and places in international competition, as exploiters and victims of colonialism, or as Gilded Age institutions that have metamorphosed spectacularly, art/museums parlay power. Where fine art was once associated with private collections, nobility, and wealth, postmodern visual culture is a phenomenon of mass access to art. Museums are reborn with the power to attract social attention and scores of culture visitors. There is also considerable financial power implicated in private and public art/museums. That power can rely on state funding and/or on wealthy individuals, foundations, and corporations. And there is a knowledge component to art/museum power that has to do with the ability to amass artworks and convince the public and professionals in the field that these works are valuable and worth seeing—a power that the art world grasps at the end of art.

Power itself, though, is notoriously difficult to handle conceptually, as IR knows better than most fields. Realist, constructivist, and feminist camps, to name just a few, endeavor to theorize and study power as a characteristic, a capacity, a relationship, a resource, a performance, and/or a discourse (e.g., Mearsheimer 2001; Nye 2004, Guzzini 1993; Barnett and Duvall 2005; Tickner 1988). Yet ongoing debates about the nature of power suggest how difficult it is even for experts to draw it definitively. "Paint power," I ask my graduate students of international relations. After some moments of merriment about this odd assignment, they produce rough sketches of hard power in action: battles, nights exploding with artillery, figures running frantically. At least two versions of upright slabs with something approximating smoke around their tops appear as power these days. Once in a while a student pens the word "Coke" or caricatures heads of state, leaving it at that. At their best, the students picture limited and obvious dimensions of power's effects, symbols, and popular representations. Rarely do they design something that even hints at the complexity of tangible and abstract power. And, crucially, few such drawings redefine the way we think of power and where and how we look for its locations, insinuations, materials, and compositions.[2] Facing us at all times, power eludes us, the many volumes written and the many pictures of it hanging in museums notwithstanding.

Joseph Nye Jr. (2004), assistant secretary of defense in the Clinton administration and Harvard professor of IR, has been promoting the idea in Washington that the key quality of power in our time is not the hard power of command or coercion that we associate with militaries and markets but the soft power of culture and values. Today's international relations hinges, he thinks, just as much on what he calls the ability to attract others as on coercing them through threats or punishments. In this regard, he is an intellectual cousin to Samuel Huntington, whose notion of clashing civilizations put culture into IR's contemporary picture of international relations. The twin towers fell because warriors armed only with box cutters had been attracted to the fundamentalist idea that the United States was the great evil-doer of our time and had to be destroyed. The final moments of that power were hard and punitive, yet the power that led up to 9/11 was an attraction-repulsion dynamic: attraction to the technology, to the ability to enroll in the West as a student, and to the ease of mobility in a place both decadent and open. On an entirely different plane, we can say that the Basque administration was attracted to the Guggenheim museum and foundation as a source of regeneration and civic pride. It then went to remarkable lengths to attract the American institution to a decaying and remote city known as a center of separatist violence. British colonialists and anthropologists were attracted to the statuary of ancient civilizations, and they used soft power to persuade local potentates to permit extraordinary removals—backed up, of course, by the harder power of empire. The 2003 war in Iraq combined hard-power militaries with armies of art defenders seeking to save art and artifacts from the warring sides.

To Nye, the main elements of soft power are nurtured and lodged in cultural institutions of religion, the media, and even the global entertainment and fashion industries. He has little to say about the power of art/museums, but then we have said a lot about them here. These popular institutions of civil society traffic in soft power. They must work with individuals, other institutions and collectivities, and oftentimes the state to get what they want and need, as well as to resist legal, financial, and competitive challenges at their doors. Museums cannot command others internationally or nationally in the sense of forcing involuntary outcomes and rules on them. For all the criticism that some in the art world hurl at the Guggenheim and Thomas Krens—in effect for not soft-pedaling museum power more internationally—Guggenheim's attractiveness is what wins it international contracts. Its resources are vast but not unlimited; it is in the realm of negotiation and management that Guggenheim rivals and perhaps betters other global art institutions. Only the Guggenheim has crossed so many borders so far and set up effectively and peacefully in places where modernist art is not expected to be—from a sheik-governed kingdom in the Middle East (soon), to a private German bank, and from a troubled region of Spain to the crass Las Vegas strip. Meanwhile, some of the more conservative art institutions, whose directors are critical of the Guggenheim approach, face scrutiny and criticism for unethical acquisition practices.

Even as museums rely on softer power, they are not averse to playing competitive hardball with one another. Power players and power brokers, they can determine value, create art stars, and decide which works can enter the art canon. Perhaps it is wise to think of power more as a continuum (Mattern 2005) or, even better from my point of view, as discourse. A discourse is an ensemble of knowledges that can become dominant in an area and shape subjectivities and behavior without overt command or coercion. That is, subjects voluntarily embrace expert standards—on art, policing, terrorism, education—or criticize within limits set by the dominant discourses. Those who see through the power of certain metanarrative discourses, such as feminists vis-à-vis patriarchal privileges or Marxists vis-à-vis capitalism, are often classed as radical, dissident, or rigid camp followers; or they are silenced and excluded. This Foucauldian understanding of power as discourse focuses on how the subject is subjected to and resists power. It complements Nye's emphasis on institutions as the progenitors of soft power (see Lukes 2005).

With an entire field of knowledge taking on a camp structure, as IR has done, the situation changes somewhat, as no one discourse is dominant enough to police the boundaries of the field. Some approaches will carry more weight with specialists in and out of the field than others, but every new camp is a dissidence tolerated by every other established camp. That is to say, every camp has discursive power. Even if some camps assert their outsider status, as feminists and postmodernists have been known to do vis-à-vis the profession of IR, they do so from a bona fide place now within a field's knowledge parameters. They are akin to avant-garde modernists, accustomed to fringe events and bad hotels, suddenly finding their work collected by Charles Saatchi and commented on in the press by art writers like Waldemar Januszczak (2005). They are in and across a border that once seemed impenetrable. So, for instance, Stella Vine, a former stripper who taught herself to paint, now sees her startling "naive" portraits hanging in the lobbies of London City companies. Princess Diana and the model Kate Moss stare out anxiously at us as we enter. They look less pulled-together in their bubble-gum-pink skins than we might expect dressed-for-success places to countenance. And yet it is the end of art—the end of "the" art canonical who's who and what's what.[3] At the end of IR, a feminist can even be elected president of the powerful International Studies Association.

Terry Eagleton (2003) has expressed concern that just as class, race, and gender enter the canons of literary and cultural studies, we become obsessed more with the body than with issues of social justice. The body we obsess over is attached to people who sort of look like us or could be us if we tried harder to match their bodies. Their bodies are seen to be heavily constructed and often badly designed as they romp through films, chick lit, Web pages, and popular magazines—the new places of cultural data. To study them, one steps over dead soldiers, nameless Iraqis, and ordinary bodies in Third World countries that relate fascinating stories about their lives through globalized channels, while unable to eat regularly (Sylvester 1999b, 2006a). All of this fits what Eagleton calls the politics of amnesia. Rephrased in Foucauldian terms, it is an acquiescence to the (soft) dominant power of popular culture/media discourse. With every exercise of power comes a countervailing power, insisted Foucault, and Eagleton urges us to resist obsessive shallowness by thinking more about the life-and-death justice issues we mask. Of course, some can become so politically focused on their own dead that they try to strip Ground Zero of other discourse-constituting meanings and artifacts.

Let us turn to artworks to illustrate the complexities of discursive power that envelop art/museums. For an exhibition held in 2000 called Encounters: New Art from Old, the National Gallery (London) invited two dozen artists to choose a work from its permanent collection as the basis for a new piece of their own. Francesco Clemente chose *An Allegory of Prudence 1565–70,* an oil painting by the greatest Old Master of the Venetian school, Titian (plate 9). It depicts ages or stages of life—youth, middle age, and old age—in the popular allegorical symbolism of that time. Three male busts perch atop the heads of three animals—a dog, a lion, and a wolf. Youthful man is put with a dog. The man at the height of power looks out over the lion's head. The old man has his wolf. Across the top of the painting, a sentence in Latin explains, "From the past the present acts prudently so as not to spoil future action." The middle-aged man of courage (who might be Titian's son) faces the spectator head on but looks slightly away, deep in thought, it can seem, about the prudence and courage associated with choosing one path over another.

Clemente's imaginative engagement with the work yields *Smile Now, Cry Later* (1998), a large (234 x 68cm) oil painting of twenty-three black men done in brut primitive style (plate 10). Each figure is skinny and naked with few bodily details other than a recognizable penis, overlong curved arms, and a cartoon mouth showing a panel of white teeth. Each also displays a piece of paper with the words "smile now," "smile later," "cry now," or "cry later," indicating the action suggested on the paper in an upturned or downturned mouth. The smiles have it in this work by a plurality of one. They are the soft-power counterpart to Titian's harder masculine representation of power advancing and retreating.

The title of Clemente's painting is one for rumination. It might come from an expression Chicanos use and even tattoo on their bodies, "Smile now, cry later." Chicanos are Mexican-Americans who display, interrogate, and contest their hyphenated identity by turning it into a performance of difference. Dave Hickey (1997) talks appreciatively about the particular performance of difference that Chicano youth have been known to attach to customized American cars. In the 1950s and 1960s, and today as well, they lowered the carriages on popular Ford and Chevy models to cover most of the tires. Then they painted the car bodies over and over. The result looked somewhat baroque—all "smooth folds of steel and the hundreds of coats of transparent lacquer [that] caught the light and held it as the cars slipped through the bright streets like liquid color—like Caravaggio meets Bernini, on wheels" (Hickey 1997, 69).

Common to "lowrider communities" in border towns like El Paso, Texas, the vehicles are/were boy-power cars, designed as much to show off identity and flamboyant masculinity as artistic skills. But it is intriguing that their colors could be soft, enticing, and pretty, even feminine. Equally intriguingly, argues Hickey, Detroit soon incorporated "the principles of lowrider into its products" (70).

In Clemente's painting, the naked figures stand as copycat individuals who entwine in a heart-shaped labyrinthine "vine" growing against a light pink background. It is not a picture of macho hard power, nor are there any beasts in their jungle. Each man is alone in his own brown-pink leaf, and yet the mutuality of autonomy comes across in the work. Superimposed with a fluid biomorphic shape—vaguely a large penis coming off a fernlike branch—the heart leaves connect. Male bonding? *Smile Now, Cry Later* is the title of a film made in 2001 that evokes a hard urban environment that two male friends struggle together to escape. The heart-shaped leaves set against a pink background, however, could tie the men into a gay community or unite them as heterosexuals seeking sentimental love. A tattoo of the common expression typically puts half the phrase on one arm and half on the other, accompanied on both sides by a pretty girl who performs the smile-frown emotion nearest her. Apparently, the bearer of the tattoo has the power to command those emotions in her, which hints at a harder power than attraction.

In both the Clemente painting and the Chicano saying and art, it is unclear what the expression or the hearts or the pink means. "Smile now, cry later" is an evocative collaged phrase, gender-bending and open to interpretation. The original Titian painting is also open to interpretation, but not in the gender essentials. It shows the passage of time inscribed on the bodies of white men, who identify with the animal natures they hover above and not with each other or with (entirely absent) women. There are no smiles on the faces there: prudence is a serious effort. There is no hint of unconventionality; the men's clothing is period and the animals are presented as beasts with partly opened mouths full of menacing teeth. Properly gendered leaders of the past, present, and future, the men have responsibility and bite, not hearts. The two paintings occupy shadowlands of each other's story, gender, allegories, and power discourses, suggesting how gender power does and does not fit dominant myths. Pictured together, that power becomes unsettled, contested, and, in postmodern terms, it is likely to be undecidable.

POWER COLLAGES:ART:IR:MUSEUMS

What if we were to collage the Titian and Clemente paintings? We could put Titian's men into the leafy labyrinth or paste cutouts of Clemente's men around the heads in the *Allegory of Prudence*. Either way or another way altogether, collage would not blend and stir one painting into another in order to achieve a new integrated whole. It would more likely present heterogeneous images that could fail initially to make sense. Upon further viewing and analysis, however, these juxtaposed images could illuminate aspects of material, political, and emotional relationships among and between men that usually go unnoticed and uncontemplated. Collage could do the same thing for shadowy mutualities of art/museums/international relations that have not been fully appreciated yet.

Collage was created to produce art while disavowing haute art traditions that seemed irrelevant to social life at the turn of the twentieth century. Picasso and Braque are credited with inventing collage around 1912 by pasting debased materials—half-smoked cigarettes and scraps of newsprint—onto the cheap wallpapers then fashionable in bourgeois homes. Varnished and framed: Voila, Art! The filth of the modern capitalist street—the stuff that clings to one's shoes or is smoked in city bars—suddenly came into art spaces that had always been expected to be relatively devoid of visible refuse. A fine-arts viewer of the time would not necessarily comprehend that outside/inside mutuality immediately. Papiers collés eluded canonical sense-making, even though modern urban life was their model—the lofty skyscrapers set against lowly scrapings, the top-hatted flaneurs in the National Gallery and the human sweat outside in Trafalgar Square, the decorative items fast off assembly lines and into middle-class homes set against the international competition in deadly mass-produced arms. The Carnegie Foundation–endowed international Peace Palace opened in The Hague in 1913, and the following year a major war broke out. Advances in photography gave us all a camera to record the truth, and we recorded as true the exoticisms we had come to associate with orientalism (Ryan 1997). Optimism and destruction, progress and waste, mess, abjection, beauty, heterogeneity, nonsense, and categorization: collage was jigsaw modernity made visual. It put modernity to us in the only way it could be assembled: as an *haute-cum-bas* experience that did not congeal, often lacked taste, to say nothing of virtue, but held a certain charm and vitality.

As an art technique, collage has been said to be "the setting of one element beside another without supplying the connection" (Shattuck, quoted in Ruzicka 1992, 126). It is mainly about juxtaposition, although little about collage is straightforward and indisputable.[4] It is not an art style as such, by virtue of eschewing coherence of meaning or wholeness of subject matter.[5] It might not offer any points of tangency or transition from one element to another; or the artist might work hard to make transitions or tangencies seem to exist. Ditto with the materials used; these often fall outside art historical standards. There are no hard-and-fast rules about form or content. Surrealists, Soviet and National Socialist governments, and artists like Hannah Hoch used collage—in Hoch's case, to mock Nazi politicians and their strutting masculinities by pasting parts of German uniforms onto folk dancing puppets. Jackson Pollock incorporated collage cutting techniques in his work. Lee Krasner cut up Pollock's and her discarded paintings and reassembled the pieces as collages. Eduardo Paolozzi's collages resemble popular scrapbook pages filled with bland advertisements of popular culture. Robert Rauschenberg applied paint to a real bed, claiming only that he had no other material to work with at the moment (Leggio 1992). Picasso's papier collé pieces of 1912 and 1913 contained newspaper clippings about conflict in the Balkans, and Gino Severini showed trench warfare (approvingly, it seems) in his collaged works.

A broad church, collage has satirized official power, inspired political allegiance or hatred, disguised messages of resistance to art traditions or to government censors, torn down icons, and ridiculed the city. Unorthodox materials have been pasted or pinned onto a range of surfaces, painted in place, assembled as photomontages, sculpted, perhaps even licked on. The point, we remember Max Ernst saying, is to create a "meeting of two distant realities on a plane foreign to them both" (quoted in Danto 1997, 18). Or more than two realities on more than one plane: only in collage, Paolozzi maintained, "can improbable events be frozen into peculiar assemblies by manipulation: time and space can be drawn together into new spatial strategy. ... [F]igures from a Turkish landscape trapped by cruelty may be released and find themselves perplexed and frightened in a French nursery flanked by a mechanical sphinx" (quoted in Taylor 2004, 139). And only in collage might we realize, as Brandon Taylor puts it, "that it is somewhere in the gulf between the bright optimism of the official world and its degraded material residue that many of the exemplary, central experiences of modernity exist" (9).

And collage continues after modernity and after art. Australian artist Imants Tillers created his Venice Biennale painting, *The Hyperborean and the Speluncar* (1986), by combining images from Greek mythology, surrealist resonances from de Chirico, and the figure of a woman lifted from a nineteenth-century British painting by Frederick Leighton (*Girls Picking Up Pebbles by the Sea,* 1871). Tillers's manipulations of time and space seem to establish a relationship between artists of different epochs. Other artists do something like this. Cy Twombly's work often references antiquity, and Anselm Keifer's mixed-media paintings gesture to German literature, philosophy, and art of other times. Such collages are powerful reminders that the usual boundaries of history, geography, and art styles and schools are littered with contradictions, overlaps, refusals of borders, and, generally, instances that are not where they are expected to be. Being not expected can land one outside the policing barricades of the moment; most of Picasso's collage art was "not exhibited for at least a decade" after it was made (Taylor 2004, 20).

The Encounters exhibition at the National Gallery carried time-travel themes of such art forward.[6] Frank Auerbach saluted John Constable's painting *The Hay Wain* (1821) through an abstract landscape of brown, green, and yellow-mustard strokes barely recognizable as trees, water, house, and sky. Louise Bourgeois turned to Turner's *Sun Rising through Vapour: Fishermen Cleaning and Selling Fish* (before 1807) and came up with a silver cone circulating blue water, which she set inside an industrial metal cage ringed by round mirrors and blue jars.[7] The late Patrick Caulfield met Zurbaran's modest still life *A Cup of Water and a Rose on a Silver Plate* (c. 1630) with a large painting evoking the interior angles of a Madrid tapas bar marketing itself through the announcement on its awning that "Hemingway Never Ate Here"—which is the title of the Caulfield painting. Its green walls, mounted buffalo head, and yellow, receding interior look nothing like the surroundings we imagine for Zurbaran's neat little cup motif; but then on a round tabletop hinged to the green wall sits a little cup. Anthony Caro encountered Duccio's *Annunciation* of 1311 through seven architectural sculptures that render in steel, wood, fiberboard, Perspex, and then sandstone the painted Italianate spaces Duccio created as the setting for Gabriel's meeting with Mary. Each sculpture rerenders the previous rerendering and lights up a different angle on the Duccio composition.

Works that unexpectedly incorporate aspects of earlier works ask the viewer/reader to reinterpret the known, see it differently, and create a new sense and sensibility after this art. Scholars of international relations work somewhat similarly when they rediscover, reinterpret, or rereference important works of their field—works by the likes of Old Masters E. H. Carr (e.g., Jones 1998), Hans Morgenthau (Tickner 1988), or Hedley Bull (Sylvester 1994a). The starting point is the old, but the analyst then veers off into new interpretations. Something emerges outside the old framework and yet remains one with it, inside. To put this differently, intense encounters with artistic and scholarly canons can go beyond the pieces and the legends at hand while simultaneously upholding them as standards against which contemporary work can still measure itself and its creativity. The borderline that seems to separate art from afterart, or the Old Master from the contemporary artist, or the power of Renaissance art from what some see as the lesser art of our times becomes a discursive wall of power that can be breached more easily than one might think.

The Power of Collage for IR

A collage that could conjoin art and international relations would not "simply" reinterpret the old. It would creatively juxtapose disparate materials, themes, and methodologies as means of contemplating and establishing redefining nexus points. A specific artwork can help us imagine the results, which is appropriate for a discussion that focuses on sight rather than linguistic skills.

Jeff Wall's *Dead Troops Talk (a vision after an ambush of a Red Army patrol, near Moor, Afghanistan, winter 1986)* (1992) is a large photograph that graphically depicts slain soldiers coming to life where they have fallen in what could be a real battle in contemporary international relations (plate 11). The men do not rise from the dead like gods, angels, heroes, or villains of war. These men are ordinary mortals. They look stunned and unhappy. They gaze disoriented, unbelieving at their monstrous wounds and those of their comrades. They marvel at their own spilled guts; they cry; they fall back in sheer exhaustion against the devastated, rocky, lifeless soil around them. The shock of killing and dying is palpable here. Wall portrays emotions that are as raw as physical wounds. And the spectator stares, looks away, stares again.

This war scene references materials of the popular media—war photographs—but does not remind us of images we have seen in the press, images that numb us, that shuffle the people fighting the wars out of the picture when they fall. We look death in the eye here and find that it initially seems obscene to linger there over the dying, wounded, frightened to death, or those so touched by war that they cannot move. Ironically, those of us most accustomed to IR's cool and distanced words of war, its strategic calculations, weapons, and war histories, might be most disinclined to take on the Wall photograph. As a topic in IR, war can seem nudged aside of late by a "security studies" camp that takes on almost everything that can render states and people insecure—from terrorism to the war on terrorism to global warming—without studying war per se. War geeks now gravitate to history, military colleges, and the few war studies departments that continue to exist. Wall's photograph helps brings war back home to IR. These uniformed soldiers are losing one of the last wars of the cold war era in a country that will recycle violence and armed conflict in 2001 and beyond. By showing dead soldiers—Soviet ones in this case—IR glimpses an aftermath of international relations that should stir us with its hard power manqué and a detritus we either cannot put into words or discursively are disallowed from mouthing in IR.

One can take *Dead Troops Talk* in a number of new directions useful in IR's aftermath. The image takes me to Judith Butler's argument in *Precarious Life* (2004, 29) that political connections with distant others take place through the commonality of vulnerable bodies in international relations: we are all vulnerable "to a sudden address from elsewhere that we cannot preempt." For soldiers, that "sudden address" is everywhere anticipated, dreaded, or manfully charged at. For the rest of us reading about battles on the streets of Falluja or bombs lobbed into Beirut, the sudden address from elsewhere unnerves, infuriates, or passes by our eyes. Most of us are not in immediate danger. Seeing dead troops realizing that they have not been able to preempt their own cessation by getting the other side first is immensely touching. It can bring on tears, a response to art that James Elkins (2004) finds all too rare today, especially among learned people.

And yet the scene is not real. These are not soldiers, and their deaths have been avoided. Wall photographed the scene in stages within a studio, using costumed actors whom he posed in various moods. The photo fragments were then assembled to look seamless, as though illustrating Butler's point that emotions of grief can "tear us from ourselves, bind us to others, transport us, undo us, implicate us in lives that are not our own, irreversibly, if not fatally" (Butler 2004, 25). Wall's dead men alive are torn from themselves and yet are bound to one another and implicated fatally in one another's war fate. This sleight-of-eye photo collage performs the kind of engaged sensibility that we rarely stage in IR treatments. The work provides a way to move toward aspects of war that other types of approaches might omit or fail to communicate adequately. It sets in motion what I call a world-traveling methodology, one that can veer from canonical scripts to face the life-and-death challenges that Eagleton, for one, finds missing in today's scholarship. The effect of this strange piece of art that does not look like a collage is to pin us to the scene through heightened sensory awareness of the precariousness of life (Sylvester 2005). Butler (2004, 151) would take that awareness further to "interrogate the emergence and vanishing of the human at the limits of what we can know, what we can hear, what we can see, what we can sense." Wall's artwork communicates clearly to me that international relations could be as much a sensory experience as pedagogical, theoretical, professional, or camp.

How different Wall's work is in form and effect from the dioramas of war that often feature in war museums. Those displays miniaturize historical battles using tiny plastic figures and props. Sometimes the point is to render a particular battle as accurately as possible, albeit relatively clinically, and other times visitors peer into the Plexiglas boxes and must imagine official war-fighting campaigns. The blood is obviously daubed onto soldiers who are usually shown fighting or marching. War dead might be lying about, but they certainly are not rising to contemplate their own demise. Jake and Dinos Chapman created a dioramic artwork they call *Hell* (1999–2000), which was subsequently destroyed in the London art-warehouse fire of 2004 and is being reconstructed in double gore. It was a swastika-shaped assemblage composed of more than five thousand toy soldiers. Each soldier engages in horrifying violence against one of his own or against a foreign enemy, whose body looks very much like his own. The murderous frenzy appears orderly and systematic when viewed from a distance, owing to the battlefield motif and the uniforms worn by all the figures. Get closer and the mise-en-scène is entirely orgiastic, pornographic. It dissolves the honored borderline separating nations, causes, soldiers, and war spectators. Everyone is inside that war assemblage, not as innocent victims but as participants in confabulations of international violence. We recall IR theorist Jean Elshtain (1987) arguing over twenty years ago that good soldiers are like good mothers in body-concerned ways.[8] The Chapmans suggest in visual mode that the good soldier is a questionable category and that it is illusory to think anyone is outside war and able to determine from a God's-eye view—perhaps a just war view—who the good within it might be.

Collage brings components of competing and complementary stories and scenes onto a plane that does not make immediate sense for any of the parts or for the viewer. In the Chapman assemblage, uniformed soldiers of two states fight each other and one another. Soldiers fight; that is their job and there is no point, the artists seem to be saying, in pretending that they will fight only other nations' soldiers and not one another, themselves, their own bodies. Soft power is not a métier here. Wall causes it to appear by collaging the hardness of war fighting with a softer but immensely power-laden reflection on war's grisly, personal, soldierly aftermath. The terminal corporeal wounds enable us to explore in more rounded terms just what it means to be a soldier, to be at war, in war, fighting a war, a casualty of war, and a perpetrator of war. It is all so germane to the real world of international relations today, where war-fighting strategies emphasize technological force and avoidance of collateral damage—until, that is, the soldiers get on the ground. Then war atrocities become visible.

So many neglected topics in IR come to mind as I look at *Dead Troops Talk* and *Hell*. Western societies persist in waging war to settle disagreements in international relations. At the same time, they strive to avoid casualties on their side. Casualties on the other side are less troublesome. But are they? Who is the casualty when an institution like war persists transhistorically and transculturally and yet has a poor record of resolving the conflicts against which it is waged? Ethical issues emerge all around. Humanitarian interventionist war today is premised on saving people in communities under attack by attacking the attacking communities. Yet when we contemplate child soldiers in Africa who, under the influence of drugs and other abuses, are trained to commit savage killings in and across local communities, we turn aghast and condemnatory. Who can kill whom, and what is the relationship between bodies that kill and the bodies of various ages they kill in various cultures? More, when public officials endorse killing heads of state or paramilitary operatives, those dead bodies rise and contemplate their wounds as martyrs or prophets or as soldiers who cannot finally and decidedly be killed. There are also stone-and-mortar victims of war. What rises again after what Robert Bevan (2006, 8) calls a war-linked "repression of architecture"?

And the "spectator," who is that person? A Buddhist acquaintance of mine does not watch TV news programs lest the latest violence in the world pollute his dwelling and spirit. He refuses to be a spectator. Journalists display the opposite tendency. They regularly go into war zones to photograph and report war's victories and tragedies. They spectate up close. So does the Red Cross as it delivers food behind the lines. So does the soldier who trains to kill, goes into combat, and watches those around him die. Everyone makes a decision to look at or look away from the composition of war. And then we might stand in front of the artworks by Wall and the Chapmans, looking at what they have rendered, the types of items they have assembled, composed, juxtaposed, and made to look unjuxtaposed. Who is touching and being touched by war and who is not? These questions inside international relations are not yet taken up adequately by a field that studies war. There is a sphere of mutuality here that art already seems to identify and can enable those with less visual acuity to see.

Some IR analysts seem ready to enter the field's conceptual and methodological no-go zones. Laura Sjoberg (2006, 211), for one, urges IR feminists to view war from positions of empathetic cooperation with those who advocate it, those who do not, and all who are affected by it. To do so would be a departure for feminist IR, which has tended to distinguish itself from other camps in in IR that are not antiwar and against all forms of violence. It is as though to study war straight up would be tantamount to condoning or even accepting it. Sjoberg objects to this distancing posture toward a major social institution that shows no signs of abating, an institution that has as much impact on women, and as much gender relevance, as any topic feminist IR does take up. She gets us thinking about feminist war theorizing and what it would and could entail. Initially, she argues, it entails empathy, "an ethical guideline to make sense of human interaction, choice, and responsibility. . . . [It] is not sharing others' experiences, nor is it pitying others' plights" (48).

Most war studies approaches downplay empathy for the hard power of realpolitik. If we started with empathy wedded to social cooperation instead, we would come up with a power-with approach that encourages dialogue among all those who will be affected by or implicated in any war under consideration. Certain dialogues might take feminists into war rather than away from it, as two chapters in Sjoberg's groundbreaking book, *Gender, Justice, and the Wars in Iraq* (2006), make clear: "Feminists Go to War" and "Feminists Fight Wars." Other dialogues will move in countervailing directions. Empathetic cooperation becomes a way into war studies that juxtaposes elements of war that we do not usually put together in IR, thereby enabling a picture to form of varied relationships in war. If people outside any war room got to have a say in war planning—ordinary people whose lives will be disrupted or put on the line—it is not likely that a resulting collage of views would duplicate what the literature of the field presents. The very ordinariness of the concerns about loss of people, resources, buildings, kindergartens, and energy supplies will compose pictures of life "in the gulf between the bright optimism of the official world and its degraded material residue." These pictures will also, undoubtedly, be full of emotion.

Picture it: We come to a war dialogue with a starting theme or belief and are made to consider a wide range of considerations that contest, pull out, contradict, and generally stretch our position. Not aiming for a single narrative picture but striving to reveal new relationships, we world-travel to a particular war's effects and affects, as described to us by those most likely to experience them. On the journey, we find ourselves shifting knowledge and identity repertories to accommodate many of the positions we hear (see Sylvester 1994b, 2002b, 2006b). The original picture of war that we brought to the dialogue might become blurry as we become more adept at what Stephanie Shields (2002:, 6) calls, simply, "taking it personally." What Sjoberg describes is a process, not "a" position. The composition it yields will be messier than the one we held in our heads at the beginning. Borders will be too many to count, per-haps, or obscured by jumbled juxtapositions that produce the crystalline clar-ity of Wall's conjoined photos.

But enough with the talking. Anne Orford (2003) is right when she says that touch is a missing aspect of politics in our overly visual—and wordy—times. We neglect to touch and be touched by what we see around us. A large hand-woven rug bears the woven images of heaving bodies. Some bodies are in motion and some huddle with others. Bodies fire weapons and bodies fall on the ground. Children's bodies reach out as some bodies incline toward them or sit crying when other bodies turn away or fail to move. Children's bodies shoot guns. Wall's soldiers from a different war are there too—dead and alive still, uniformed, stunned, bewildered. All the bodies on the rug touch other bodies in a writhing *horror vacui,* or fear of empty space, that we have to look at hard to see and trace. When it hits us, the body collage of war can touch us emo-tionally; yet we also want a touch that is physical. So, raise the many inter-twined people filling the rug and bid spectators to touch these bodies while they look at the piece. Doing so, they enter the picture as participants in the touching dialogue of war. We touch figures touching others in war and are touched physically by them. The touching, intervening, and customizing of the collage is akin to continuing a human-art-war dialogue with the eyes and the emotions. It is a process that achieves creative insight through juxtaposition more so than by maintaining skepticism on borders, where Eagleton, keeping company with postmodernist colleagues, says creativity is supposed to be.

One more element is required to complete the collage: a mirror about one foot off the ground placed around the rug at a three-foot distance from it. Now we spectators cannot approach the rug—whether we touch it our not—with-out seeing bits of ourselves collaged oddly to it. Flesh and fabric paste onto war. Our feet, our legs, and our hands touch war bodies and become body parts of war. The process enacts human mutuality rather than strategic interactions. For IR specialists among the touchers, the engagement with art puts us in sensory contact with a core topic of our field in ways that highlight bodily vulnerabil-ities, our own included. Art specialists who touch the work bring their bodies directly into a larger political dialogue that is closely proximate to international relations. No one is where she or he expects to be, but we are somewhere that opens up sights, insights, priorities, relationships, and power discourses for fur-ther contemplation and creative output.[9]

The Power of the Art/Museum Collaged to IR

Mary Poovey (2004) anticipated a range of connections around art and international relations when she briefly mused about the need to look at abstractions such as nationalism or globalization as forms of interaction among social collectives, individuals, and cultural as well as political institutions. She does not mention art museums, but there certainly is considerable interaction in those places. People picnic at the museum. They dance there. Some sing or put on plays in the exhibition rooms.[10] Great philosophers book in to speak. The Hell's Angels roar up to rescue the American flag from "desecration" in the Phoenix Art Museum exhibition, The Flag in Art (1996).[11] Others jump into Tracy Emin's *Bed*.[12] The art museum is the new town square, the new salon, the new fun place, a free space of ideas and play. The museum also renovates old cellar rooms to handle cappuccino machines and racks of lamb stacked on eggplant: reservations recommended. It directs the flow of gallery traffic and ushers spectators into films and lectures. Usually it smiles benignly at the buskers, mimes, and occasional motorcycles outside. Striving social classes give something back to the art museum for all its efforts: trust. They trust that this is one institution that will, that must, and that usually does reflect as well as shape their values (Cuno 2004b). Feel the buzz.

Of course, the art museum is not a freewheeling space. It is a power space like any other social institution. To David Carr (2001, 30) the museum is an "entity that emanates dense waves of power, value and authority. It is endowed with power by its treasures and by its control of knowledge and information." "It" is moved and controlled and fought over and funded or not, which is to say that a number of social forces and processes spin their interests in and around the art, the buildings, and the policies. Chief curators count in this picture as powerful individuals, but so do big collectors, corporate donors, museum directors, town administrators, media, artists, spectators, art historians, publishers, and restaurateurs. Add to all this the soft discursive power, value, and authority some art museums can carry into international relations, and there can be little surprise that museums land in spots far from national starting places. The Guggenheim travels with foreign architect and foreign art, spends millions, soaks up millions, and reinvests all those millions locally and at home. Foreign troops arrive to fight a war and decidedly not to see the splendid art museums. Commanded to take art seriously in Baghdad (perhaps), they show artlessness by trampling Babylon. MOMA does a photographic exhibition on mankind during the cold war and ends up leading the viewer down the path of American international power. *Madonna of the Pinks* becomes the quintessential Renaissance babe to save, to keep, to possess, to cage in a London museum. The Parthenon marbles hang about oblivious to the incessant debate about how to establish the proper national and institutional home for them and for other ancient art. At Ground Zero, multiple groups grapple for the right to define the power, value, and authority of resurrected or submerged twin towers of international relations.

"People are turning to the museum, says the former Director of the Art Institute, Chicago, for 'a center that holds,' a place that will provide continuity from the past to the present, and a structure with which to confront the future" (Wood 2004, 113).[13] Maybe, but they also like the escalator rides up the side of the Pompidou Center and admire the view over a martini at London's National Portrait Gallery or from a hillside perch at the Getty. The art museum is a living collage of our time, the art of the museum. It is dense and encompassing, powerful, and disparate. It is most certainly not a center that holds together better than other social institutions of the time. Try to paint "it." Try to sculpt "it." A piece called *They Want to Be Anything but Art Museums* would play up Roberta Smith's (2000, 1) claim that some art institutions give up on their core mission as they strive to become social hangouts. Something called *Memory Bank* could affix the great works across art history and hope to suggest a space dedicated to "the immortality of human aesthetic achievement" (Wood 2004, 113).

Then again, a collage of the art museum could start with Richard Hamilton's shimmering fiberglass and cellulose rendering of the exterior of *The Solomon R. Guggenheim Museum* (1965–1966). Hamilton's work is of particular interest when thinking about how juxtaposition could enable us to face the art/museum without giving it a single narrative location or meaning in the contemporary world. His painting *The Saensbury Wing* (1999–2000) (also called *Sainsbury Wing*), was featured in the Encounters exhibition (plate 12). It is a painting from a computer-generated image that takes inspiration from Peter Saenredam's *Interior of the Grote Kerk at Haarlem* (1636–1637). Instead of redoing a Dutch church, Hamilton shows, in sharp perspectival manner, the interior entry to the Sainsbury Wing of the National Gallery, as seen from the top of its grand staircase. His view strips away most people, most artworks, and some of the proportions and architectural details that Robert Venturi and Denise Scott Brown designed for the real Sainsbury Wing. The reworked arches, columns, and sweeping skeletal spaces enter into a call-and-response relationship to Saenredam's golden-age *Grote Kerk*. If we look down the church/museum corridor, as Hamilton's technique directs us to do, we also see that a large Renaissance painting by Cima, which has hung at that end of the Sainsbury Wing, is replaced by Hamilton's own oil painting after a computer-generated image of a Republican inmate in Long Kesh high-security prison near Belfast. Called *The Citizen* (1982–1983), the piece is as dramatically mannered as any Caravaggio. Its defiant glare challenges the viewer, warns her, eyes her.

In Hamilton's *Saensbury Wing*, though, there is no milling crowd or dogs sniffing the interior columns with prurient interest. Other than *The Citizen*, only one figure appears in the work, a young woman standing in the right foreground under an empty, black, diamond canvas. She seems serious about being there and has paused in her pursuits to read what could be a gallery guide. The thing is, she has no clothes on. Standing there naked, she looks confidently contemporary, and yet she could be someone right out of a Renaissance painting in the Sainsbury Wing. Perhaps she has stepped daintily from a Cranach work in order to read the guide's rendition of herself and then defy the painter's and the curator's sense of her place. Certainly she is not able to look at the many other works that would usually flank hers—they are not where they are expected to be. Neither is she. Has she stepped out of another time and another framed action to be humanly in our spaces (Morphet 2000)?

Along with the prisoner-citizen painting behind her, she is rendered in pinky flesh tones while all else in the work is grayish. Perhaps the two real people are in an artificial space called art. *The Citizen* is self-dramatizing, as if he has finally found the commanding power place he was always supposed to have. She is not like that at all. Absorbed by something outside herself, she calmly stands, balanced and at ease. Her demeanor seems right, the naked presentation of her less so. The New York–based feminist art-activist group the Guerrilla Girls (1995) used to hang posters near art museums asking, Do women have to be naked to enter the museum? Apparently so at the end of art no less than during its heyday. *The Citizen* is certainly getting a good look at her and so, complicitly, are we.

Hamilton's composite art/museum emphasizes a designed space where canonical art is scanty on the walls, spectators are few, the architecture is the thing, and some art tropes never change. We can wonder whether we should be there at all, before a space that has been stripped of all excess except the excess of the artist. The imagined museum is not exactly a rendition of the old art institution as a temple few enter, even though it is admirably quiet there, something Paul Virilio (2003) might appreciate. It is not the real Sainsbury Wing of the National Gallery, with its design flourishes, social bustle, and teeming art. *The Saensbury Wing* is more of an aftermath of art/museums. It shows little we would call art except a work by the maker of the rejiggered building. This institution is not about saving art, as we have seen museums do under a variety of rationales; this space has shed art. People, too. One spectator looks at something in her hand instead of at the one piece of art on display behind her, or the magnificent minimalist Renaissance architecture all around her. The other gazes out at us with unflinching eyes. He famously wants Britain to declare him a political prisoner, a citizen from another land altogether; he has smeared his own excrement on the wall to his left in protest. He looks like an Irish Jesus, bare chested and barely modest in draped towel. The other observer, the soft-power woman, is modest in her self-containment but not in other ways.

With its predominantly gray and white tones, punctuated only twice with human colors, *The Saensbury Wing* can be cold and foreboding. If the flesh woman in the front of the painting makes her way down the columns to the back, will the citizen's skin redden hotly? Will he jump out of the painting and grab her, take her prisoner, a hostage in the name of another land that has fought to be free? He is a terrorist, after all—or so it was said of all Irish Republican Army members. In IR, we know quite a bit about terrorism. We study it in the international places we think it threatens, which so far does not include art/museums. Has the anti-Christ figure of our time now infiltrated a London museum? Are we saving the nation for terrorist art/saving art for those who smear excrement about? Hickey might hope so. Danto might find fear and terror embedded mostly in the questions asked about who controls art/museums today. Face the Hamilton piece again: Who is the stranger in the picture—the young woman, the citizen, the architect, the artist, the museum staff, us? Is nowhere safe from international relations?

Suddenly, Hamilton's museum can feel gendered, claustrophobic, prison-like, and eerily violent. There does not seem to be a way in or a way out of it. It is quiet, yes; but it is in need of some pity, which Virilio might also urge. Indeed, something about the emptiness and quiet suggests a voice or two commanded into silence. We are not in a lifestyle destination here. It is not a place people throng to or fully trust. Maybe it is not even a place of art at all so much as a composite of materials, technologies, images, time frames, country references, international relations, and schools of art history remembered and airbrushed. An afterland, good and bad, it is a place where big issues dwell, as in the world around, unresolved but illuminated. If we can face this art/museum and its evocations of international relations, we are in the world. For Elkins (2004), the trick is to look without trying too hard to decipher meanings. For Orford (2003), it is to find a way to touch a scene. For Butler (2004), the politics of connecting with distant others through the commonality of vulnerable bodies is the thing. For nameless others, the challenge is to stop hearing the echo of falling towers and finally wash that taste of soot and dust out of the mouth.

We can enter into situations or spaces or knowledges that differ from our usual contexts for thinking about art or about international relations and, instead of refusing their relevance to our area, engage with their differences creatively. That is the borderline I want to highlight skeptically and then cross. Hickey (1997) is right, in my view, when he talks about the importance of customizing, whether it is customizing received artworks, consumer items (cars), academic fields, or institutions. Collage is the customizer's dream and reality. It traverses boundaries without setting up exclusive enclaves. Picture it: The camps of IR set about lighting the evening fires around which they will discuss, each in its own way, the ongoing fighting in the Middle East. The lights of the British Museum go off, and the night guards come on to secure art of the Middle East from robbers and slashers. Danto (2001, xxix) ventures out that same evening to "an installation by Haim Steinbach at the Sonnabend Gallery in SoHo. ...[A] room was lined with mostly empty steel shelves of the kind we might see in a storeroom. On one there was a pair of running shoes. On another a television set with a grainy screen. In one corner there was a random stack of drab office chairs, beneath which there was a pile of sand. There was something melancholy about it, and my companion observed that it looked just like some political headquarters in the Negev." "Museums live in a world that is not immune from politics," opines Glenn Lowry, the director of MOMA. "In fact, they are deeply woven into that world" (Lowry 2004, 196). The challenge is to see the weavings.

Lowry continues, "But I think there is always a danger when museums engage in a larger social or political agenda. It disengages them from the practice of art history." *The Citizen* glares down the corridor. The woman has had enough chill and quietly steps out of his view and into a large Pollock painting she has been reading about all this time in her guide to MOMA. Still naked, she wraps her body in the dense, thick colors and feels more secure than she did before. She has saved herself after art, she thinks, has escaped the demanding gaze of the tormented citizen–political prisoner and that stench of shit. The swirling, looping colors comfort and cushion her. Stretching out now to read about MOMA and the cold war, bright yellows pulled right up to her chin, she faces us briefly and smiles. It is noon in New York and the place is jammed.

Notes

Chapter 1

1. Museum restaurants add to the bazaar effect. Celebrity chefs Wolfgang Puck and Marc Aumont consider museums ideal venues to showcase their food-design talents (Severson 2006, 30), and even the most pedestrian of museum restaurants can return up to 25 percent of their gross revenues to the museum.

2. Jonathan Jones (2007, 24), one of the regular art writers for the *Guardian* newspaper, captures that disdain. Reviewing the exhibition Tutankhamun and the Golden Age of the Pharaohs, which came to London's O2 (Millennium Dome) in late 2007, he says:

> I would love to be positive. To caution you not . . . to despair when you go inside and drift down a shopping-mall line with sad cafes before entering the show via an escalator that makes it just like going to the adjacent multiplex cinema. Not to listen to the horrible music that plays not merely in the show's corridors but in its actual galleries. Not to be disgusted by the banal architecture that effortlessly recreates the feeling of a posh hotel lobby. Not to be distracted by all the films, overcalculated lighting effects and fake pillars. I would love to say, in short: ignore the trappings of the exhibition, and focus on the objects, for they will more than repay the effort. But . . . I feel angry to have seen it—angry with myself for not heeding the warning signs, those vulgar ads and cheap publicity stunts. I should have stayed away.

3. Annual attendance at the Victoria and Albert Museum in London went from 456,000 in 1857 to over a million in 1870 (McClellan 2003b, 8–10).

4. The discipline-defining debates of IR are controversial, both in the matter of whether they constituted real debates and in what they covered and omitted. See Schmidt 1998 and Sylvester 1994a.

5. Among the camps are oldies of the field—e.g., the English school, intelligence studies, international organization, foreign policy analysis, international law, peace studies, environmental studies, scientific IR—and newer camps of feminist theory and gender studies, global development, postcommunist states, comparative interdisciplinary studies, human rights, and international political sociology. In addition to organized camps there are many traditions of research that need no formal organization to be heard. Realism—the emphasis on state struggles for power or survival—carries on,

now splintered into classical, neo, and constructivist schools. There is a liberal camp, which brings together fragments of neoliberalism, institutionalism, and constructivist institutionalism. There are strategic studies and new security studies. Poststructuralism, postcolonial studies, and feminist constructivism overlap and exist separately. Regional "schools" flourish—not only the English school (which studies aspects of international society) but also the Copenhagen school of security studies and the mathematically oriented rational choice American school; meanwhile, the British International Studies Association has a thriving poststructuralist working group and a smaller art-and-politics camp. International political economy holds down a campsite and so does the related and enormous area of globalization studies (both with proliferating graduate programs).

6. I say "reasonably comfortable," as I have found that critical IR groups can be excruciatingly ill at ease around feminists. Feminists might be invited to present work at critical IR conferences or workshops, but feminist writings are not often engaged and feminists themselves are not usually placed within the pantheon of critical IR's important scholars. This tendency is especially evident in critical security circles in Europe. See discussion in Sylvester 2007b.

7. It is said, though, that Baudrillard finds the art in the mental moment that transpires prior to snapping a photograph. This cannot be exhibited, so his photographs themselves cannot be art, even though MOMA, the Whitney, and other museums vie to purchase them (Lotringer 2005, 17).

8. There are other views on the end of the museum. Douglas Crimp (1993) thinks, for example, that the art/museum ended when photography was pried away from its material and technological context and brought into the museum as "art."

9. Although quality is slippery and contentious in the realm of contemporary art. See Jones 2007, 11.

Chapter 2

1. It is curious that Neil MacGregor (2004a, 22), director of the British Museum, glosses over the selective entry requirements of the early museum, writing that "from the beginning, the British Museum was for all studious and curious people. . . . It was a museum for the public and for the citizen." He repeats this theme in a more recent piece, rather injudiciously called "The Whole World in Our Hands" (MacGregor 2004b).

2. There are still at least two countries within the United Kingdom, as living in Cumbria, a border county with Scotland, makes quite clear. The nation to the immediate north takes its difference seriously, to the point of periodically contemplating separation from England. See the engaging account of historical border-living by the Scottish Cumbrian Eric Robson (2006).

3. Donald Preziosi (1996, 284) calls this "the disciplining of whole populations through a desire-driven interaction with objects."

4. The museum was clearly nudged to do this by the scathing Edwards Report of 1996, a consultancy study on management that accused the museum of making its col-

lections speak for themselves and of not doing enough to attract and excite audiences or stimulate public enthusiasm. For a discussion of the report, see Zan 2000.

5. The museum has been closed to the public since 1991, by decision of Saddam Hussein. He and his family regularly "visited" the museum in the intervening years to take objects for their homes. There are plans to open two rooms to the public soon. See discussion in chapter 3.

6. An April 21, 2007, statement by the museum declares:

> The Trustees have for years been looking to see if there is any reasonable ground on which a way forward with Greek colleagues might be constructed. To date, this has sadly not proved possible. Among many problems has been that successive Greek government have publicly disputed the Trustees' unquestionable legal ownership of the Sculptures. This has made any meaningful discussions virtually impossible. . . . The Trustees have lent often to Greece, especially in the recent Athens Olympic year of 2004, but they have never received a normal loan request for any of the Parthenon sculptures. What successive Greek governments have always sought is the permanent removal of all of the sculptures to Athens. The Trustees do not foresee ¶a situation where they could possibly accede to such a request. (British Museum, 2007)

7. Some say the Delian League could have ended for reasons of a peace treaty with Persia. Similarly, there are accounts suggesting that very little foreign money found its way into the Parthenon building project. See Boedeker and Raaflaub 1998.

8. Yet, even Thucydides warned angry Athenians about the risks of imperialism. Writing a judgment of Pericles, Thucydides says of Pericles' warnings to Athenian citizens: "He told them that if they would be quiet and take care of their navy, and not seek to expand the empire during this war or endanger the city itself, they should have had the upper hand. But they did the opposite on all points." (Quoted in Woodruff 1993, 57).

9. For a good overview of the debates on cosmopolitanism versus communitarianism as they unfold in IR, see Hutchings 1999. Critics of cosmopolitanism that distrust certain organizational forms of power include Dillon (1998), Lipschutz and Conca (1994), and Dryzek (1995). There are also critics of the communitarian sense that a community is self-evident and relatively fixed rather than a constructed and changing political invention and intervention into subjectivity (e.g., Jabri 1998; Mouffe 1993).

Chapter 3

1. Over 500,000 properties are protected by state conservancy regulations. My Grade II–listed Georgian house in Cumbria, for example, cannot be structurally altered, even to install energy-saving windows, without local government approval. There is nothing like that intensity of state protection for artworks held in national museums.

2. D. H. Lawrence declared American painting wedded to Puritanism's dread of lush beauty, a problem that "held back" British art during and following the Cromwell

era (1653–1658), although the Puritan-embodying art of the United Provinces was apparently an exception (Duncan 1999, 316).

3. Carey (2005) notes a variety of prejudices about art appreciation. It is thought that art appreciation can diminish class conflict and promote gentler civilization. It can supposedly tap dimensions of consciousness otherwise inaccessible. It is said to enhance learning so viewers can reach truer, more transcendent and unsullied knowledge. On one or more of these grounds, most states use taxpayer moneys to support the arts. Yet Carey reminds us that Hitler loved the arts and wanted to shape the German nation around a particular politicized aesthetics. (Camp executioners enjoyed classical music played by camp inmates before and during the gassings.) Art and violence have gone together as easily as art and gentle civilization. Indeed, we sometimes call the awesome violence of certain aesthetic representations "the sublime."

4. Getty Center docent, March 26, 2006, Los Angeles.

5. Carrier (2006, 171) prefers to say that "after the Getty, traditional museums feel intolerably busy."

6. There is also likely to be an element of deep-rooted anti-Americanism in such assessments. To the degree that the Getty institutions are staged in a theme-park way, they trigger British and European disdain of America's globalized popular culture. See Markovits 2007.

7. It needs to be reiterated, though, that America's early patrician elites effectively kept out nouveau riche interests in art museums until the late nineteenth century. See Bennett 1995, 115–16.

8. The Web site is saatchigallery.com/yourgallery. It attracted 1,750 contributing artists in its first month, averaging 1.4 million hits a day (Gibson 2006, 11). The site has added an online art mag-blog called Your Gallery.

9. Other influential British collectors of contemporary art include Anita and Poju Zabludowicz and Muriel and Fred Salem, plus around fifty solid dealers who have emerged in London since the 1990s. Alongside the celebrity artists they promote and big collectors like Saatchi, these dealers are so powerful that their events can put public art museums in the shadows. Perhaps, one commentator says, it is "unrealistic to expect public museums and galleries to operate independently" (Rawsthorn 2006, 28).

10. These tanks meant war business, unlike the decommissioned tank set in the forecourt of the British Museum in 1989, which was a very telling advertising hook for the exhibition Treasures for the Nation.

11. Similar local entrepreneurism has been evident at newly found archaeological sites in Iran and is expected in Cambodia as soon as mines are cleared from certain areas of the country (*Art Newspaper* 2004c).

12. These and other Iraqi archives entered the United States under a 1965 program that guarantees to protect State Department–approved cultural objects loaned from foreign countries. Once objects are inside the United States, though, it is allowable for individuals to claim rightful ownership of certain items. A spate of such claims could cause the collection to disappear as quickly as the war threatened to do. The National Archives and Records Administration therefore issued a statement expressing hope that claims of private or national ownership would be held off by the Coalition Authority, the political entity that had custodianship over the items at the time (*Art Newspaper* 2004a:10).

13. Anticipating a war in Iraq, the *Art Newspaper,* the leading international trade paper for art professionals, offered this headline for its November 2002 (no. 130) issue: "Iraq's History Is Our History Too."

14. If the British are more interested in their history than their present, the same cannot be said of American museums. In 2003, contemporary art acquisitions led in the ranks of all U.S. museum acquisitions, with work by Matthew Barney (e.g., the Cremaster Cycle, 1994–2002) proving the most popular (*Art Newspaper* 2004e).

Chapter 4

1. Even MOMA, however, has not always been immune to the appeal of Old Masters. In 1939, it took on the exhibition Italian Masters, which had been bound for the Metropolitan Museum of Art before foundering on a disagreement with the Italian government. MOMA endeavored to fit this unusual program into its remit by mounting a concurrent exhibition, Modern Masters.

2. Derek Gillman (2006, 23), the former director of the Pennsylvania Academy of Fine Arts and current director and president of the Barnes Foundation, writes: "While America has many import and export controls, it has yet to implement one that constrains the flow of art on the grounds of national interest, and is unaccustomed to rhetoric over the 'loss of national treasures.'" It can happen, though, as the curious case of the Gilbert Stuart portrait of George Washington, known as the Lansdowne portrait, shows. The owners in Scotland reluctantly lent the portrait for the opening of the Smithsonian's National Portrait Gallery in 1968, on a temporary six-month permit only. Three decades later the portrait was still there, clearly in breach of the original terms, and the owners would agree to part with it only for $20 million. The Smithsonian found itself unable to raise the funds, whereupon the portrait was saved by the Donald W. Reynolds Foundation. It was a much-hailed intervention for what came to be known, unusually, as a national treasure (see Christman 2002).

3. This is not an entirely new phenomenon. Arthur Danto (1997, 176) reminds us that the Brooklyn Museum, which opened in 1897, was mostly building and little art: "There was something almost touching in the disparity between its architectural proclamation of grandeur and the limited extent of its fine arts holdings."

4. For an overview of modern art theory and practice, see Chipp 1992; Crow 1996; Collings 2000; Hughes 1991; Lynton 1989; Dawtrey, Wood, Jackson, and Meecham 1996.

5. Lee Hall (2000, 112), former president of the Rhode Island School of Design, writes of American abstractionists as "an inadvertent community of artists interested in disparate aspects of modernism [who] viewed themselves as individualistic, held together only casually by shared concerns, greatly separated in matters of style and direction in art."

6. The one major exception is Frances Stonor Saunders (1999; 2000), who maintains the more radical interpretation of MOMA's early role in promoting abstract expressionism. As the former arts editor of Britain's *New Statesman* and a continuing film documentarist, her radical line in *The Cultural Cold War: The CIA and the World of Arts and Letters* has a following in the United Kingdom but less of one in the United States. She has been accused of writing a definitive book on the subject without con-

sulting key sources, such as the Bertrand Russell Archives (Blitz, 2001–2002). Writing in *Art Forum,* Robert Simon (2000, 1) concludes that "Saunders winds up presuming exactly what needs to be carefully argued: that there is a more or less tight causal link between the initiatives of powerful elites—the directives and intentions of both institutional and individual players—and the cultural object, its conditions of production, the systems of its display and distribution, its reception, content, and form."

7. Artist expatriates from India (e.g., Avinash Chandra) and China (e.g., Li Yuan Chia) brought elements from their cultures to their art too, changing modernism, shaping it, giving it regional meaning (Araeen 1989).

Chapter 5

1. Personal correspondence with Zulaika, 2007.

2. There was more at stake than Krens's personal reputation. His apparent use of deaccessioning moneys to fund renovations led to an ethics investigation by the Association of Art Museum Directors in 2003. He was cleared of charges.

3. The first expansion occurred in New York City itself with the opening in 1992 of a Guggenheim branch in Soho. The museum, designed by Arata Isozaki, was on three loft floors of a nineteenth-century landmark on Broadway. This project failed in 2001 after several efforts to boost flagging attendance by bringing in a trendy exhibition, renovating to lessen the museum space, appealing to a corporate backer, and even removing the admission charge. Over the years, a number of announced or anticipated Guggenheim franchise deals have fallen through before they were realized: in Rio de Janeiro, Taiwan, Sydney, Edinburgh, Hong Kong, and Venice to name a few.

4. In this respect, it is noteworthy that one of the strongest recent attacks on Krens and the Guggenheim devolves into a polemic, in part because the researcher does not lay out the checkered history of art patronage before lambasting what she calls, as the title of her book, *Privatising Culture: Corporate Art Intervention since the 1980s.* See Wu 2000.

5. Lisa Dennison, a longtime curatorial force at Guggenheim, then became its director. In mid-2007, she resigned that post and moved to Sotheby's. The new director of the Guggenheim Foundation and Museum was announced in September 2008 as Richard Armstrong, former director of the Carnegie Museum of Art, Pittsburgh. Armstrong is expected to strengthen ties among the existing Guggenheim museums and develop collaborative projects with other major international art museums, such as the Tate.

6. Zulaika questions whether this fee structure is generalizable or was specific to the Bilbao case. When he conducted research in Salzburg on the failed effort to partner with Guggenheim, those involved were "flabbergasted," to use his word, by the amount Bilbao was asked to contribute (personal correspondence, 2007). And in fact, the *Art Newspaper* (2007a, 32) puts the original capital costs covered by the Basque administration at $124.8 million.

7. Krens, however, oversaw art commissions for the Deutsche Guggenheim branch—by the likes of Gerhard Richter, Rachel Whiteread, and Jeff Koons—that have now become part of the larger Guggenheim collection.

8. He has since set up a programming partnership with the Kunsthistorisches Museum in Vienna.

9. Zulaika doubts that Guggenheim ever paid "one single penny" of the remaining 5 percent that fell to it, not even the costs of Krens's various trips to Bilbao (personal correspondence, 2007).

10. Gehry (2000) contrasts his interest in creating a building that would do something for Bilbao with the architectural approach seen in MOMA's recent renovations. The new MOMA, he says, "does everything possible for art, but it doesn't deal with the city. It doesn't deal with those other issues."

11. Keeping company with ETA on the terrorist list of 1998 was Cambodia's Khmer Rouge and Peru's Shining Path, but not the Irish Republican Army.

Chapter 6

1. McKinsey & Co., the consulting firm David Rockefeller hired in 1959 to study the World Trade Center idea, concluded that most companies would gain little by locating within a unified complex.

2. The two European empires continued to clash, though, for years. The Dutch retaliated for the loss of Manhattan by pushing the British out of Surinam. Several years later, a Dutch fleet sailed into New York Harbor, retook Manhattan, and held it for fifteen years. In 1788, the British regained it but then lost the country to its settlers.

3. J. P. Morgan built a neoclassical revival–style bank in the area in 1913. It still stands, despite the twenty-pound TNT bomb that exploded outside it in 1920, turning bank windows into a kind of "snow" that pitted the facade. Thirty people died in the initial explosion, another ten died in subsequent days, and more than three hundred people were injured. Eric Darton (1999, 14) recounts the aftermath: "'Public outrage' over the bombing served as a timely pretext for the mass roundup of radicals— particularly foreigners—followed by a cycle of deportations, extraditions, indictments, false confessions, and jailhouse suicides. . . . Finally, in 1930, the massive ten-year manhunt ground to a halt, petering out in a maze of blind alleys. None of the perpetrators of the so-called Broad Street massacre was ever identified." At that time, the foreign bombers were assumed to be communists.

4. This enthusiasm for renewal was enabled by the Federal Housing Act of 1949 and its Title I provisions for governments to engage in "slum clearance."

5. I thank Stephen Chan for drawing my attention to these linguistic points.

6. George W. Bush made this clear in the speech he delivered to the Republican Party convention in late August 2004, calling America "liberty central."

7. Airlines, however, may impose their own "rules" on passengers, such as the widespread practice of warning passengers that they may not congregate in groups near the toilets or other places on the plane.

8. She has since extended her analysis into a booklength discussion, *Terror in the Skies* (Jacobsen 2005). Not reassured by the outcome of that flight, especially after interviewing a range of security experts, she concludes that what she saw was a probe or practice run for a real terrorist attack. She claims that the subsequent investigation into the activities of the fourteen "strange" travelers was botched by all participating

government agencies, including the Los Angeles Police Department, the FBI, and the Federal Air Marshals.

9. That architect abandoned Yamasaki's concerns about the psychological effects of large glass expanses on people inside the buildings. The new 7 World Trade Center is sheathed now in 538,420 square feet of glass, which gives it more than 12 acres of "transparency" (Dunlap 2004). It is a decidedly boring building.

10. Martin Filler writes in the *New York Review of Books* (2005, 7) that "cities in Europe and Japan would look quite different if places where thousands of innocent civilians died in World War II had been left vacant as memorials." He claims that the "unprecedented nature of such carnage in the United States has made opposition to the families seem not merely insensitive but politically suicidal."

11. I am reminded of H. G. Wells's possibly apocryphal comment as he contemplated wrecking New York in his *War in the Air* (1908): "What a ruin it will make." Cited in Bevan 2006, 66.

12. As of August 14, 2007, the organization had raised $300 million for the memorials, only $50 million short of its goal of raising enough to support capital and planning costs, with an initial endowment to support operations. Construction of the footings started in 2006. The steel girders were in place by 2007, and an opening in 2009 is expected.

13. It is telling, however, that the brokerage firm of Goldman Sachs elected to build its $2.4 billion headquarters across from the World Trade Center site. Ground Zero, the former disaster area turned site of memory, will likely attract many such firms.

Chapter 7

1. Eagleton does say in *After Theory* (2003, 40) that a border is a place of resourcefulness, "if not always a painless one." But he does not dwell there. Four years later, he expresses clear concern about the brutality of some creative border places and the destructiveness of some acts of resourceful imagination (lecture at Lancaster University, November 5, 2007; also, Eagleton 2005).

2. Jonathan Jones (2006) makes a similar point with respect to artworks trying to capture twenty-first-century war.

3. Januszczak (2005) writes of Vine's work in a way that guarantees success at the end of art: "It's all done pretty crudely. There's not much give in Vine's fingers. Her emotional range covers a narrow band on the Bridget Jones spectrum. She copies her images from existing sources. Her colours are a cake-maker's—girlie pinks, Alice-band blues—and the way she writes on her pictures has been learnt from a bakery. But there's something there, nevertheless: a combination of empathy and cynicism that can be startling."

4. Roland Barthes (1985, 211) has argued that collages "do not juxtapose, they conglomerate." Christine Poggi (1992, xiii) claims that collage is "an alternative to the modernist tradition in twentieth-century art." My account is indebted to two sources. One is the analysis of collage by Brandon Taylor (2004), who argues convincingly that collage is the making of modern art. The other is the edited volume from the MOMA series Studies of Modern Art that accompanied the museum's 1961 exhibit The Art of

Assemblage (Elderfield, 1992). These volumes are in exquisite and bridging "touch" with each other across the time gap.

5. There is some controversy on this point as well. The British art critic Lawrence Alloway argued that some collages exhibit artistic wholeness by assimilating disparate pieces into an organized work, thus achieving a new aesthetic unity. Joseph Ruzicka's (1992) edited transcript of a symposium held at MOMA in 1961, The Art of Assemblage, provides insight into this and other controversies.

6. David Carrier (2006, 50) uses the term "time-travel" to refer to museums enabling art viewers to travel back in time to places and moments difficult for us to imagine. He says that "when we look at old works of art . . . we identify with the viewers who originally experienced them, thus extending the span of our own lives." It is his response to the museum skeptics who insist that once the context of an artwork is gone, the museum cannot be said to be preserving the work. I am using time-travel only a bit differently to refer to some collage compositions that juxtapose varying epochs or styles of art in ways that show continuities as well as differences.

7. We must note, though, that Bourgeois was one of only three women artists invited to do an Encounter work. The other two were Paula Rego and, working with Claes Oldenburg, Coosje Van Bruggen. None of the works that inspired the contemporary artists in the show was done by women. For a sharp gender critique of the exhibition, see McQueen 2001.

8. For a discussion of this analogy, see Sylvester 1994b.

9. For further discussion, see Sylvester 2005. This rug is inspired by an artwork done by Dominique Blain, a French Canadian artist. Hers weaves life-size images of land mines so cleverly into the design of a seemingly "oriental carpet" that it takes serious concentration to pick them up. Once viewers realize what they are seeing, they often back away, not wanting to be blown up or implicated in acts of war. The rug collage I imagine operates in quite the opposite manner; it does not trick the viewer into a recoil but rather welcomes touch. Its raised figures are meant to be compellingly tactile.

10. I have happened on serious drama taking place in the galleries of the Walters Art Museum, Baltimore, as well as chamber music in the National Gallery of Australia and the Yale Center for British Art.

11. They carefully folded up every flag that seemed inappropriately exhibited and handed it to the curator. They said they were veterans of the Vietnam War and were upset at the idea that the symbol of a country they fought for would be shown trailing out of urinals onto the floor or made to be walked on as art. The juxtaposition of many motorcycle engines outside, many men dressed in black leather clomping about, and their largely respectful mien in the subdued spaces of the museum—to say nothing of the iconic American flag—made an instant collage. It is one I will never forget.

12. During the 1999 Turner Award Exhibition, two art students took their clothes off and jumped into Emin's My Bed, a controversial, life-size, unmade bed as artwork, scattered with the aftermaths of many bedtime activities. They claimed to be extending the work and making it more interesting.

13. James N. Wood later became president and CEO of the J. Paul Getty Trust.

References

Abrams, M. H. 1989. *Doing Things with Texts: Essays in Criticism and Critical Theory.* New York: W. W. Norton.

Adams, Georgina. 2005a. "The Baneful Effects of Lavish Spending." *Art Newspaper,* no. 157 (April), 31.

———. 2005b. "The Art Market: Boom or Bubble?" *Art Newspaper,* no. 164 (December).

Aguilar, Palomar. 1998. "The Memory of the Civil War in the Transition to Democracy: The Peculiarity of the Basque Case." *West European Politics* 21.

Ahmed, Sara. 2000. *Strange Encounters: Embodied Others in Post-Coloniality.* London: Routledge.

Allen, Brian. 2003. "Saving Art for the UK." *Art Newspaper,* no. 139 (September), 25.

Al-Radi, Selma. 2003. "War and Cultural Heritage: Lessons from Lebanon, Kuwait and Iraq." Lecture delivered at Museum The Prinsenhof, Delft. The Hague: Prince Claus Fund, 26 September.

Alternatives: Social Transformation and Humane Governance. 2000. Special issue, Poetic World Politics, 25, 3.

Alternatives: Global, Local, Political. 2006. Special issue, Art and Politics, 31, 1.

Altwick, Richard. 1999. "National Monuments." In Boswell and Evans 1999, 240–57.

Anderson, Benedict. 1991. *Imagined Communities: Reflections on the Origins and Spread of Nationalism.* London: Verso.

Anderson, Elijah. 1990. *Streetwise: Race, Class and Change in an Urban Community.* Chicago: University of Chicago Press.

Appadurai, Arjun. 1993. "Disjuncture and Difference in the Global Cultural Economy." In *Colonial Discourse and Post-Colonial Theory: A Reader,* ed. Patrick Williams and Laura Chrisman, 324–39. London: Harvester Wheatsheaf.

Appiah, Kwame Anthony. 2006. *Cosmopolitanism: Ethics in a World of Strangers.* New York: Norton.

Appleyard, Bryan. 2006. "The Look We Love." *Sunday Times Culture,* March 26, 4–5.

———. 2007. "A World of Its Own," *Sunday Times Culture,* May 6, 4–7.

Araeen, Rasheed. 1989. *The Other Story: Afro-Asian Artists in Post-War Britain.* London: South Bank Centre.

Archibugi, Daniele. 2004. "Cosmopolitan Democracy and Its Critics: A Review." *European Journal of International Relations* 10, no. 3:437–73.

Arnold, Dana. 2003. Series editor's preface to *Art and Its Publics: Museum Studies at the Millennium,* ed. Andrew McClellan, ix–x. Oxford: Blackwell Publishing.

Arruti, Nerea. 2003. "Reflecting Basqueness: Bilbao from Mausoleum to Museum." *International Journal of Iberian Studies* 16, no. 3:167–75.

Art Monthly. 1999. "Art and the New Pilgrimage." Theme issue, no. 119 (May).

Art Newspaper. 2002. "Iraq's History Is Our History Too." No. 130 (November), 1, 4.

———. 2003a. "We Serve All Cultures, Say Big, Global Museums." No. 132 (January), 1, 6.

———. 2003b. "International Outrage as Great Museum Is Sacked." No. 136 (May), 1, 6.

———. 2003c. "National Gallery Reaches Out to the Underprivileged in Bid to Save Raphael." No. 138 (July–August), 8.

———. 2003d. "Seized: Over 600 Objects Looted from Iraq." No. 139 (September), 1, 3.

———. 2003e. "The Future of Raphael's Madonna Still Hangs in the Balance." No. 139 (September), 9.

———. 2003f. "Senior Cultural Adviser Comes under 'Friendly Fire.'" No. 140 (October), 1, 5.

———. 2003g. "The Numbers Are In, but the Hunt for Objects Contitnues." No. 140 (October), 5.

———. 2003h. "Keeping Art in the UK." No. 141 (November), 5.

———. 2003i. "Picking Up the Pieces." No. 142 (December), 22.

———. 2003j. "Sharing Is the Winning Motto." No. 142 (December), 25.

———. 2004a. "Saddam's Secret Hoard of Jewish Manuscripts." No. 143 (January), 10.

———. 2004b. "Saved from the Looting but Damaged by Flooding." No. 143 (January), 10.

———. 2004c. "London and Paris Markets Flooded with Looted Iranian Antiquities." No. 143 (January), 9.

———. 2004d. "Looters Hot on the Heels of the Bomb Disposal Experts." No. 144 (February), 24.

———. 2004e. "Contemporary Art Leads Museum Acquisitions in 2003." No. 146 (April), 22–26.

———. 2004f. "Britain to Ratify Hague Convention." No. 148 (June), 4.

———. 2004g. "We Have Seen the Active Destruction of the Archaeological and Historical Period." No. 151 (October), 7.

———. 2005a. "Museums Closed and Looting Rampant." No. 155 (February), 4.

———. 2005b. "The Rise and Rise of Damien Hirst." No. 155 (February), 1.

———. 2005c. "Fifteen Years Reporting the International Art World." No. 164 (December), 29.

———. 2007a. "The Bilbao Effect: From Poor Port to Must-See City." No. 184 (December), 32–33.

———. 2007b. "How to Achieve the Bilbao Effect." No. 184 (December), 33.

Ashley, Richard. 1989. "Living on Border Lines: Man, Poststructuralism, and War." In *International/Intertextual Relations: Postmodern Readings of World Politics,* ed. James Der Derian and Michael Shapiro, 259–321. Lexington, MA: Lexington Books.

Ashley, Richard, and R. B. J. Walker. 1990. "Speaking the Language of Exile: Dissident Thought in International Studies." *International Studies Quarterly* 34, no. 3:259–68.

Ashton, Dore. 1972. *The New York School: A Cultural Reckoning.* Berkeley and Los Angeles: University of California Press.

Atick, Richard. 1999. "National Monuments." In Boswell and Evans 1999, 240–57. London: Routledge.

Baggini, Julian. 2004. "Folkestone Revisited." *Guardian,* June 24, G16–17.

Balibar, Etienne. 1995. "Ambiguous Universality." *Differences: Journal of Feminist Cultural Studies* 7, no. 1:48–74.

Ballard, J. G. 2007. Introduction to "Great Modern Buildings, Guggenheim Bilbao, Frank Gehry." *Guardian* (October).

Barkawi, Tarak, and Mark Laffey. 2002. "Retrieving the Imperial: Empire and International Relations." *Millennium* 31, no. 1:109–27.

Barnett, Michael, and Raymond Duvall. 2005. "Power in International Politics." *International Organization* 59, no. 1:39–75.

Barthes, Roland. 1973. "The Great Family of Man." In *Mythologies,* trans. Annette Lavers, 101–2. St. Albans, UK: Paladin Books.

———. 1985. *The Responsibility of Forms.* Trans. Richard Howard. Berkeley and Los Angeles: University of California Press.

Barzun, Jacques. 1959. *The House of Intellect.* New York: Harper.

Baudrillard, Jean. 1982. "The Beaubourg Effect: Implosion and Deterrence." *October* 20 (Spring): 3–13.

———. 2005. *The Conspiracy of Art.* Ed. Sylvere Lotringer. Trans. Ames Hodges. Foreign Agents series. New York: Semiotext(e).

Beard, Mary. 2002. *The Parthenon.* London: Profile Books.

Beckett, Andy. 2003. "Can Culture Save Us?" *Guardian, G2,* June 6, 5.

Beigbeder, Frederic. 2005. *Windows on the World.* Trans. Frank Wynne. London: Harper Perennial.

Beitz, Charles. 1999. "International Liberalism and Distributive Justice: A Survey of Recent Thought." *World Politics* 51, no. 2:269–96.

Bell, Clive. 1969. "The Aesthetic Hypothesis." In Tillman and Cahn 1969.

Belting, Hans. 1987. *The End of the History of Art.* Trans. Christopher Wood. Chicago: University of Chicago Press.

———. 2003. *Art History after Modernism.* Chicago: University of Chicago Press.

Benjamin, Walter. 1992. "The World of Art in the Age of Mechanical Reproduction." In *Illuminations,* 217–51. London: Fontana.

Bennett, Catherine. 2004. "Real Blood for Saatchi's New Bloods." *Guardian,* April 29, 5.

Bennett, Tony. 1995. *The Birth of the Museum: History, Theory, Politics.* London: Routledge.

Bevan, Robert. 2006. *The Destruction of Memory: Architecture at War.* London: Reaktion Books.

Bhabha, Homi. 1994. "Dissemination." In *The Location of Culture,* 139–70. New York: Routledge.

Bjelajac, David. 2000. *American Art: A Cultural History.* London: Laurence King.

Blitz, David. 2001–2002. "Cultural Cold War." *Russell,* n.s 21 (Winter): 176–80.

Bloom, Lisa, ed. 1999. *With Other Eyes: Looking at Race and Gender in Visual Culture.* Minneapolis: University of Minnesota Press.

Boedeker, D., and K. Raaflaub, eds. 1998. *Democracy, Empire, and the Arts in Fifth-Century Athens.* Cambridge, MA: Harvard University Press.

Bogdanos, Matthew. 2005. *Thieves of Baghdad*. London: Bloomsbury.

Boswell, David, and Jessica Evans, eds. 1999. *Representing the Nation: A Reader*. London: Routledge.

Bourdieu, Pierre. 1984. *Distinction: A Cultural Critique of the Judgment of Taste*. Trans. Richard Nice. Cambridge, MA: Harvard University Press.

Bourdieu, Pierre, and Alain Darbel, with Dominique Schnapper. 1991. *The Love of Art: European Art Museums and Their Public*. Trans. Caroline Beattie and Nick Merriman. Oxford: Polity Press.

Bradley, Kim. 1997. "The Deal of the Century: Planning Process for Guggenheim Museum Bilbao, Spain." *Art in America* 85 (July): 48–55.

British Museum. 2007. Statement on Parthenon Sculptures, April 7. www.britishmuseum.org. Accessed November 5, 2007.

Brooks, Peter. 1992. "Gauguin's Tahitian Body." In Broude and Garrard 1992, 330–45. New York: Icon Editions, 330–45.

Brooks, Richard. 2003. "Who Needs Old Masters Anyway?" *Guardian*, November 16, 7.

Brotton, Jerry. 2006. *The Sale of the Late King's Goods: Charles I and His Art Collection*. London: Macmillan.

Broude, Norma, and Mary Garrard, eds. 1992. *The Expanding Discourse: Feminism and Art History*. New York: Icon Editions.

Brown, Chris. 1995. "International Political Theory and the Idea of World Community." In *International Relations Theory Today*, ed. Ken Booth and Steve Smith, 90–109. University Park: Pennsylvania State University Press.

Build the Memorial. 2007. "Foundation to Become National September 11 Memorial & Museum at the World Trade Center." Press release, August 14. www.buildthememorial.org. Accessed January 5, 2008.

Bulletin of the Museum of Modern Art. 1942. 10, no. 1 (October–November).

Bullough, Edward. 1969. "Psychical Distance." In Tillman and Cahn 1969.

Butler, Judith. 2004. *Precarious Life: The Powers of Mourning and Violence*. London: Verso.

Camilleri, J., and Richard Falk. 1992. *The End of Sovereignty? The Politics of a Shrinking and Fragmented World*. Aldershot, UK: Elgar.

Campbell, Matthew. 2004. "Iraq's Culture Cops Go Hunting Looters." *Guardian*, January 11, 2004, 29.

Carey, John. 2005. *What Good Are the Arts?* London: Faber and Faber.

Carpenter, Charli. 2003. "'Women and Children First': Gender, Norms, and Humanitarian Evacuation in the Balkans 1991–95." *International Organization* 57 (Fall): 661–94.

Carr, David. 2001. "Balancing Act: Ethics, Mission, and the Public Trust." *Museum News,* September/October, 30.

Carrier, David. 2006. *Museum Skepticism: A History of the Display of Art in Public Galleries*. Durham, NC: Duke University Press.

Caute, David. 2003. *The Dancer Defects: The Struggle for Cultural Supremacy during the Cold War*. Oxford: Oxford University Press.

Caygill, Marjorie. 2003. *The Story of the British Museum*. 3rd ed. London: British Museum Press.

Ceballos, Sara Gonzalez. 2003. "The Role of the Guggenheim Museum in the Development of Urban Entrepreneurial Practices in Bilbao." *International Journal of Iberian Studies* 16, no. 3:177–86.

Chakrabarty, Dipesh.2000. *Provincializing Europe*. Princeton, NJ: Princeton University Press.

Chan, Stephen.1997. "Too Neat and Under-Thought a World Order: Huntington and Civilizations." *Millennium* 26, no. 1:137–40.

———. 2003. "The Performativity of Death: Yukio Mishima and a Fusion for International Relations." *Borderlands e-Journal* 2, no. 2. www.borderlandsejournal.adelaide.edu.au/issues/vol2no2.html.

Chapman, Jake. 2003. Interview for "A Bigger Splash: What Would You Buy with £25m?" *Guardian*, November 13, 8–9.

Chave, Anna. 1993. "Pollock and Krasner: Script and Postscript." *RES* 24 (Autumn): 95–111.

Chin, Christine. 1998. *In Service and Servitude: Foreign Female Domestic Workers and the Malaysian "Modernity" Project*. New York: Columbia University Press.

Chipp, Herschel B. 1992. *Theories of Modern Art: A Source Book by Artists and Critics*. Berkeley and Los Angeles: University of California Press.

Christman, Margaret. 2002. "The Story of the Lansdowne 'Washington.'" In *George Washington: A National Treasure*, by Richard Brookhiser, Margaret C. S. Christman, and Ellen G. Miles. Washington, DC: Smithsonian Institution.

City Broadsheet (New York). 2006. March, 1.

Coalition of 911 Families. 2002. "Coalition of 911 Families Memorial Position." www.coalitionof911families.org/CoalitionFamilies.html. Accessed August 14, 2007.

Cockcroft, Eva. 1985. "Abstract Expressionism, Weapon of the Cold War." In Frascina 1985, 125–33.

Collings, Matthew. 2000. *This Is Modern Art*. London: Weidenfeld Nicolson Illustrated.

Conn, Steven. 1998. *Museums and American Intellectual Life, 1876–1926*. Chicago: University of Chicago Press.

Connaisance des Arts. 1999. Special issue on Guggenheim Bilbao.

Constantinou, Costas. 1996. *On the Way to Diplomacy*. Minneapolis: University of Minnesota Press.

———. 2001. "Hippopolis/Cynopolis." *Millennium* 30, no. 3:785–804.

Conversi, Daniele. 1997. *The Basques, the Catalans and Spain: Alternative Routes to Nationalist Mobilization*. Reno: University of Nevada Press.

Coombes, Annie. 1994. *Reinventing Africa: Museums, Material Culture and Popular Imagination in Late Victorian and Edwardian England*. New Haven: Yale University Press.

Cordone, Pietro. 2003. "The Aftermath of Conflict: The Coalition Is Failing to Protect Iraq's Heritage." *Art Newspaper*, no. 140 (October), 25.

Cotter, Holland. 2007. "Leaving Room for the Troublemakers." *New York Times*, March 28, H1, H35.

Coulter, Ann. 2006. *Godless: The Church of Liberalism*. New York: Crown Forum.

Craven, David. 1996. "The Latin American Origins of Alternative Modernism." *Third Text* 36:29–44.

Crimp, Douglas. 1993. *On the Museum's Ruins*. Cambridge, MA: MIT Press.

Crow, Thomas. 1996. *Modern Art in the Common Culture*. New Haven: Yale University Press.

Cuno, James, ed. 2004. *Whose Muse? Art Museums and the Public Trust*. Princeton, NJ: Princeton University Press.

———. 2004a. "The Object of Art Museums." In Cuno 2004, 49–75.

———. 2004b. Introduction to Cuno 2004, 11–25.

Daily Mail Special Exhibition Number. 1908. London, July–October.

Danto, Arthur. 1997. *After the End of Art: Contemporary Art and the Pale of History.* Princeton, NJ: Princeton University Press.

———. 2001. *The Madonna of the Future: Essays in a Pluralistic Art World.* Berkeley and Los Angeles: University of California Press.

———. 2002. "A Commentary on the End of Art: What You Think Is What It Is." *Art Newspaper,* no. 125 (May), 31.

———. 2003. "No End in Sight." *Art Newspaper,* no. 139 (September), 33.

Darby, Phillip. 1997. *At the Edge of International Relations: Postcolonialism, Gender and Dependency.* London: Pinter.

Darton, Eric. 1999. *Divided We Stand: A Biography of New York's World Trade Center.* New York: Basic Books.

Dawtrey, Liz, Paul Wood, Toby Jackson, and Pam Meecham, eds. 1996. *Investigating Modern Art.* New Haven: Yale University Press.

De La Puente, Joaquin. 2002. *Guernica: The Making of a Painting.* Madrid: Silex.

De Leeuw, Ronald. 2003. "Director, the Rijksmuseum, Ronald de Leeuw: Let's Get Together over Our Export Laws." *Art Newspaper,* no. 142 (December), 26.

Deleuze, Gilles. 1994. *Difference and Repetition.* Trans. Paul Patton. New York: Columbia University Press.

De Ros, Xon. 2002. "The Guggenheim Museum Bilbao: High Art as a Popular Culture." In *Constructing Identity in Contemporary Spain: Theoretical Debates and Cultural Practices,* ed. Jo Lavanyi, 280–93. Oxford: Oxford University Press.

Derrida, Jacques. 2003. "Following Theory." In *Life.after.theory,* ed. Michael Payne and John Schad, 1–51. London: Continuum.

Der Spiegel 2002. *Inside 9-11: What Really Happened.* New York: St. Martin's Press.

Dillon, Mick. 1998. "Criminalising Social and Political Violence Internationally." *Millennium* 27, no. 3:543–67.

Discover America Advocacy Campaign. 2007. "Unwelcoming USA Losing Tourists." Yahoo.com News. November 2.

Dobrzynski, Judith. 2000. "Hip versus Stately: The Tao of Two Museums." *New York Times.com,* February. Accessed May 18, 2008.

Doss, Erika. 1991. *Benton, Pollock and the Politics of Modernism: From Regionalism to Abstract Expressionism.* Chicago: University of Chicago Press.

Doty, Roxanne. 1996. *Imperial Encounters.* Minneapolis: University of Minnesota Press.

Dower, John. 1999. *Embracing Defeat: Japan in the Aftermath of World War II.* London: Penguin.

Drayton, Richard. 2005. "Shock, Awe and Hobbes Have Backfired on America's Neocons." *Guardian,* December 28, 26.

Dryzek, John. 1995. "Political and Ecological Communication." *Environmental Politics* 4, no. 4:13–30.

Duncan, Carol. 1992. "The MOMA's Hot Mamas." In Broude and Garrard 1992, 347–58.

———. 1995. *Civilizing Rituals: Inside Public Art Museums.* London: Routledge.

———. 1999. "From the Princely Gallery to the Public Art Museum: The Louvre Museum and the National Gallery, London." In Boswell and Evans 1999, 304–31. London: Routledge.

Dunlap, David W. 2004. "Defying Terror, Towers Are Wrapped in Glass." *International Herald Tribune*, September 7, 2.

Eagleton, Terry. 2003. *After Theory*. London: Allen Lane, Penguin.

———. 2005. *Holy Terror*. Oxford: Oxford University Press.

Edkins, Jenny. 2003. *Trauma and the Memory of Politics*. Cambridge: Cambridge University Press.

Edkins, Jenny, Veronique Pin-Fat, and Michael Shapiro, eds. *Sovereign Lives: Power in Global Politics*. London: Routledge.

Elderfield, John, ed. 1992. Preface to *Essays on Assemblage*, 7–9. New York: Museum of Modern Art.

———. 1994. Preface to *The Museum of Modern Art at Mid-Century: At Home and Abroad*, 6–11. New York: Museum of Modern Art.

Elkins, James. 2003. *Visual Culture: A Skeptical Introduction*. London: Routledge.

———. 2004. *Pictures and Tears*. New York: Routledge.

Elshtain, Jean Bethke. 1987. *Women and War*. New York: Basic Books.

Enloe, Cynthia. 1989. *Bananas, Beaches and Bases: Making Feminist Sense of International Relations*. London: Pandora Press.

———. 1993. *The Morning After: Sexual Politics at the End of the Cold War*. Berkeley and Los Angeles: University of California Press.

Evans, Graeme. 2003. "Hard-Branding the Cultural City—from Prado to Prada." *International Journal of Urban and Regional Research* 27, no. 2:417–40.

Evans, Jessica. 1999a. "Introduction: Nation and Representation." In Boswell and Evans 1999, 1–8.

———. 1999b. Introduction to part 4. In Boswell and Evans 1999, 365–70.

Falk, John H. 1998. "Visitors: Who Does, Who Doesn't and Why." *Museum News*, March–April.

Family Steering Committee for the 911 Independent Commission. 2002. "Questions Unanswered." www.911independentcommission.org/questions.html. Accessed August 14, 2007.

Featherstone, Mike. 1991. *Postmodernism and Consumer Culture*. London: Sage.

Filler, Martin. 2005. "Why the Ground Zero Design Is So Bad." *New York Review of Books,* February 24, 6–11.

Finley, M. I. 1981. *Economy and Society in Ancient Greece*. London: Chatto and Windus.

Finnemore, Martha, and Kathryn Sikkink. 1998. "International Norm Dynamics and Political Change." *International Organization* 52, no. 4:887–917.

Flanders, Judith. 2006. *Consuming Passions: Leisure and Pleasure in Victorian Britain*. London: HarperPress.

Foucault, Michel. 1966. *The Order of Things*. New York: Vintage Books.

———. 1983. *This Is Not a Pipe*. Berkeley and Los Angeles: University of California Press.

Franc, Helen. 1994. "The Early Years of the International Program and Council." In *The Museum of Modern Art at Mid-Century: At Home and Abroad*, ed. John Elderfield, 109–49. New York: Museum of Modern Art.

Franco-British Exhibition Official Guide. 1908. London.

Frascina, Francis. 1985. *Pollock and After: The Critical Debate.* London: Paul Chapman.

Freeland, Cynthia. 2003. *Art Theory: A Very Short Introduction.* Oxford: Oxford University Press.

Frost, Mervyn. 2003. "Tragedy, Ethics and International Relations." *International Relations* 17, no. 4:477–95.

Fuchs, Doris. 2005. "Commanding Heights? The Strength and Fragility of Business Power in Global Politics." *Millennium* 33, no. 3:771–801.

Fukuyama, Francis. 1989. "The End of History?" *National Interest* 16, no. 3:3–18.

———. 1992. *The End of History and the Last Man.* London: Penguin Books, 1992.

Gablik, Suzi. 2004. *Has Modernism Failed?* London: Thames and Hudson.

Gadamer, Hans-Georg. 1999. *Truth and Method.* Ed. J. Wiensheimer and D. Marshall, trans. New York: Continuum.

Gauguin, Paul. 1972. *Noa Noa.* Ed. and trans. Nicholas Wadley. London: Jonathan Griffin.

Gehry, Frank. 2000. Interview by John Tulsa for BBC Radio 3 series *Great Artistic Figures.* May 7, BBC Archives.

Gellner, Ernst. 1983. *Nations and Nationalism.* Oxford: Blackwell.

George, Donny. 2004. Quoted in Matthew Campbell, "Iraq's Culture Cops Go Hunting Looters." *Guardian*, January 11, 29.

Getty, J. Paul. 1976. *As I See It.* London: W. H. Auden.

Getty Museum. 2005. http://www.getty.edu/visit/places/architecture.html. Accessed December 14, 2005.

Gibson, Owen. 2006. "Saatchi Site Seeks Arctic Monkeys of Art World." *Guardian*, May 25, 11.

Gillespie, Angus. 1999. *Twin Towers: The Life of New York City's World Trade Center.* New York: New American Library Trade.

Gillman, Derek. 2006. *The Idea of Cultural Heritage.* Leicester, UK: Institute of Art and Law.

Glancey, Jonathan. 2004. "'You've Got to Have Faith.'" *Guardian, G2,* August 4, 8–9.

———. 2005. "In Case of War: Nominations Sought for List of Cultural Treasures to Be Saved at All Costs." *Guardian*, September 4, 3.

———. 2007. "Acropolis Now." *Guardian, G2,* December 3, 23–25.

Glanz, James, and Eric Lipton. 2003. *City in the Sky: The Rise and Fall of the World Trade Center.* New York: Times Book, Henry Holt.

Glas, Eduardo Jorge. 1997. *Bilbao's Modern Business Elite.* Reno: University of Nevada Press.

Goodnough, Robert. 1951. "Pollock Paints a Picture." *Art News,* May, 38–41, 60–61.

Gordenker, Leon, and Thomas Weiss, eds. 1996. *NGOs, the UN and Global Governance.* Boulder, CO: Lynne Rienner.

Graham, Brian, G. J. Ashworth, and J. E. Tunbridge. 2000. *A Geography of Heritage: Power, Culture and Economy.* London: Arnold.

Greenberg, Clement. 1971. Art and Culture: Critical Essays. Boston: Beacon Press.

———. 1985. "Avant-Garde and Kitsch." In Frascina 1985, 21–23.

Greenfield, Jeanette. 1995. *The Return of Cultural Treasures,* 2nd ed. London: Cambridge University Press.

Guerilla Girls. 1995. *Confessions of the Guerilla Girls.* London: Pandora.

Guilbaut, Serge. 1983. *How New York Stole the Idea of Modern Art: Abstract Expressionism, Freedom, and the Cold War.* Trans. Arthur Goldhammer. Chicago: University of Chicago Press.

Guzzini, Stefano. 1993. "Structural Power: The Limits of Neorealist Power Analysis." *International Organization* 47, no. 3:443–78.

Hall, Lee. 2000. *Elaine and Bill: Portrait of a Marriage; The Lives of Willem and Elaine de Kooning.* New York: Cooper Square Press.

Hameed, Abdul Aziz. 2005. Quoted in "Museums Closed and Looting Rampant." *Art Newspaper,* no. 155 (February), 4.

Hansen, Lene. 2006. *Security as Practice: Discourse Analysis and the Bosnian War.* London: Routledge.

Harbison, Robert. 1997. *Eccentric Spaces.* New York: Alfred A. Knopf.

Harootunian, Harry. 2004. "Theory's Empire: Reflections on a Vocation for *Critical Theory*." *Critical Inquiry* 30, no. 2:396–402.

Haskell, Francis. 2000. *The Ephemeral Museum: Old Master Paintings and the Rise of the Art Exhibition.* New Haven: Yale University Press.

Hauptman, William. 1973. "The Suppression of Art in the McCarthy Decade." *Artforum* 12, no. 2: 48.

Heinich, Nathalie. 1988. "The Pompidou Centre and Its Public: The Limits of a Utopian Site." In *The Museum Time-Machine: Putting Cultures on Display,* ed. Robert Lumley, 199–212. London: Routledge.

Held, David. 2003. "Cosmopolitanism: Globalisation Tamed?" *Review of International Studies* 29, no. 4:465–80.

———. 1995. *Democracy and the Global Order: From the Modern State to Cosmopolitan Governance.* Cambridge: Polity Press.

Henderson, Gregory. 1983. "Korean Art in Western Collections: 6 and 7, The Collection of the Gregory Hendersons." *Korean Culture* 4, no. 3:3–15 and no. 4:28–37.

Heywood, Paul. 1995. *The Government and Politics of Spain.* New York: St. Martin's Press.

Hickey, Dave. 1997. *Air Guitar: Essays on Art and Democracy.* Los Angeles: Art Issues Press.

Higgins, Charlotte. 2005. "Plea for Titian: National Gallery Fails to Win Lottery Aid to Keep £66.5m Masterpiece." *Guardian,* September 6, 7.

———. 2006. "Buried Treasure." *Guardian, G2,* April 20, 6–11.

Hinsley, Curtis. 1991. "The World as Marketplace: Commodification of the Exotic at the World's Columbian Exposition, Chicago, 1893." In *Exhibiting Cultures: The Poetics and Politics of Museum Display,* ed. Ivan Karp and Steven D. Lavine, 344–65. Washington, DC: Smithsonian Institution Press.

Hitchens, Christopher. 1998. *The Elgin Marbles: Should They Be Returned to Greece?* London: Verso.

Holo, Seima Reuben. 1999. *Beyond the Prado: Museums and Identity in Democratic Spain.* Liverpool, UK: Liverpool University Press.

Hooper-Greenhill, Eilean. 1994. *Museums and the Shaping of Knowledge.* London: Routledge.

Horgan, John. 1997. *The End of Science: Facing the Limits of Knowledge in the Twilight of the Scientific Age.* New York: Broadway Books.

Hornby, Joan. 1988. "The Korean Collection at the National Museum of Denmark." *Korean Culture* 9, no. 4:14–22.

Hoving, Thomas. 2005. "Getting It Right at the Getty." www.latimes.com, September 27. Accessed October 1, 2005.

Howard, Michael. 2006. "Saviour of Iraq's Antiquities Flees to Syria." *Guardian*, August 26, 17.

Hubbard, Phil. 1996. "Urban Design and City Regeneration: Social Representations of Entrepreneurial Landscapes." *Urban Studies* 33, no. 8:1441–61.

Hughes, Robert. 1991. *The Shock of the New*. New York: McGraw-Hill.

Hume, David.1969 (1757). "The Standard of Taste." In Tillman and Cahn 1969, 115–30.

Hunt, Tristan. 2005. "Greedy Old Masters." *Guardian*, August 12, 21.

Huntington, Samuel. 1996. *The Clash of Civilizations and the Remaking of World Order*. New York: Simon and Schuster.

Hutchings, Kimberly. 1999. *International Political Theory*. London: Sage.

Inayatullah, Naeem. 2003. "Present Dangers." *Borderlands e-Journal* 2, no. 2. http://www.borderlandsejournal.adelaide.edu.au/issues/vol2no2.html.

Inayatuallah, Naeem, and David L. Blaney. 2004. *International Relations and the Problem of Difference*. London: Routledge.

International Freedom Center. 2005. "Content and Governance Report." September 23. New York: IFC.

Jabri, Vivienne. 1998. "Restyling the Subject of Responsibility in International Relations." *Millennium* 27, no. 3:591–611.

———. 2003. "Pinter, Radical Critique and Politics." *Borderlands e-Journal* 2, no. 2. http://www.borderlandsejournal.adelaide.edu.au/issues/vol2no2.html.

Jabri, Vivienne, and Eleanor O'Gorman, eds. 1999. *Women, Culture and International Relations*. Boulder, CO: Lynne Rienner.

Jackson, Richard. 2005. *Writing the War on Terrorism: Language, Politics, and Counter-Terrorism*. Manchester, UK: Manchester University Press.

Jacobsen, Annie. 2004. "Could It Happen Again?" *Sunday Times*, July 25, sec. 4, 1–2.

———. 2005. *Terror in the Skies: Why 9/11 Could Happen Again*. Dallas: Spence Publishing.

Jameson, Frederic. 1991. *Postmodernism, or, The Cultural Logic of Late Capitalism*. Durham, NC: Duke University Press.

Januszczak, Waldemar. 2005. "The Picture of Health?" *Sunday Times Culture Magazine*, November 27, 17.

Jencks, Charles. 2002. Quoted in "No Logo, No Global?" *Art Newspaper*, no. 129 (October).

Jenkins, Ian. 1992. *Archaeologists and Aesthetes in the Sculpture Galleries of the British Museum, 1800–1939*. London: British Museum Press.

———. 2001. *Cleaning Controversy: The Parthenon Sculptures 1811–1939*. British Museum Occasional Papers 146. London.

Jesse, Neal, and Kristen Williams. 2004. *Identity and Institutions: Conflict Reduction in Divided Societies*. Albany: State University of New York Press.

Jones, Anny Brooksbank. 2003. "Challenging the Seductions of the Bilbao Guggenheim." *International Journal of Iberian Studies* 16, no. 3:159–65.

Jones, Charles. 1998. *E. H. Carr and International Relations: A Duty to Lie*. Cambridge: Cambridge University Press.

Jones, Jonathan. 2003. "I Have Seen the Future and It Bounces." *Guardian*, November 11, 12–13.

————. 2006. "The Shame and the Glory." *Guardian Weekend Magazine*, September 2, 28–33.

————. 2007. "Tomb Raiders." *Guardian, G2*, November 15, 23–26.

Kagan, Robert. 2003. *Paradise and Power: America and Europe in the New World Order*. London: Atlantic Books.

Kant, Immanuel. 1790. *The Critique of Judgment*. Trans. James Creed Meredith. Oxford: Clarendon Press, 1969.

Kantor, Sylvia Gordon. 1999. *Alfred H. Barr Jr. and the Intellectual Origins of the Museum of Modern Art*. Cambridge, MA: MIT Press.

Kaprow, Allan. 1993. *Essays on the Blurring of Art and Life*. Berkeley and Los Angeles: University of California Press.

Keating, M. 1995. "Europeanism and Regionalism." In *The European Union and the Regions,* ed. B. Jones and M. Keating, 1–22. Oxford, Clarendon Press.

Keating, Michael, and Monika de Frantz. 2003. "Culture-Led Strategies for Urban Regeneration: A Comparative Perspective on Bilbao." *International Journal of Iberian Studies* 16, no. 3:187–94.

Kennan, George. 1956. *International Exchange in the Arts*. New York: International Council of the Museum of Modern Art.

Kimmelman, Michael. 1994. "Revisiting the Revisionists: The Modern, Its Critics, and the Cold War." In *The Museum of Modern Art at Mid-Century: At Home and Abroad,* ed. John Elderfield, 38–55. New York: Museum of Modern Art.

————. 2004. "The Cold War over the Arts." Review of *The Dancer Defects,* by David Caute. *New York Review of Books* no. 51, May 27, 9. www.nybooks.com/articles/17118. Accessed August 5, 2007.

————. 2006. "Is It All Loot? Tackling the Antiquities Problem." *New York Times,* March 29.

Kleinfelder, Karen. 1993. *The Artist, His Model, Her Image, His Gaze*. Chicago: University of Chicago Press.

Knight, Christopher. 1994. "These Are the Only Women Running Major Art Museums in the United States. Can You Believe It?" *Los Angeles Times,* March 27.

Kodat, Catherine Gunther. 2004. "High Art in Low Times." *Boston Review* 29, October/November. http://bostonreview.net. Accessed August 5, 2007.

Kolker, Robert. 2005. "The Grief Police." *New York,* November, 28.

Kopper, Hilmar. 1999. "1 + 1 = 3." Essay on the Deutsche Guggenheim Berlin Web site, http://www.deutsche-bank-kunst.com/guggenheim/e/.

Kozloff, Max. 1973. "American Painting during the Cold War." *Artforum* 11, no. 9: 43–54.

Kramer, Hilton. 1955. "Exhibiting the Family of Man: The World's Most Talked-About Photographs." *Commentary,* October, 366–67.

Krens, Thomas. 1999. Interview with *Connaissance des Arts. Connaissance des Arts,* special issue on Guggenheim Bilbao, 1999: 14–20.

————. 2000a. "Partnership in Patronage." An essay appearing on the Deutsche Guggenheim Berlin Web site, http://www.deutsche-bankkunst.com/guggenheim/e/.

————. 2000b. "Developing the Museum for the 21st Century: A Vision Becomes a Reality." In *Visionary Clients for New Architecture,* ed. Peter Noever. New York: Prestel.

Kuh, Katharine. 2006. *My Love Affair with Modern Art: Behind the Scenes with A Legendary Curator.* Ed. Avis Berman. New York: Arcade Publishing.

Kurlansky, Mark. 2000. *The Basque History of the World.* London: Vintage.

Kuspit, Donald. 2000. *The Rebirth of Painting in the Twentieth Century.* Cambridge: Cambridge University Press.

————. 2004. *The End of Art.* Cambridge: Cambridge University Press.

Langewische, William. 2003. *American Ground: Unbuilding the World Trade Center.* New York: North Point Press.

Le Carré, John. 2001. "The War That Came In from the Cold." *Australian,* October 20, 7, 10.

Leggio, James. 1992. "Robert Rauschenberg's *Bed* and the Symbolism of the Body. *Essays on Assemblage,* ed. John Elderfield, 79–117. New York: Museum of Modern Art.

Leja, Michael. 1993. *Reframing Abstract Expressionism: Subjectivity and Painting in the 1940s.* New Haven: Yale University Press.

Lewison, Jeremy. 1999. *Interpreting Pollock.* London: Tate Gallery Publishing.

Libeskind, Daniel. 2002. Roundtable on the Future of Museums: "No Logo, No Global?" *Art Newspaper,* no. 129 (October), 19.

————. 2004. *Breaking Ground.* London: John Murray.

Lipschutz, Ronnie, and K. Conca, eds. 1994. *The State and Social Power in Global Environmental Politics.* New York: Columbia University Press.

Lisle, Debbie. 2007) "Benevolent Patriotism: Art, Dissent and the American Effect." *Security Dialogue* 38, no. 2:233–50.

Lotringer, Sylvere. 2005. "The Piracy of Art." In *The Conspiracy of Art,* by Jean Baudrillard, ed. Sylvere Lotringer, 9–21. Foreign Agents Series. New York: Semiotext(e).

Lowry, Glenn. 2004. Speaking in "Round Table Discussion." In Cuno 2004, 171–201.

Luke, Timothy. 2002. *Museum Politics.* Minneapolis: University of Minnesota Press.

Lukes, Steven. 2005. "Power and the Battle for Hearts and Minds." *Millennium* 33, no. 3:495–522.

Lynes, Russell. 1973. *Good Old Modern: An Intimate Portrait of the Museum of Modern Art.* New York: Atheneum.

Lynton, Norbert. 1989. *The Story of Modern Art.* London: Phaidon.

MacGinty, Roger. 2004. "Looting in the Context of Violent Conflict: A Reconceptualisation and Typology." *Third World Quarterly* 25, no. 5.

MacGregor, Neil. 2004a. "Not Only of the World, but for the World." *Art Newspaper* no. 143 (January), 22.

————. 2004b. "The Whole World in Our Hands." *Guardian Review,* July 24, 4–6.

————. 2003. "A Pentecost in Trafalgar Square." In Cuno 2004, 27–48.

Maleuvre, Didier. 1999. *Museum Memories: History, Technology, Art.* Stanford, CA: Stanford University Press.

Marandel, Jean-Patrice, and George Goldner. 2003. Quoted in "Sharing Is the Winning Motto." *Art Newspaper,* no. 142, December, 25.

Marchand, Marianne, and Ann Sisson Runyan, eds. 2000. *Gender and Global Restructuring: Sightings, Sites and Resistances.* Boulder, CO: Lynne Rienner.

Mari-Molinero, Clare, and Angel Smith, eds. 1996. *Nationalism and the Nation in the Iberian Peninsula: Competing and Conflicting Identities.* Oxford: Berg.

Markovits, Andrei. 2007. *Uncouth Nation: Why Europe Dislikes America*. Princeton, NJ: Princeton University Press.

Masters, Cristina, and Elizabeth Dauphinee. 2007. *The Logic of Biopower and the War on Terror*. London: Palgrave.

Mattern, Janice Bially. 2005. "Why 'Soft Power' Isn't So Soft: Representational Force and the Sociolinguistic Construction of Attraction in World Politics." *Millennium* 33, no. 3:583–612.

Maurice, Clare, and Richard Turnor. 1992. "The Export Licensing Rules in the United Kingdom and the Waverley Criteria." *International Journal of Cultural Property* 1.

McCann, David. 2003. *Dancer: A Novel*. New York: Metropolitan Books.

McCarthy, Rory, and Maeev Kennedy. 2005. "The Wrecking of Babylon: U.S.-Led Forces Leave a Trail of Destruction and Contamination in Architectural Site of World Importance." *Guardian*, January 15, 1.

McClellan, Andrew, ed. 2003a. Introduction to *Art and Its Publics: Museum Studies at the Millennium*, xiii–xviii. Oxford: Blackwell Publishers.

McClellan, Andrew. 2003b. "A Brief History of the Art Museum Public." In *Art and Its Publics: Museum Studies at the Millennium*, 1–49. Oxford: Blackwell Publishers.

McKibben, Bill. 2001. *The End of Nature*. New York: Peter Smith.

McKillop, Beth. 1992. *Korean Art and Design*. London: Victoria and Albert Museum.

McMahon, Barbara. 2005. "Getty Museum Knowingly Bought Archaeological Treasures Stolen from Italy, Investigation Claims." *Guardian*, September 27, 15.

McNeill, D. 2000. "McGuggenisation? National Identity and Globalisation in the Basque Country." *Political Geography* 19, no. 4:473–94.

McQueen, Alison. 2001. "Gendered Encounters." Review of *Encounters: New Art from Old*, by Richard Morphet. *Art Journal*, June 22, 103–4.

Mearsheimer, John. 2001. *The Tragedy of Great Power Politics*. New York: W. W. Norton.

Medhurst, Ken. 1982. "Basques and Basque Nationalism." In *National Separatism*, ed. C. H.Williams, 236–37. Vancouver: University of British Columbia.

Melikian, Sourcen. 2003. "National Gallery Fights for Raphael." *International Herald Tribune*, August 2–3, 7.

Medrano, Juan Diez. 1995. *Divided Nations: Class, Politics, and Nationalism in the Basque Country*. Ithaca, NY: Cornell University Press.

Merryman, John. 1986a. "Two Ways of Thinking about Cultural Property." *American Journal of International Law* 80: 831–53.

———. 1986b. "Who Owns the Elgin Marbles?" *ARTnews*, no. 85 (September), 107.

Millard, Rosie. 2002. *The Tastemakers: U.K. Art Now*. London: Scribner.

Millennium. 2001. Special issue, Image and Narratives in World Politics, vol. 30, no. 3.

———. 2006. Special issue on the sublime, vol. 34, no. 3.

———. 2007. Special issue, "Theory of the 'International' Today," vol. 35, no. 3.

Miller, Dorothy. 1946. *Fourteen Americans*. New York: Museum of Modern Art.

Mitchell, W. J. T. 2004. "Medium Theory: Preface to the 2003 *Critical Inquiry* Symposium." *Critical Inquiry* 30, no. 2:324–35.

Moon, Katherine. 1997. *Sex among Allies: Military Prostitution in US-Korea Relations*. New York: Columbia University Press.

Morphet, Richard. 2000. "Richard Hamilton." In *Encounters: New Art from Old*, 142–51. London: National Gallery.

Moss, Stephen. 2005. "The Tycoon Who Wants to Save the World." *Guardian, G2*, September 23, 9–11.

Mouffe, Chantal. 1993. *The Return of the Political.* London: Verso.

Moulaert, Frank, Arantxa Rodriquez, and Erik Swyngedouw. 2003. *The Globalized City.* Oxford: Oxford University Press.

Moustakas, John. 1989. "Group Rights in Cultural Property." *Cornell Law Review* 74.

Mulvey, Laura. 1989. *Visual and Other Pleasures.* Bloomington: Indiana University Press.

Nagel, Susan. 2004. *Mistress of the Elgin Marbles: A Biography of Mary Nisbet, Countess of Elgin.* New York: William Morrow.

Noever, Peter. 1993. *The End of Architecture.* New York: Prestel.

Nye, Joseph, Jr. 2004. *Soft Power: The Means to Success in World Politics.* New York: Public Affairs Press.

Odysseos, Louiza. 2001. "Laughing Matters: Peace, Democracy and the Challenge of the Comic Narrative." *Millennium* 30, no. 3:709–32.

Oguibe, Olu. 1994. "A Brief Note on Internationalism." In *Global Visions: Towards a New Internationalism in the Visual Arts,* ed. Jean Fisher, 50–59. London: Kala Press.

———. 1995. *Uzo Egonu: An African Artist in the West.* London: Kala Press.

———. 2004. *The Culture Game.* Minneapolis: University of Minnesota Press.

Orford, Anne. 2003. *Reading Humanitarian Intervention: Human Rights and the Use of Force in International Law.* Cambridge: Cambridge University Press.

Orton, Fred, and Griselda Pollock. 1996. *Avant-Gardes and Partisans Reviewed.* Manchester, UK: Manchester University Press.

Payne, Stanley. 1975. *Basque Nationalism.* Reno: University of Nevada Press.

Peaceful Tomorrows. 2004. "Mission." www.peacefultomorrows.org/mission.html. Accessed August 14, 2007.

Pears, Ian. 1988. *The Discovery of Painting: The Growth of Interest in the Arts in England, 1680–1768.* New Haven: Yale University Press.

Penttinen, Elina. 2007. *Globalization, Prostitution and Sex-Trafficking.* London: Routledge.

Phillips, Christopher. 1981. *Steichen at War.* New York: Harry N. Abrams.

———. 1984. "In the Family Way." *Afterimage* 11, no. 10:10–13.

Plaza, Beatriz. 2006. "The Return on Investment of the Guggenheim Museum Bilbao." *International Journal of Urban and Regional Research* 30, no. 2:452–67.

Poggi, Christine. 1992. *In Defiance of Painting: Cubism, Futurism, and the Invention of Collage.* New Haven: Yale University Press.

Pogrebin, Robin. 2006. "Alice Greenwald, 9/11 Museum Director, Girds for Challenge," *New York Times,* April 22. http: www.nytimes.com/2006/04/22. Accessed February 1, 2007.

Polcari, Stephen. 1993. *Abstract Expressionism and the Modern Experience.* Cambridge: Cambridge University Press.

Pollock, Griselda. 1992. "The Gaze and the Look: Women with Binoculars; A Question of Difference." In *Dealing with Degas: Representations of Women and the Politics of Vision,* ed. Richard Kendall and Griselda Pollock, 106–30. New York: Universal.

Pommier, Edouard. 1989. *Le problème du musée à la veille de la Révolution.* Montargis: Musée Girodet.

Poovey, Mary. 2004. "For What It's Worth . . ." *Critical Inquiry* 30, no. 2:429–33.

Portal, Jane. 2000. *Korean Art and Archaeology.* London: Thames and Hudson.

Preziosi, Donald. 1996. "Collecting/Museums." In *Critical Terms in Art History,* ed. Robert Nelson and Richard Shiff, 407–18 . Chicago: University of Chicago Press.

Prior, Nick. 2002. *Museums and Modernity: Art Galleries and the Making of Modern Culture.* Oxford: Berg.

———. 2003. "Having One's Tate and Eating It: Transformations of the Museum in a Hypermodern Era." In *Art and Its Publics: Museum Studies at the Millennium,* ed. Andrew McClellan, 51–74. Oxford: Blackwell Publishing.

Rappolt, Mark. 2003. "The Medium Is the Message." *Modern Painters,* Autumn, 26–29.

Rawsthorn, Alice. 2006. "Private Art on Public View." *Guardian,* May 24, 28.

Rice, Danielle. 2003. "Museums: Theory, Practice, and Illusion." In *Art and Its Publics: Museum Studies at the Millennium,* ed. Andrew McClellan, 77–95. London: Blackwell.

Richmond, Yale. 2003. *Cultural Exchange and the Cold War: Raising the Iron Curtain.* College Park: Pennsylvania State University Press.

Robinowitz, Dorothy. 2004. "The 9/11 Widows." *Wall Street Journal,* April 14, A14.

Robins, Kevin. 1999. "Tradition and Translation: National Culture in Its Global Context." In Boswell and Evans 1999, 15–32.

Robson, Eric. 2006. *The Border Line.* London: Francis Lincoln.

Roe, Jae-Ryung. 2001. *Contemporary Korean Art.* Canberra: Craftsman House.

Rogers, Josh. 2006. "An Underground Memorial Loses Some of Its Upside." *Downtown Express: The Newspaper of Lower Manhattan,* March 10–16, 1, 6.

Rosenberg, Harold. 1952. "The American Action Painters." *Art News,* December, 22–23, 48–50.

Rosenblum, Robert. 1982. "A Curator's Choice 1942–1963: A Tribute to Dorothy Miller." New York: Rosa Esman Gallery.

Rubin, William. 1996. "Reflections on Picasso and Portraiture." In *Picasso and Portraiture,* ed. William Rubin, 13–109. New York: Museum of Modern Art.

Russell, John Malcolm. 1997. *From Nineveh to New York.* New Haven: Yale University Press.

Ruzicka, Joseph, ed. 1992. "Transcript of the Symposium [The Art of Assemblage]." In *Essays on Assemblage,* ed. John Elderfield, 124–50. New York: Museum of Modern Art.

Ryan, James. 1997. *Picturing Empire: Photography and the Visualization of the British Empire.* London: Reaktion Books.

Rykwert, Joseph. 2000. *The Seduction of Place: The City in the Twenty-First Century.* New York: Pantheon Books.

Saatchi, Charles. 2003. "Museums and Contemporary Art: The 'White Cube' Is Dead." *Art Newspaper,* no. 141, November, 24.

Said, Edward. 1978. *Orientalism.* New York: Vintage.

Saltz, Jerry. 2006. "One Year After: Is MOMA a Madman That Thinks It Is King?" *Modern Painters,* December 2005–January 2006, 40–41.

Sandeen, Eric. 1995. *Picturing an Exhibition: The Family of Man and 1950s America.* Albuquerque: University of New Mexico Press.

Saunders, Frances Stonor. 2000. *The Cultural Cold War: The CIA and the World of Arts and Letters.* New York: New Press.

Schneider, Keith. 2006. "Adding Profits to the Gift Shop." *New York Times,* March 29, 31.

Schubert, Karsten. 2000. *The Curator's Egg: The Evolution of the Museum Concept from the French Revolution to the Present Day*. London: One-Off Press.

Sekula, Allan. 1983. "The Traffic in Photographs." In *Modernism and Modernity*, ed. Benjamin Buchloh, Serge Guilbaut, and David Solkin, 121–54. Halifax: Press of the Nova Scotia College of Art and Design.

Serota, Nicholas. 2000. *Experience or Interpretation: The Dilemma of Museums of Modern Art*. London: Thames and Hudson.

———. 2003. "Tate Director, Nicholas Serota: Recent Art Is Patrimony Too." *Art Newspaper*, no. 142 (December), 23–24.

Settis, Salvatore. 2004. "History in the Making." *Guardian*, January 19, 15.

Severson, Kim. 2006. "Go for the van Gogh, but Stay for the Smoked Eel with Jalapeno." *New York Times*, March 29, 30.

Shapcott, Richard. 2002. "Cosmopolitan Conversations: Habermas, Gadamer and the Cosmopolitan Project." *Global Society* 16, no. 3:221–43.

Shapiro, Michael, and Hayward Alker, eds. 1996. *Challenging Boundaries: Global Flows, Territorial Identities*. Minneapolis: University of Minnesota Press.

Shields, Stephanie. 2002. *Speaking from the Heart: Gender and the Social Meaning of Emotion*. Cambridge: Cambridge University Press.

Shiner, Larry. 2003. *The Invention of Art: A Cultural History*. Chicago: University of Chicago Press.

Shorto, Russell. 2005. *The Island at the Centre of the World: The Untold Story of Dutch Manhattan and the Founding of New York*. London: Black Swan.

Simon, Robert. 2000. "Front Matters." Review of *The Cultural Cold War*, by Frances Stonor Saunders. *Artforum*, Summer, 1–3. Available at findarticles.com. Accessed April 8, 2007.

Sjoberg, Laura. 2006. *Gender, Justice, and the Wars in Iraq: A Feminist Reformulation of Just War Theory*. New York: Lexington Books.

Smith, Anthony. 1999. "History and Modernity: Reflections on the Theory of Nationalism." In Boswell and Evans 1999, 45–60.

Smith, Judith, ed. 1998. *Arts of Korea*. Exhibition catalog. New York: Metropolitan Museum of Art.

Smith, Roberta. 2000. "Memo to Art Museums: Don't Give Up on Art." *New York Times*, December 3, sec. 2, p. 1.

Smith, Steve. 2003. "Singing Our World into Existence: International Relations Theory and September 11." Presidential Address for the International Studies Association, Portland, Oregon, February.

Solomon, Deborah. 2002. "Is the Go-Go Guggenheim Going, Going?" *New York Times Magazine*, June 30, 36.

Solomon-Godeau, Abigail. 1992. "Going Native: Paul Gauguin and the Invention of Primitivist Modernism." In Broude and Garrard 1992, 313–30.

Solway, Diane. 1998. *Nureyev: His Life*. London: Phoenix.

Staniszewski, Mary Anne. 1998. "Exhibition as National Covenant: 'The Road to Victory.'" In *The Power of Display: A History of Exhibition Installations at the Museum of Modern Art*, 207–60. Cambridge, MA: MIT Press.

Steichen, Edward. 1955. *The Family of Man*. Prologue by Carl Sandburg. Exhibit catalog. Museum of Modern Art, New York. New York: Maco Magazine Corp.

Sylvester, Christine. 1994a. *Feminist International Relations in a Postmodern Era*. Cambridge: Cambridge University Press.

———. 1994b. "Empathetic Cooperation: A Feminist Method for IR." *Millennium* 23, no. 2:315–36.

———. 1995. "African and Western Feminisms: World-Traveling the Tendencies and Possibilities." *Signs: Journal of Women in Culture and Society* 20, no. 4:941–69.

———. 1996. "Picturing the Cold War: An Eye Graft/Art Graft." *Alternatives* 21, no. 4:393–418.

———. 1998. "Handmaids' Tales of Washington Power: The Abject and the Real Kennedy White House." *Body and Society* 4, no. 3:39–66.

———. 1999a. "(Sur)real Internationalism: Emigres, Native Sons and Ethical War Creations." *Alternatives: Social Transformation and Humane Governance* 24, no. 2:219–63.

———. 1999b. "Development Studies and Postcolonial Studies: Disparate Tales of the 'Third World.'" *Third World Quarterly* 20, no. 4:703–21.

———. 2001. "Art, Abstraction, and International Relations." *Millennium* 30, no. 3:535–54.

———. 2002a. *Feminist International Relations: An Unfinished Journey.* Cambridge: Cambridge University Press.

———. 2002b. "Internations of Feminism and International Relations." In Sylvester 2002a, 287–316. ———. 2002c. "Picturing the Cold War: An Eye Graft/Art Graft." In Sylvester 2002a, 122–46.

———. 2003. "Global Development Dramaturgies/Gender Stagings." *Borderlands* 2, no. 2. www.borderlandsejournal.adelaide.edu.au/issues/vol2no2.html.

———. 2004. "Fictional Development Sovereignties." In Edkins, Pin-Fat, and Shapiro 2004, 141–61.

———. 2005. "The Art of War/The War Question in (Feminist) IR." *Millennium* 33, no. 3:855–78.

———. 2006a. "Bare Life as a Development/Postcolonial Problematic." *Geographical Journal* 172, no. 1:66–77.

———. 2006b. "Bringing Art/Museums to Feminist International Relations." In *Feminist Methodologies for International Relations,* ed. Brooke Ackerly, Maria Stern, and Jacqui True, 201–20. Cambridge: Cambridge University Press.

———. 2007a. "Whither the International at the End of IR?" *Millennium* 35, no. 3:551–73.

———. 2007b, "Anatomy of a Footnote." *Security Dialogue* 38, no. 4:547–58.

Sylvester, David, with Clement Greenberg. 1950. "The European View of American Art." *Nation*, November 25, 490–93.

Szarkowski, John. 1994. "'The Family of Man,'" In *The Museum of Modern Art at Mid-Century: At Home and Abroad,* ed. John Elderfield, 12–37. New York: Museum of Modern Art.

Tadiar, Neferti Zina M. 1998. "Prostituted Filipinas and the Crisis of Philippine Culture." *Millennium* 27, no. 4:927–54.

Taylor, Brandon. 2004. *Collage: The Making of Modern Art.* London: Thames and Hudson.

Taylor, Matthew, Josh Spero, and Charlotte Higgins. 2007. "Prices Soar As World's Super-Rich Invade London Art Market." *Guardian*, June 23, 14.

Thomas, Nicolas. 2004. *Discoveries: The Voyages of Captain Cook.* London: Penguin.

Thompson, David. 2004. "Death of the Gallery." *Guardian*, April 15, 23.

Tickner, Ann. 1988. "Hans Morgenthau's Principles of Political Realism: A Feminist Reformulation." *Millennium* 17, no. 3:429–40.

———. 1992. *Gender in International Relations: Feminist Perspectives on Achieving Global Security*. New York: Columbia University Press.

Tillman, Frank, and Steven Cahn, eds. 1969. *Philosophy of Art and Aesthetics: From Plato to Wittgenstein*. New York: Harper and Row.

Venturi, Robert, Denise Scott Brown, and Steven Izenour. 1972. *Learning from Las Vegas*. Cambridge, MA: MIT Press.

Vidarte, Juan Ignacio. 1999. Foreword to *Guggenheim Bilbao*, special issue of *Connaisannce des Arts*: 4–11.

Vidler, Anthony. 2000. *Warped Space: Art, Architecture, and Anxiety in Modern Culture*. Cambridge, MA: MIT Press.

Virilio, Paul. 2003. *Art and Fear*. Trans. Julie Rose. London: Continuum.

Wallach, Alan. 2000. "Class Rites in the Age of the Blockbuster." *Harvard Design Magazine* 11, Summer: 48–54.

Watson, Peter. 1992. *From Manet to Manhattan: The Rise of the Modern Art Market*. London: Hutchison.

Wells, H. G. 1908. *The War in the Air*. London: Harmondsworth.

Wheen, Francis. 2004. *How Mumbo-Jumbo Conquered the World: A Short History of Modern Delusions*. London: Fourth Estate.

Williams, Sharon. 1978. *The International and National Protection of Movable Cultural Property: A Comparative Study*. Dobbs Ferry, NY: Oceana Publications.

Wood, James N. 2004. "The Authorities of the American Art Museum." In Cuno 2004, 103–28.

Woodruff, Paul, trans. 1993. *Thucydides: On Justice, Power, and Human Nature*. Indianapolis: Hackett.

Woolf, Marie. 2007. "Britain to Woo World with First Cultural Envoy." *Sunday Times,* December 30, 4.

Wright, Patrick. 1999. "Trafficking in History." In Boswell and Evans 1999, 115–50.

Wu, Chin-tao. 2002. *Privatising Culture: Corporate Art Intervention since the 1980s*. London: Verso.

Wullschlager, Jackie. 2003. "Driven to Abstraction." *Financial Times*, November 1–2, W7.

Zan, Luca. 2000. "Management and the British Museum." *Museum Management and Curatorship* 18, no. 3:221–70.

Zelevansky, Lynn. 1994. "Dorothy Miller's 'Americans,' 1942–63." In *The Museum of Modern Art at Mid-Century: At Home and Abroad,* ed. John Elderfield, 57–107. New York: Museum of Modern Art.

Zulaika, Joseba. 1997. *Crónica de una seducción: El museo Guggenheim Bilbao*. Madrid: Editorial Nerea)

———. 1999. "'Miracle in Bilbao': Basques in the Casino of Capitalism." In *Basque Cultural Studies,* ed. William Douglass, Carmelo Urza, Linda White, Joseba Zulaika, 262–74. Reno: University of Nevada.

———. 2003. "In Love with 'Puppy': Flowers, Architecture, Art and the Art of Irony." *International Journal of Iberian Studies* 16, no. 3:145–58.

Index

MEDIA_{and}POWER

David L. Paletz, series editor

Paradigm Publishers is proud to announce a new book series that publishes work uniting media studies with studies of power.

In keeping with Paradigm's mission, the series is innovative and original. It features books that challenge, even transcend, conventional disciplinary boundaries, construing both media and power in the broadest possible terms. At the same time, books in the series are designed to fit into several different types of college courses: in political science, public policy, communication, journalism, media, history, film, sociology, anthropology, and cultural studies.

Intended for the scholarly, text, and trade markets, the series should attract authors and inspire and provoke readers. Series editor David L. Paletz is Professor of Political Science and Director of the Film/Video/Digital Program at Duke University, and former editor of *Political Communication*. He is known for his research on media and power and his encouragement of original work from others.

Published in the Series

Spinner in Chief: How Presidents Sell Their Policies and Themselves, Stephen J. Farnsworth

The Age of Oprah: Cultural Icon for the Neoliberal Era, Janice Peck

Art/Museums: International Relations Where You Least Expect It, Christine Sylvester

Mousepads, Shoeleather and Hope: Lessons from the Howard Dean Campaign for the Future of Internet Politics, Zephyr Teachout and Thomas Streeter, et al.

Forthcoming in the Series

From Cronkite to Colbert: The Evolution of Broadcast News, Geoffrey Baym

Creative Destruction: Modern Media and the End of the Citizen, Andrew Calabrese

Media and Conflict: Escalating Evil, Cees J. Hamelink

Netroots: Online Progressives and the Transformation of American Politics, Matthew R. Kerbel

Sex and Violence: The Hollywood Censorship Wars, Tom Pollard

Unleashing the Power of Social-Issue Documentaries: Strategies for Political Impact, David Whiteman